D1594254

Blake's Night Thoughts

Blake's Night Thoughts

Jeremy Tambling

© Jeremy Tambling 2005

First published 2005 by
PALGRAVE MACMILLAN
Houndmills, Basingstoke, Hampshire RG21 6XS and
175 Fifth Avenue, New York, N.Y. 10010
Companies and representatives throughout the world

PALGRAVE MACMILLAN is the global academic imprint of the Palgrave
Macmillan division of St. Martin's Press, LLC and of Palgrave Macmillan Ltd.
Macmillan® is a registered trademark in the United States, United Kingdom
and other countries. Palgrave is a registered trademark in the European
Union and other countries.

ISBN 1–4039–4284–6 hardback

This book is printed on paper suitable for recycling and made from fully
managed and sustained forest sources.

A catalogue record for this book is available from the British Library.

Library of Congress Cataloging-in-Publication Data
Tambling, Jeremy.
   Blake's night thoughts / Jeremy Tambling.
      p. cm.
   Includes bibliographical references and index.
   ISBN 1–4039–4284–6
   1. Blake, William, 1757–1827—Criticism and interpretation.
   2. Blake, William, 1757–1827—Knowledge—Psychology.
   3. Blake, William, 1757–1827—Psychology. 4. Thought and
   thinking in literature. 5. Mental illness in literature.
   6. Psychology in literature. 7. Melancholy in literature.
   8. Night in literature. I. Title.

   PR4148.P8T36 2004
   821'.7—dc22
                                                    2004051503

10   9   8   7   6   5   4   3   2   1
14 13 12 11 10 09 08 07 06 05

Contents

Preface

Books have multiple sources. *Blake's Night Thoughts* aims at a close reading of Blake, by focusing on a preoccupation in his work, which also seems a condition marking it, and the sources of interest which have prompted its writing include several I know and can date, and just as many others which must remain forgotten or unconscious. So, as I complete it I am not sure why it took so long to start writing, because it has been something I wanted to do almost since first reading some of the *Songs of Innocence and Experience* (a school experience) and realizing also while an undergraduate, and working intensively with, amongst all the other sources, D.J. Sloss and S.R. Wallis's edition that to write on Blake meant also the Blake that goes beyond those poems. I have been reading and teaching Blake, both very concentratedly and in dispersed moments since then. Some work has been done while engaged in other areas – two of which, however, have been most apt for the study of Blake. One was working on Dickens, between whom and Blake connections have sometimes been made, and the other working on Dante. To read Dante requires thinking about Blake's own complex response to Dante in, for instance, his illustrations.

I have several grateful acknowledgements. As an undergraduate, I enjoyed Philip Brockbank on Blake, and F.R. Leavis, whose wrestlings with Blake in seminars held me fascinated: utterly committed, he also seemed to be held back from developing writing on Blake in a way which I have attempted to think further about it in this book. (And Leavis was not alone in this: there is no Blake in Empson, or in the 'New Critics', or in Paul de Man, or in Geoffrey Hartman, or in Hillis Miller.) The book has benefitted from readings of chapters by Ackbar Abbas in Hong Kong, Chris Barlow in Colchester, and Steve Clark in Japan: I thank the latter in particular for his generosity with his time, and for organizing, with Masashi Suzuki, the 'Blake in the Orient' conference in Kyoto in November 2003: I met many Blake scholars there and I learned much. Conversations and specific points of help have come, past and present, from Bob Pattison in undergraduate years and after, Stanley Gardner, David Bindman, and, in Hong Kong, David Clarke, Georg Predota, David Pomfret, and Ron Hill. The death of Graham Martin in early 2004 ends conversations enjoyed for over twenty years, and walks in London which were always a source of stimulus and encouragement.

When it comes to walking London, I would also thank Colin Davies for spirited companionship on so many idiosyncratically chosen itineraries. Part of the material on Dante and Blake, now dispersed in the book, comes from my essay 'Dante and Blake: Allegorizing the Event' edited by Nick Haveley (London: Macmillan 1998), pp. 33–48, and a draft of Chapter 7 called 'Illustrating Accusation: Blake on Dante's *Commedia*' in *Studies in Romanticism* 37 (1998), 395–420. I am grateful for permissions to reprint. I thank the University of Hong Kong for giving me a University-funded research grant which, lasting through the period of writing, has been very enabling. The book is dedicated to Pauline, Kirsten, and Felix, with thanks for everything, and in the context of this book, for the way they have all followed Blake around.

A Note on Texts

Having always used Blake edited by Geoffrey Keynes (Oxford: Oxford University Press 1966), this appears in the text as K. But references also appear to the edition by David Erdman (E): *The Complete Poetry and Prose of William Blake*, new and revised edition (Berkeley University of California Press 1982). Unlike Keynes, this modernizes neither spelling nor punctuation, and quotations are taken from it. I have drawn on the notes in the edition of W.H. Stevenson, *The Poems of William Blake* (London: Longman 1971), based on the Erdman text and dating back to 1965, and they appear as S.

The Blake reader needs the illustrations, and I have given references here to the editions brought out by the William Blake Trust in conjunction with Princeton University Press and the Tate Gallery (1991–1995) under the editorship of David Bindman, giving citations by the initial of the editor and page reference to their text:

vol. 1: *Jerusalem* ed. Morton Paley (P)
vol. 2: *Songs of Innocence and Experience* ed. Andrew Lincoln (L)
vol. 3: *The Early Illuminated Books* (*All Religions are One, There is No Natural Religion, The Book of Thel, The Marriage of Heaven and Hell, Visions of the Daughters of Albion*) ed. Morris Eaves, Robert N. Essick and Joseph Viscomi (EEV)
vol. 4: *The Continental Prophecies* ed. D.W. Dörrbecker (D)
vol. 5: *Milton* ed. Robert N. Essick and Joseph Viscomi (EV)
vol. 6: *The Urizen Books* ed. David Worrall (W)

For *The Four Zoas*, which Erdman, Keynes and Stevenson print differently from each other, my preference has been Keynes's version because while it may not always help with variant readings, it does not impose an interpretation of the text as Erdman does in conflating the two versions of Night the Seventh. Keynes makes the text more unified, narrating more consistently than is possible either from the standpoint of what the text offers, which has the status of night thoughts, or from the state of the text. For this text I have given page numbers, following and using Cettina Tramontano Magno and David V. Erdman (eds), '*The Four Zoas' by William Blake: Photographic Facsimile of the Manuscript with*

Commentary on the Illuminations (Lewisburg, Pa.: Bucknell University Press 1987) cited as ME. References in the text are to the manuscript's page-number, to Keynes's night and line number, and then the pagination in E and K.

References to Blake's art follow Martin Butlin's edition and catalogue numbering in *The Paintings and Drawings of William Blake*, 2 vols, plates and text (1981), appearing as B. *William Blake's Designs for Edward Young's Night Thoughts* ed. John E. Grant, Edward J. Rose, Michael J. Tolley, and David Erdman (1980) is used for the numbering of Blake's illustrations here, marked G.

Four other abbreviations:
BR: G.E. Bentley Jr, *Blake Records* (1969)
PE: David Erdman, *Blake: Prophet Against Empire: A Poet's Interpretation of the History of his Own Times* (1954: 2nd edition, 1969)
Phillips: Michael Phillips, *William Blake: The Creation of the Songs from Manuscript to Illuminated Printing* (2000)
SP: G.E. Bentley Jr, *The Stranger from Paradise: A Biography of William Blake* (2001)
Milton's *Paradise Lost* is quoted from the edition by Alastair Fowler (2nd edition, 1997), Shakespeare from the various Arden second editions.

1
Introduction: 'The Sun is Gone Down'

> the bright morn
> Smiles on our army, and the gallant sun
> Springs from the hills like a young hero
> Into the battle, shaking his golden locks
> Exultingly...
>
> ('King Edward the Third' 3.1–5, E. 427, K. 21)

Blake's art celebrates dawn, the theme of the picture 'Albion Rose' or 'Glad Day', which is inscribed: 'Albion rose from where he labourd at the Mill with Slaves / Giving himself for the Nations he danc'd the dance of Eternal Death' (E. 671, K. 160). The lyric 'And did those feet' from the Preface to *Milton* anticipates day, its 'dark Satanic mills' (E. 95–6, K. 480–1) like Albion's mill, representing 'the same dull round' (E. 2, K. 97).[1] C.H. Parry (1848–1918) set it in 1916 for the patriotic 'Fight for Right' movement of Sir Francis Younghusband (1863–1942), a British army officer and explorer, responsible for the invasion of Tibet in 1903, and touched with a belief in world religion. Parry repeated the performance for a Women's Demonstration meeting at the Albert Hall in 1917, while at a Suffrage Demonstration concert on 13 March 1918, Millicent Fawcett wanted it as the Women's Voters Hymn. The Women's Institute took it up when it started in 1924. Elgar rescored it in 1922 for the Leeds Festival, and since 1953 it has been sung at the last night of the Promenade concerts, so associating Blake with Thomson's 'Rule Britannia' (1740).[2]

Robert Bridges, who inspired Parry, had wanted Blake's lyric as a new national anthem, as it were, celebrating the day. Its use by British

Conservative and Labour Parties, or in film promoting Britain (Hugh Hudson's *Chariots of Fire*, 1981), has made it secular, Christian, pacific, patriotic, nationalistic. It gave the title to F.R. Leavis's *Nor Shall My Sword: Discourses on Pluralism, Compassion and Social Hope* (1972), an attack on 'technologico-Benthamism', marshalling Blake against Bentham, simplifying Blake, underestimating Benthamism. The unison song monumentalizes Blake, minimizing the complexity of 'Mental Fight', contesting 'clouded hills' and '*dark* Satanic mills'. 'Dark', with its cognates, spreads over eight pages in the Blake Concordance.[3] 'Dark Satanic mills' fuses two moments from *Samson Agonistes*: 'Eyeless in Gaza, at the mill with slaves' (41) and 'O dark, dark, dark, amid the blaze of noon' (80). 'Dark' comments on both the mills and the blind prisoner.

Blake as the artist of night appears in illustrations for Edward Young's poem *Night Thoughts*. Blake has been discussed in relation to night in pastoral poetry, including Spenser and Milton, as by David Wagenknecht, who draws on Blake's woodcuts to an edition of Virgil's pastoral poems of 1825.[4] These influenced artists who followed Blake: John Linnell (1792–1882), who associated himself with him in 1818, and Samuel Palmer (1805–1881), later Linnell's son-in-law. Palmer was born in London's Old Kent Road to a bookseller and to the daughter of a Baptist banker, William Giles, whose son, John, became both stockbroker and painter, one of the group called 'The Ancients'. Palmer's father, who became a Particular Baptist minister in Shoreham outside London, was another. So were Francis Oliver Finch (1802–1862), George Richmond (1809–1896), Edward Calvert (1799–1883), and the Tatham brothers, Frederick and Arthur. The latter became a clergyman, the former (1805–1878) followed the preacher Edward Irving (1792–1834), under whose influence he destroyed some of Blake's work in his possession.[5] Linnell, a Baptist, joined the newly formed Plymouth Brethren during the years 1843–1848, and wrote scholarly if amateur pieces on the Bible. Palmer too, a member of the established Church, was intensely religious. Linnell and Palmer both finished outside London in prosperous and middle-class Redhill and Reigate, towns outside London's destabilizing urbanism.[6] In terms to be discussed in Chapter 6, neither allowed themselves to be mad enough.

Blake's woodcuts, with crescent and full moons, 'visions of little dells, and nooks, and corners of Paradise', as Calvert called them (*BR* 271, B. cat. 769), emerge as white from the black, dominant background. Night, rejecting 'gaudy daylight' – Palmer's description of Blake's woodcuts (*BR* 271) – seems to be more real than day. Palmer cites *Macbeth* – 'The West yet glimmers with some streaks of day' – for his pen and brush work 'Late

Twilight' (1825),[7] which shows a crescent moon in the centre, and a shepherd asleep.[8] A full moon appears in 'Coming from Evening Church', an oil work of 1830. The church nestles below high hills (associated in other works with massy bright clouds), which, with the moon, make a feminine landscape enfolding the peasants 'in fruitful and deep delved womb' so that everything of value within the valley is 'almost buried from the sight / Of travellers on the higher ground'.[9] Night, female, burying, concealing, recalls:

> There is a place where Contrarieties are equally True
> This place is called Beulah, It is a pleasant lovely Shadow
> Where no dispute can come. Because of those who Sleep.
> Into this place the Sons & Daughters of Ololon descended
> With solemn mourning into Beulahs moony shades & hills ...
> (*Milton* 2.1–5, E. 129, K. 518)

Beulah goes further than Generation, and much further than Ulro, which is night because it is a period of 'sleep' (*Jerusalem* 4.1, E. 146, K. 622). But Beulah's Paradise stops short of Eternity.[10] Absence of vision means absence of tension in the treatment of the rural poor, a trait increasing throughout the century.[11] In 1846, Samuel Palmer illustrated Dickens's *Pictures from Italy*. The choice of topos is significant. Palmer, though he returned to London from Shoreham, stressed the pastoral, and could not have illustrated Blake's, or Dickens's, London.[12]

Palmer's smiling half-moons recall Blake's 'Night' in *Songs of Innocence*, where 'The moon like a flower, / In heavens high bower; / With silent delight, / Sits and smiles on the night' (E. 13, K. 118). Night and moon are differentiated, or the moon as the trace of the sun makes the night something else, indicative of 'immortal day', which also appears in the poem. 'Night', however, takes up some six pages of the Blake Concordance. There is also 'night fear', something dreaded, to be escaped from, in *The French Revolution* (233, E. 296, K. 144). These evocations of night evoke half of what night means in Blake, but the other half is more the terrain of 'night thoughts'. This night that remains in shadow I will introduce through Blake's Ugolino, from Dante's *Inferno*.

Ugolino and Urizen

The eighteenth century translated the narrative of Ugolino over thirty times, including that by Gray, the first part of Dante to receive such attention. The first, Jonathan Richardson in *A Discourse on the Dignity, Certainty, Pleasure and Advantage of the Science of a Connoisseur* (1719), influenced Sir Joshua Reynolds's *Discourses* (1769–1790). The complete *Inferno* first appeared in Henry Boyd's English translation in 1785, but Reynolds painted Richardson's Ugolino in 1773. He faces the front, ignoring the pleas of his youngest son, while his other sons evoke Michelangelesque terror in poses recalling Carracci's *Pietà*. The painting suggests that non-classical note in Reynolds: awareness of the monstrous, which made the painting the subject of criticism for lack of taste.[13] It is a night-thoughts scene; dawn coming through the barred window high up in the painting's centre is superfluous.

Paget Toynbee quotes the *Quarterly Review* of 1832 that 'Dante was brought into fashion in England by Sir Joshua Reynolds.' William Hayley (1745–1820), an early translator of Dante, addressed Reynolds: 'Thy Ugolino gives the heart to thrill / With pity's tender looks and horror's icy thrill' (*An Essay on Painting*, 1778). Fuseli's pen and wash drawings of Dante, including Ugolino (Rome, 1774), led to a further painting of the theme in 1806.[14] Before Blake illustrated Dante's *Commedia*, he made pencil-and-ink sketches of Ugolino and his sons between 1780 and 1785 – while two illustrations of the early 1790s – in *For Children: The Gates of Paradise*, no. 12, and *The Marriage of Heaven and Hell*, Plate 16 – relate to the episode.[15]

Dante's meeting with Ugolino (*Inferno* canto 32, 124–39 to 33, 1–90) is in the ice of the ninth, last circle of hell, reserved for traitors. Ugolino, crouched behind his enemy the Archbishop Ruggieri, gnaws the nape of his neck. He tells of his death by starvation at the hands of Ruggieri when he and his sons were locked up in a 'muda', a tower for keeping hawks. With the connivance of the people of Pisa, the key was thrown away, the father and sons left to starve. Criticism has often suggested that, on the basis of his last line 'poscia, piú che' l dolor, poté 'l digiuno' (afterwards hunger had more power than grief, *Inferno* 33.75),[16] Ugolino committed technophagia while starving, blind: gnawing at the bodies of his dead children.

Ugolino begins saying that Dante wills that he would renew his desperate sorrow by telling his story, but the renewing reiterates, in his repetition of the event, the sense of the future eaten by the past. Though he solicits Dante's weeping, he does not, perhaps cannot, weep,[17] while Dante's reaction is as aggressive as Ugolino wishing for Pisa to be engulfed by its rivers being dammed up, an image of incorporation, of consuming, equivalent to the image of technophagia. He continues the barbarism by which the future is eaten up, taken away. Not dissociating himself from Ugolino, he becomes like him, recording his hatred of Pisa in the present tense, as what he thinks now. The text does not move away from that state, which remains to haunt its affirmations. Perhaps he can feel no more, like Ugolino, whose silence in the prison is self-repressive: 'I did not weep, so stony I grew within...' ('Io non piangea, sì dentro impetrai' [33.49]). Repressed feeling fits melancholia, where the sight of the dying children, whose faces repeat his own misery, works on his damaged narcissistic sense, driving him inward towards further melancholia.[18] He produces in turn no affect in Dante except stoniness, blankness and melancholia. Ugolino, spectrous figure of melancholia, passes that state on, as engulfing, cannibalistic, and all-consuming. Ugolino's perceptions are night thoughts. In his account of his allegorical dream in the prison, allegory is a veil that covers, like the veil 'where the Dead dwell' in For the Sexes: The Gates of Paradise. Ugolino describes the dream as tearing the veil of the future. It shows him as a wolf, with wolf cubs, being hunted down by dogs. Tearing the veil and tearing the flesh are similar, while there is also fear of being eaten, becoming a body in pieces, the corps morcelé.[19] In the doubleness of wolf and whelps / father and sons, Ugolino cannot read himself as a wolf, but the dream, of being devoured by hunting bitches, finds a fragmentary fulfilment in starvation, and in the father becoming cannibalistic and dog-like.[20]

The vividness of Ugolino for Blake shows in his presence in Plate 12 of For the Sexes: The Gates of Paradise, sitting, his knees up, in a foetal, melancholic position – like others of the figures in those plates, reminiscent of the circle which, for Blake, suggests God's oppression as enforcing identity: 'If you have formed a Circle to go into / Go into it yourself & see how you would do' (E. 516, K. 557). 'Does thy God, O Priest, take such vengeance as this?', addresses Ruggieri, but in the 1818 Gates, an 'I' assumes responsibility for having enclosed the father and the Sons 'in depths of dungeons'. Ugolino is imprisoned by a Urizenic 'I', rationalistic, cold figure of law-making and abstraction, identified with the Priest and state power. The 'I' is a repressive Dantean poet needing redemption since he has been a Urizen himself.[21] The figures in The Gates compare with plate 16 of The Marriage of Heaven and Hell, which shows almost the same, save that in the Gates each character is isolated, and here they are pulled together. The illustration is placed above a passage describing the 'Giants who formed this world into its sensual existence and now seem to live in it in chains', these being the products of the 'cunning of weak and tame minds which have the power to resist energy'.

Thus one portion of being, is the Prolific. the other, the Devouring: to the devourer it seems as if the producer was in his chains, but it is not so, he only takes portions of existence and fancies that the whole.

(E. 40, K. 155)

Ugolino is a giant, embodiment of kinetic energy, but Erdman, discussing the plates draws attention to his eyes, mesmerised, unseeing, non-visionary, darkened. In copy G of the plate, 'we see below his open left hand a bloody red lump gleaming on the floor, flesh he has tried eating'.[22] He embodies prolific energy, tormented by the unseen devourers like Fuseli's Ugolino: 'a man of wonder and admiration, of resentment against man and devil, and of humiliation before God; prayer and parental affection fills the figure from head to foot' (E. 768, K. 864).[23] Yet Ugolino is also the devourer, and the duality of creating and devouring, where the Devourer thinks the producer is in his chains, and 'the Prolific would cease to be Prolific, unless the Devourer, as a sea, recieved the excess of his delights', gives priority to reason, or restraint, or destruction, which Blake depicts. Making Ugolino the devourer makes him Urizen, with whose features there is a fit, and whose name may even evoke Dante's creation. The stoniness fits Urizen too. Blake's comments on the *Commedia* to Crabb Robinson (1775–1867) make Dante Urizenic a vengeful Ugolino. Awareness of his stoniness of being works in the *Commedia*, when Beatrice says Dante is mentally 'made of stone' ('fatto di pietra', *Purgatorio* 33, ll. 72–3).[24] In the portrait of Dante for Hayley's library, Dante is at the centre, as though on a classical medallion, with bay leaves around him, looking right to where an Ugolino figure cradles one child, another sitting by his side. To his left is a prison fetter. The imperial motif implies power-relationships, linking Dante, Ugolino, and Urizen.

The Ugolino episode seems a crux within Blake, a source of a conflictual reading, as much as a crux within Dante. As a reflection on the power of ruin and fragmentation, it makes Dante as an allegorist in the mode of Walter Benjamin in his pairing of allegory with melancholy. Benjamin's crux text is Dürer's *Melencolia I*: Blake's print of that he kept until he died (*SP* 392).[25] The conflictual state of Ugolino and his sons in the prison makes for 'night thoughts', where desire for the morning and its reason contrasts with night and its reason, which is inseparable from a non-differentiated madness and death. Night, which makes the self lose its sense of itself, making it in reaction obsessional, paranoid, as with Ugolino, makes it impossible to read the scene in one way. Hence the diverse reactions to the art the episode inspired, beginning with Blake, in whose case it seems that the artist will not dissociate himself from the masculine melancholic prisoner, hero and entrapped at once. But night thoughts question masculinity and gender.

Night and gender

Night in Blake may be false consciousness, expressed in terms of a female-to-male encouragement to war; as seen in the illustration for 'Now comes the night of Enitharmon's joy' where a warrior-form like a crusader is worshipped by female angels.[26] But more:

> Now comes the night of Enitharmons joy!
> Who shall I call? Who shall I send?
> That Woman, lovely Woman! may have dominion?
> Arise O Rintrah thee I call! & Palamabron thee!
> Go! tell the human race that Womans love is Sin!
> That an Eternal life awaits the worms of sixty winters
> In an allegorical abode where existence hath never come:
> Forbid all Joy, & from her childhood shall the little female
> Spread nets in every secret path.
>
> (*Europe* 5.1–9, E. 62, K. 240)

It is a double message: sexuality must be repressed and the body made no more than that of a worm at a moment when it is also to be elevated by the exalted place given to the female. Christianity becomes the religion of deferred gratification.[27] In her sleep, lasting for eighteen hundred years of Christianity, Enitharmon laughs to see:

> Every house a den, every man bound; the shadows are filld
> With spectres, and the windows wove over with curses of iron:
> Over the doors Thou shalt not; & over the chimneys Fear is written:
> With bands of iron round their necks fasten'd into the walls
> The citizens: in leaden gyves the inhabitants of suburbs
> Walk heavy; soft and bent are the bones of villagers.
>
> (12.25–31, E. 64, K. 243)

She seems to have plunged each house in the city, the suburbs, and the villages into night. She presides over both 'the sports of night' and 'the night of holy shadows/And human solitude' (13.13, 18, 19), which imply the subject reduced to autoeroticism or produced as the masturbating subject. Enitharmon shows religion as feminine, and as seductive but also denying, anticipating Vala (*The Four Zoas*) and her function in relation to sexual love. Her character as the 'female will' (the will being phallic) is problematic because, while she poses the question why the woman has no other existence than as a deceptive agency of the male, that role has become significant: she represents a power given to her by the masculine Spectre, whose failure she indicates.

The language in *Europe* compares with 'The Garden of Love' (*Songs of Experience*), whose illustration shows mourners at an open grave, while the poem is in the space below the grave mouth, below which briars grow over graves. The mourners' colours and the dark background behind them makes the top half of the page belong to a state near to night:

> I went to the garden of love,
> And saw what I never had seen:
> A Chapel was built in the midst,
> Where I used to play on the green.
>
> And the gates of this Chapel were shut,
> And Thou shalt not. writ over the door;
> So I turn'd to the Garden of Love,
> That so many sweet flowers bore.
>
> And I saw it was filled with graves,
> And tomb-stones where flowers should be:
> And Priests in black gowns, were walking their rounds,
> And binding with briars, my joys & desires.[28]
>
> (E. 26, K. 215)

The title of the poem implies values remembered in the 'garden bright' of 'A Little Girl Lost' (E. 29, K. 219) and looked for in 'The Little Girl Lost' when the 'desart wild / Become[s] a garden mild' (E. 20, K. 112). In the first stanza, the garden supports play. In the second, 'which so many sweet flowers bore' implies cultivation that seems to arise spontaneously, and which can be held non-possessively in conditions of play on 'the green' – as in 'The Ecchoing Green' (E. 8, K. 116), which echoes in the first line of the 'Nurse's Song' of *Songs of Innocence*, 'When the voices of children are heard on the green' (E. 15, K. 121).[29]

The 'garden of love', the activity of playing on the green and the 'sweet flowers' exist in a continuum. But now the Chapel is 'in the midst' and the grounds cannot be entered because of the gates, while the door into the Chapel has 'Thou shalt not' written over it. The verb in 'So I *turn'd* to the Garden of Love', one of the richest in Blake, along with 'return', comes at the turn of the twelve-line poem, implying a poetic change, turning as troping. The garden now cultivates graves and tombstones, deathly promptings to melancholia in such eighteenth-century grave-yard poets as Gray and Young. Perhaps the turn in the poem is temporal, corresponding to a change between Elizabethan (so many 'sweet flowers') and eighteenth-century poetry; the question being: what can be produced within the culture of rationalism (no nonconformist enthusiasm here) which so values death? – the subject's own death, the death it deems proper to itself.[30] So Gray's *Elegy in a Country Churchyard*, only partly oppositional to that culture, teaches the 'rustic Moralist to die' (line 100).

After the 'turn', priests in night-like black gowns walk their rounds like beadles or police-officers, followed by the turning, internal rhyme. 'Bind-ing with briars my joys & desires' indicates not so much the flowers of the second stanza, as the subject's thoughts which must be acknowledged (*my* joys) and which are now bound to sticks to keep them straight (S. 212). The image is familiar from Foucault's *Discipline and Punish* which includes illustrations of the training of young plants in such a manner. The subject is under surveillance from its own superego, its own priests. The last internal rhyme makes the briars the name to give to desires constructed as onanistic and bound, where binding intensifies the eroticism of those desires, seen in the illustration as graves, bound. Binding, as in Blake's *Night Thoughts* no. 96 where an angel flies down to touch on the back of a crouched figure weeping by a grave criss-crossed with briars like a chain, is repeated, backwards and forwards.[31] Binding keeps the dead body in place. Perhaps 'binding' associates with Freud's *Beyond the Pleasure Principle* on the binding that the death drive accomplishes, working on what he calls 'primary processes' at work in the organism. Here, the act of binding, which is an act of repetition as education is, confers identity, making the primary processes identifiable separate drives.[32]

The walled Chapel replaces the green which had no boundaries, while the graveyard replaces the garden. In the Chapel, the heart is shut up, distinguishing between what is inside and what is outside, the proper and the improper. The barred gates and interdiction over the door announces that the ego has enclosed the other within itself. The psychoanalysts Nicholas Abraham and Maria Torok call this 'incorpor-ation'. It is a way of denying a loss – such as the death of the other – which would damage narcissism.[33] The Chapel *denies* the presence of death in its permanence of structure, while the graves show the *production* of death, in which the joys and desires are part, since they are seen by the priest as deviant, or harmful to the touch. The Chapel's architecture represents Freudian repression, but the 'turn' generates the production of the subject, Foucault's topic.

Responding to the night of graveyard poetry, 'The Garden of Love' becomes a 'night' poem, as much as Christianity is the night of Enitharmon's joy. Perhaps Blake can never leave this ground. In 'The Ecchoing Green' (*Songs of Innocence*), 'The sun doth descend, / And our sports have an end'. These 'sports', different from Enitharmon's 'sports of night', echo in the last lines 'And sport no more seen, / On the darkening Green' (E. 8, K. 116), so 'green' must darken to something else, turning away from 'The Ecchoing Green'.

The loss of the value of 'green' appears as it turns from the sense of 'fresh', to 'envious', in the first verse of 'Nurse's Song' (*Songs of Experience*):

> When the voices of children, are heard on the green
> And whisprings are in the dale:
> The days of my youth rise fresh in my mind,
> My face turns green and pale.
>
> Then come home my children, the sun is gone down
> And the dews of night arise
> Your spring & your day, are wasted in play
> And your winter and night in disguise.
>
> (E. 23, K. 212)

The day-vision is supplemented by something else coming from underneath, from 'the dale', which, in the poem's symmetry, 'rises' up as with the 'dews of night', markers of sex or death. Perhaps whisperings imply the unconscious, as they imply memory which rises fresh in her mind as whisperings. The word 'rise' connects with 'And the dews of night arise' so that memories are dew-like, markers of the night. The days of her youth exist symmetrically with the third line of the second verse, where 'day' and 'play' rhyme so as to weaken both words. The nurse's face turns green and pale, and her change of colours necessitates the poem's last word, 'disguise', half-rhyming with 'night' and associated with it, as night is with winter. Play and disguise relate to each other, the latter a more extreme version of the former. The nurse is outwardly divided in the colours her face has turned to, and inwardly divided between voices and whisperings, her present and the days of her youth. The latter are perhaps remembered in the illustration, where, amid autumn grapes, she tends the hair of a richly dressed boy. Perhaps she is also figured in the girl reading in the doorway. Self-divided, she says there is nothing but disguise, in weaker or stronger forms. 'Disguise', like night, occludes identity which it replaces. Perhaps disguise is gender-related. The voices of children on the public space of the green take no account of the perhaps covert whisperings in the dale (hidden, deceptive, perhaps indicating sexual awareness). Their play is a waste in that they miss its undercurrents: their sun has gone down already. The poem *Songs of Innocence* contests that view twice over, first by the nurse's sense that the day will be renewed:

> Come come leave off play, and let us away
> Till the morning appears in the skies.
>
> (E. 15, K. 121)

Second, by the children's refusal to believe that the light has faded away: 'it is yet day / And we cannot go to sleep'.

In *Songs of Experience*, the nurse's last two lines evoke childhood and age, following the pattern of the children and the older nurse, or they imply that winter and night are already upon the children, as the days of the nurse's youth retain the cold force of night dew. The children, ungendered in the poem, take no account of the whisperings, so missing everything that comes between spring and winter, and which is also absent in the poem. They miss the significance of the sexual, which means that both their presents and futures are disguised from them, or are lived in disguise (the condition of playing on the green), or that their gender-positions are a disguise, or that their days will close with the disguise, like the nurse, of publicly unacknowledged desire. Even the nurse's identity is a disguise. Unnamed, she exists only in her function, like the shepherd or the chimney sweeper in other *Songs*. Disguise relates to the wish to see gendered identity as complete, but gender splits the fantasised identity seen as bisexual in Lacan's mirror-stage. The split subject of sexuality associates with the night of identity-loss.

'The Garden of Love' shows the loss of the 'green' to the suburb, making the poem part of the social history of building London. Blake knew himself part of a cultural history, focused in his relation to London and the changes taking place within it and in the sense of the power of the urban to form character. Living in a history of urban capitalist modernizing, he was conscious of being placed outside history by the market-place and by Britain becoming politically reactionary. Another reason for linking Blake and night, then, relates to the city. Night is a characteristic mode of city-existence, whose crises, as perceived then, are only partly resolvable by day. Taken symbolically, the city is always a night-state, deranging the senses: the day makes no difference. The point applies to both Blake and, only a few years later, Dickens.[34] With low-density housing, and an early tendency to spread out from old city walls – OED credits Chaucer for the word 'suburbs' to describe Southwark, the area south of London bridge – London is unlike either Paris, whose central planning was begun by Napoleon, or New York. London could never have been Benjamin's 'capital of the nineteenth century' for its lack of centre and, perhaps, its Evangelicalism, on which Dickens comments as in his account of a London Sunday evening where everything is 'locked and barred' (*Little Dorrit* 1.3). In Baudelaire's Paris, Haussmann's metropolitan improvements changed everything for the third Napoleon; for Blake, Nash's London was restructuring the West End for the Prince Regent, who modelled himself on the first Napoleon. Despite urban improvements, whose aim is to make the city less subject to the night, the city gives no single place to the subject, its nature being to de-structure. In Blake, it must be read doubly, being the city built by Urizen, and by Los (and then called Golgonooza, as in Night the Fifth of *The Four Zoas*). And Urizen and Los may not be separate identities. Madness and gender, fixed or unfixed, interrelate: the city generates 'night thoughts'.

Night and madness

On 16 January 1826, Blake wrote in an autograph album, 'William Blake, one who is very much delighted with being in good Company. Born 28 Nov.r. in London & has died several times since' (E. 698, K. 781).[35] Here, Blake accepts posthumous existence, and death is not that which confirms the self's single identity, nor is identity something singular. It pluralizes, responding to the idea that 'everyone is a little group', as Deleuze and Guattari say in a passage which could apply to Blake's Four Zoas: 'neither men nor women are clearly defined personalities, but rather vibrations, flows, schizzes and "knots"'.[36] The Four Zoas relate to the four elements, who appear in the figures of water (which in *The Four Zoas* becomes Tharmas), earth (which becomes Los, in his identity as Urthona), air (Urizen), and fire (Luvah). They are seen similarly in the plates that illustrate the emblem-book, *For the Sexes: The Gates of Paradise*, and as separated they show an alienating breakdown into individual subjectivity. Nietzsche writes in *The Birth of Tragedy* of the dismemberment of Dionysos: 'dismemberment – the truly Dionsyiac suffering – was like a separation into air, water, earth, and fire, and . . . individuation should be regarded as the source of all suffering and rejected'.[37] Yet the precision of four, plus the emanations of these four in Blake is not quite Deleuzian; it clings to the idea of discrete identities, so that while identity becomes plural it does not cease to be identity. That doubleness is part of Blake's night thinking.

Blake does not want to be thought of in terms of an authorizing identity when he says of his 'designs': 'And tho I call them Mine I know that they are not Mine' (letter to Dr Trusler, 16 August 1799, E. 701, K. 792). Death is the name for those breaks within the subject, which make it discontinuous with itself and which see the subject as marked by absence. In Emmanuel Levinas, death is that which disconfirms a sense of self, self as a 'totality'. In *The Writing of the Disaster* Blanchot 'call[s] disaster that which does not have the ultimate for a limit: it bears the ultimate away in the disaster' (28). The writing of the disaster is a 'break with every form of totality' (75), a break with language as communicative, or systematizing, where it is inevitably a exclusion of what Levinas calls 'the absolutely other'. Levinas replaces 'totality' with 'infinity', saying:

> The relation with infinity will have to be stated in terms other than those of objective experience, but if experience precisely means a relation with the absolutely other, that is with what always overflows thought, the relation with infinity accomplishes experience in the fullest sense of the word.[38]

What 'overflows thought' is of the night, night thoughts. The argument linking Blake not to a totality but to infinity means that any transmission of knowledge can only be fragmentary, or allegorical, for only this could resist the sense that the 'totality' can be known. Hence Los's drive towards systematicity cannot be taken as commitment to a complete mythic cycle, though he says in *Jerusalem*:

> I must Create a System, or be enslav'd by another Mans
> I will not Reason & Compare: my business is to Create
> (*Jerusalem* 10.20, 21, E. 153, K. 629)

Los's affirmation of the power of a system, which may be a system of thought, is part of an ambiguity inherent in Blake. Part of it looks towards the day, desiring single identity, and the power to form, while something else dreads single identity as a disguise while also dreading something else which may be associated with melancholia tending to madness, which is both that identity petrified into hardness and the loss of such identity. Madness in Blake, and, possibly, Blake's madness, appears as a form of energy which exists in a complex relation to the state of being formed into a discrete identity, and as a fascination with 'other' states. The label of madness particularly attached itself to Blake after the 1790s, from *The Four Zoas* and after, but it is a fascination or danger at work throughout.

Blanchot refers to Blake's madness, implicitly, in *Le pas au-delà* (1973), discussing Freud's 'Beyond the Pleasure Principle'. Supplementing Freud, he asks what Nietzsche – a writer Freud avoids – would say was 'beyond' that pleasure principle. The answer is that the 'eternal return' (which because it cannot return to the 'same' place, destroys the thought of identity and of chronological sequence) is 'beyond'. Blanchot's comment implies Blake:

> Nietzsche, certainly, can be born before Hegel, and when he is born, in fact, it is always before Hegel; from this comes what one is tempted to call his madness: the relationship necessarily premature, always anticipated, always not now, thus without anything that can assure it by founding it on an actuality – whether this be of now, of the past (original) or of the future (prophetic). When one is content to say that madness is a reason ahead of reason, one wrongs both madness and reason. Even the maxim: 'they were mad so that we no longer had to be', which Nietzsche might have accepted, still supposes simple temporal relations, always unifiable and reconcilable in the conception of a time essentially unique, itself, in as much as it is thought, withdraws from its own becoming, since it is dependent on a grand system. In this light, he is crazy who is wise before being so, before the letter. But the other madness – that which has no name to enclose it – would be an infinitely multiple relation that, even if called temporal, would hide itself from all that would subject it to time, even as outside of time. Madness is called so only by the language of the Law which, at best, assigns it the role of that which would precede it, that which would always be before the law, although the law in itself implies the impossibility of anything that could be anterior to it. That is why there is not madness, but there *will be* madness, the existence of this as a real possibility always having to be put in parentheses and under a conditional without condition. Which 'madness' admits as well, since the parenthesis is its madness in which it would like to put everything, including itself.[39]

If Blake is here, it is for the paraphrase of 'If others had not been foolish, we should be so' (*The Marriage of Heaven and Hell* 9.13, E. 37, K. 152), where folly includes madness. It is like other Proverbs of Hell – 'The road of excess leads to the palace of wisdom', or 'What is now proved was once, only imagin'd', or (though there is no chronology implied here) 'Every thing possible to be believ'd is an image of truth' (7.3, 8.12, 18, E. 35, 36, 37, K. 151). Blanchot concedes the value of the statement, but it makes him suggest that Blake was not mad enough. If others had not been foolish, we would be so now. The argument vindicates madness but serves the history of reason. This madness, a 'reason ahead of reason', compares with the '*other* madness' which serves neither linear chronology nor a developmental history. The first madness, as with the Proverbs of Hell, may be tolerated. But the other madness is also in Blake: it marries heaven and hell, but not with the sense that these are discrete entities, but categories riven by the night, and his writing of the night exists, like Nietzsche's, in a text excluding chronology, identity, and a present.

This introductory detail enables my mapping of what lies ahead. In Chapter 2, pursuit of Blake and the undoing power of the night goes through the *Songs of Innocence and of Experience*. Chapters 3 and 4 survey the nocturnal in Blake through the perspective of Young's *Night Thoughts*, looking at Young (1683–1765) and the indeterminateness implied in his title, examining Blake's illustrations to these, and two poetic responses: *For the Sexes: The Gates of Paradise* and *The Four Zoas*. The text has both a dream and a social context, and Chapter 5 follows the latter by relating Blake's night to London, while Chapter 6 integrates this urban context with madness in Blake. Yet 'madness' cannot be taken here in either a clinical or a positivist sense, nor can it be taken as something that can be easily delimited from other states, such as melancholia. In any case, madness is over-determined, being both the power of the Spectre, and something else which contests that. Chapter 7 looks at night, the city and the Blakean unconscious within the illustrations for Dante made in London in 1824: it sees changes in the way night is conceptualized as threatening Blake's night, and it thinks finally of London after Blake.

There are readings here of poems which do not stand alone, but which, while they are structures of total complexity, are also fragments of each other, interrelating through common uses of words. Not just the expression of single dramatic voices, they evoke more than 'contrary states of the human soul'. Heidegger, discussing Georg Trakl, another poet of Night, says that 'every great poet creates his poetry out of one single poetic statement only' adding that 'the poet's statement remains unspoken. None of his individual poems, nor their totality, says it all. Nonetheless, every poem speaks from the whole of the one single statement, and in each instance says that statement.' Further, 'the sole statement lies in the realm of the unspoken'.[40]

Heidegger's position may seem complacent, but it is interesting to take it as making a poem a fragment of what must always be subject to deferral, since language 'flatly refuses to express itself in words' (*On the Way to Language* p. 81). The unsaid, the reserve, may be seen in Levinas's thought as the infinite, the *il y a*, or what, in Chapter 3, appears as Blanchot's 'other night', an idea which comes from Levinas who makes the night the period of insomnia:

> Vigilance is quite devoid of objects. That does not come down to saying that it is an experience of nothingness, but that it is as anonymous as the night itself. Attention presupposes the freedom of the ego which directs it; the vigilance of insomnia which keeps our eyes open has no subject. It is the very return of presence into the void left by absence – not the return of *some thing*, but of a presence; it is the reawakening of the *il y a* in the heart of negation'.[41]

The *il y a* is the moment of haunting, in a time when the distinction between living and dead breaks down. Levinas cites passages in Shakespeare where the spectre is the shadow between being and nothingness (*Existence and Existents* p. 62). Shakespeare's spectres haunt Blake's night thought. An association of ideas seems possible – between the spectre as an absence, nonetheless felt, and dominating the more for not being present; and the night as the reserve, the other, the *il y a*, producing that which is spectral. The poem as a fragment – the point holds for the Prophecies, nearly all, in their own terms, fragmentary – emanates from nothing other than what cannot be brought into presence. In the *Songs of Innocence and of Experience*, to which I now turn, the feeling of reading across from text to text, as everywhere in Blake, takes away the power of any night/day antithesis that seems to be offered; night affects them in every way.

2
'In the Silent of the Night'

Nocturne

In Thomas Mann's novel *Doctor Faustus* (1947), the composer Adrian Leverkühn turns away from setting German texts in favour of those of Verlaine and 'his particular favourite, William Blake'.[1] Mann's understanding of Blake came from W.H. Auden (who said that 'the whole of Freud's teaching may be found in *The Marriage of Heaven and Hell*'),[2] and his choice of poems from the *Songs of Experience* is created by their subject: night. Leverkühn is writing a Nocturne. Piano pieces called Nocturnes were first written by the composer John Field (1782–1837), influential on Chopin, and they appear around 1812. But in Mann's Blake, the night is not just part of a mood, but active, troubling, disorganizing.

The 'Introduction' to *Songs of Innocence*, in a move which goes from piping to singing to writing, confirms that these songs are to be sung, leaving the music uncomposed on the page but picked up in the poem's visual quality. Zeitblom, narrating Adrian Leverkühn's life, writes:

> As for Blake's singular poetry, he had composed music for the famous verses about the rose that grows sick from the dark love of the worm that has found its way to her crimson bed. And then the uncanny sixteen lines of 'A Poison Tree', in which the poet waters his wrath with tears, suns it with smiles and deceitful wiles, until its tree bears a bright apple that poisons the friend who steals it – and whom the hater is glad to see lying dead beneath the tree the next morning. The poem's wicked simplicity was perfectly recreated in the music. But I was even more deeply impressed, on the very first hearing, by a song based on words by Blake: the dream of a chapel all of gold before which people stand, weeping, mourning, worshipping, but

not daring to enter in. There now rises up the figure of a serpent, who knows how to force and force and force his way into the shrine, who draws his slimy length along the jewelled pavement, until he reaches the altar, where he vomits his poison out on the bread and on the wine. 'So', the poet concludes, with the desperate logic of therefore and thus, 'I turned into a sty and laid me down amid the swine'. The fearful nightmare of that vision, its growing horror, its sickening defilement, and its final fierce renunciation of a humanity degraded by the very sight – it was all reproduced with amazing urgency in Adrian's music (176).

Leverkühn sets three texts: first, 'The Sick Rose' (E. 23, K. 213), given with its draft from the Notebook:

> O Rose thou art sick.
> The invisible worm,
> That flies in the night
> In the howling storm:
>
> Has found out thy bed
> Of crimson joy:
> [O, dark secret love
> Doth life destroy. – *del*.]
> And [his – *del*.] [her] his dark secret love
> Does thy life destroy.
>
> (E. 23, K. 175, 213)

The second, 'A Poison Tree', 'Christian Forbearance' in the draft:

> I was angry with my friend;
> I told my wrath, my wrath did end.
> I was angry with my foe:
> I told it not, my wrath did grow.
>
> And I waterd it in fears,
> Night & morning with my tears:
> And I sunned it with smiles,
> And with soft deceitful wiles.
>
> And it grew [by] both day and night.
> Till it bore an apple bright.
> [And I gave it to my foe – *del*.]

And my foe beheld it shine,
And he knew that it was mine.

And into my garden stole,
When the night had veild the pole;
In the morning [Glad] glad I see;
My foe outstretchd beneath the tree.

(E. 28, K. 165, 218)

Zeitblom, a humanistic narrator, defines the texts with terms such as 'wicked simplicity' and 'uncanny', and reads the poem about the dream of the chapel and the serpent, trying to follow the events, but unable to, so that he is left with nightmare, horror, defilement, and renunciation of humanity. The poem, untitled, appears in the 1793 Notebook:

I saw a chapel all of gold
That none did dare to enter in
And many weeping stood without
Weeping mourning worshipping

I saw a serpent rise between
The white pillars of the door
And he forcd & forcd & forcd,
[Till he broke the pearly door – *del*.]
Down the golden hinges tore

And along the pavement sweet
Set with pearls & rubies bright
All his slimy length he drew
Till upon the altar white

Vomiting his poison out
On the bread & on the wine
So I turnd into a sty
And laid me down among the swine

(E. 467–8, K. 163, 467)

In these three poems, the worm finds its way to a crimson bed; the friend steals the apple; and the serpent forces his way into the shrine. Each transgresses within the spaces of the bed, the garden and the shrine, transgression generating action. Poison links these texts, as does the power of attraction (the rose, the apple, the chapel) which is meretricious like the attractions of the commodity in capitalism. In the first poem, poison appears through the trace of sickness in the rose; the second has poison in the 'apple bright'; and in the third, the serpent vomits its poison out.

When 'the rose...grows sick from the love of the worm that has found its way to her crimson bed', Zeitblom makes the rose a *fleur du mal* who loves the worm, detaching the rose's sickness from the worm's penetration.[3] The plate shows a caterpillar, in the top left-hand corner, about to consume a leaf, so that the destruction of the rose is not confined to the worm, which may be subordinate to night, the powerful force at work. In 'A Poison Tree', the poison relates to the wrath of the narrator, and to the poison (envy) in the thief who would steal the apple. In 'I saw a chapel all of gold', the brightness – like the rose's crimson – may also produce a poison, in repelling worshippers, who stand at a distance 'weeping' – a word repeated – and mourning, which is 'worshipping'. The chapel's bread and wine is part of a phantasmagoria which includes pearls and rubies, white pillars, and white altar. The serpent's poison is secondary to the first unstated poison associated with the chapel. In each case the transgressiveness relates to another, earlier transgression, as Blake wrote: 'All Penal Laws court Transgression & therefore are cruelty & Murder' (E. 618, K. 393). This foreshadows Bataille.[4] Law invites and depends upon transgression, for until it is transgressed there is no attraction to it. Law and rule and regularity go together in Bataille, while evil is the heterogeneous, irregular (a word Bataille takes from Sade):

> Sade realised that irregularity was the basis of sexual excitement. The law (the rule) is a good one, it is Good itself (Good, the means whereby the being ensures its existence), but a value, Evil, depends on the possibility of breaking the rule. Infraction is frightening – like death: and yet it is attractive, as though the being only wanted to survive out of weakness, as though exuberance inspired that contempt for death which is necessary once the rule has been broken. These principles are bound up with human life. They are at the basis of Evil, of heroism or of sanctity.
>
> (186–7)

Bataille opposes rule to value. Law can never give values, in upholding blind universal rules. Value comes from the heterogeneous, whose mobility and power of disruption break the rule. Bataille associates irregularity with exuberance ('Exuberance is beauty', E. 38, K. 152) and excess. Evil, provoking fear and repulsion, preserves limits, while in its character as excessive and exciting, it shatters them. 'The attraction of irregularity sustains the attraction of the rule' (187).

The 'real' violence lies in the original symbolizing: the rose, which may imply virginity, or Mary, or Christianity, or woman as she is sacralized within patriarchal Christianity, or the sexual parts of the woman; or the apple, whose resonances are of the garden of Eden and which question why the fruit should have been placed there in the first instance, and why in 'my garden', which emphasises private property, productive of a transgressive desire. Or the symbol of the chapel, whose exclusionariness, which may also imply that the woman's body is the chapel of gold[5] (like the garden and the apple), making rule-abiding people wretched, while inviting spoliation, which, through the repeated 'forc'd', is presented as a rape, the excess of language commenting, perhaps, on the psychopathology of the visionary speaker ('I saw . . . I saw').[6]

Leverkühn's texts ask where transgression begins. The poems are images of each other and imaginations of disgust. The speaker addresses the rose, not the worm, as if turning upon the vulnerable thing, and the tone of the first line includes fascination, disgust, blame, accusation, prurience. Contrarily, the apostrophe also implies an attempt to speak to a person, recalling 'O Rose of May! / Kind sister, sweet Ophelia' (*Hamlet* IV. vi. 156–7) as Laertes marks his sister's madness. And the rose cannot, or does not, reply, so its labelling – perhaps accusing – as 'sick' needs reading critically. Does 'found out' imply the voyeur's, or the detective's pleasure? In 'A Poison Tree', the speaker's attitudes make the poem (as seen in 'And', repeated seven times), grow into the poison tree. The poem is also the confession, or representation of the 'I'. Everything is infected, so that even the first lines, about finishing with anger, seem unreal; can there be a distinction between the friend and the foe, or an anger which finishes and one which cannot? The 'I' – angry at the start, tearful in the midst, and glad at the end – gives an account of himself which is alienated; he cannot comment on what he has done. Taking his subjectivity as a supreme good, he says nothing else about himself. That may be the irony behind 'Christian Forbearance': he forbears acknowledging what he has done. But the title also refers to his passivity, remembering that for the religious 'Good is the passive that obeys Reason' – i.e. the rule – (E. 34, K. 149), while 'Active Evil is better than Passive Good' (E. 592, K. 77). In the third poem, the speaker's responses, having seen the chapel and the people outside, and the serpent's entry are equally strange. He sees the serpent which is 'slimy', vomit up its poison as though, after its violence, it too is disgusted with the fakery of the religion on offer, or must surrender to it, eliminating its poison in the face of

the other poison.[7] That induces the response: 'So I turn'd into a sty /
And laid me down among the swine'. Is the serpent an aspect of the
self, which induces another nauseated reaction which produces further
degradation? Or is the identification with the swine, quoting the prodigal
son (Luke 15), preferential to the ugliness of the chapel all of gold which
the serpent can make no impact upon?[8]

'In the morning glad I see / My foe outstretched beneath the tree'
indicates the pleasure that comes from not ending wrath against the
enemy who must be destroyed by the richness of the apple bright, which
is designed to cause envy. There is a pleasure in the destructive forces of
capitalist competition – which constitutes some people as natural enemies
and produces the apple bright. 'Christian Forbearance' implies the
history of envy, *ressentiment*, productive of revenge, Nietzsche's theme in
The Genealogy of Morals. *Ressentiment* comes from the spirit of capitalist
competition which enables the subject to feel glad in inducing envy, so
it produces capitalist competition in its turn.[9] More could be said on the
anger in 'A Poison Tree' which is also called 'wrath' (and linked with
another Blakean word implying loss of control, 'rage'). In 'A Poison Tree',
the foe, who cannot be taken on openly, becomes in his turn calculatedly
deceitful, like the 'I' who speaks; hence he steals into the garden, for 'he
knew that it was mine'. The *ressentiment* of the speaker produces a like
envy, a desire to cannibalize, to eat the fruit, like the worm in the bud.
Freud sees love incorporating and devouring, so abolishing the object's
separate existence, and he calls this ambivalent, hardly to be distinguished from hatred.[10] That relates back to the friend/foe antithesis of
the beginning, perhaps showing that the division is unsustainable. The
sexual implications of the devouring, since it seems two males are
involved, are suggestive, though the poem also implies that a woman is
seducing the man, for the 'apple bright', not said to be poisonous,
tempts like the rose's 'bed of crimson joy'; and since the foe who steals
partakes of Eve's character, original fruit-taker, the foe is feminized.

The three texts develop the fragment of a narrative, working through
the rose and the worm which destroys, the apple, and the foe who
would lay waste and who is destroyed, the chapel all of gold and the
serpent. The first speaker is fascinated, appalled. The second is fascinated
by his foe (the condition of hatred) and by himself. The third becomes
revolted by what he has seen. Set by Leverkühn, the songs bring Blake's
lyrics into the awarenesses of male sexuality associated with modernism:
they make problematic what they also reveal, the power of male paranoid fears, which in the twentieth century appeared, as *Doctor Faustus*
shows, in the politics of fascism.

That these are night poems becomes more significant when Leverkühn reverts to Blake:

and had set to music a very strange poem by this author he so loved: 'Silent Silent Night', with its four stanzas, each of three lines ending on one rhyme, the last of which reads, curiously enough:

> But an honest joy
> Does itself destroy
> For a harlot coy.

The composer had provided these elusively scandalous verses with very simple harmonies, which in comparison to the musical language of the whole seemed more ragged, more eerie and 'false' than the most audacious dissonances, and which in fact allowed the triad to come to monstrous fruition. 'Silent Silent Night' is for piano and voice, whereas Adrian provided two hymns by Keats (the eight stanzas of 'Ode to a Nightingale' and the shorter 'Ode on Melancholy') with an accompaniment by string quartet – to be sure, leaving far behind, and below, any traditional meaning of the term 'accompaniment'. For in fact this consisted of an extremely ingenious form of variation, in which not a single note by the voice or the four instruments did not belong to the theme. Holding sway here, without interrruption, is the tightest linkage of the voices, so that it is not a relationship between melody and accompaniment, but in the strictest sense between constantly alternating principal and secondary parts (279).

'Silent Silent Night' comes from Blake's 1793 Notebook (E. 471, K. 168). Adrian also sets, in addition to Blake and Keats's two night poems, Klopstock's 'The Festival of Spring' (*Die Frühlingsfeyer*), a text whose 'spirit of humble glorification' (290) relates to the Romanticism which Adrian plays with, since he allows no dominance by the voice (expression of personal subjectivity) over the accompaniment. In contrast to Blake and Keats, Friedrich Gottlieb Klopstock (1724–1803), the 'high-soaring poet' (287), is the poet 'expressing and arousing enthusiastic reverence'. Mann and his Nietzschean composer read Blake as the opposite of Klopstock; hence, in this 'elusively scandalous' Blake poem, first in the set of 'Romantic' texts which are set by Adrian, the scandal is in the rhyme words, apparently confirming universal harmony while subverting it.

Silent Silent Night
Quench the holy light
Of thy torches bright

For possessd of Day
Thousand spirits stray
That sweet joys betray

Why should joys be sweet
Used with deceit
Nor with sorrows meet

But an honest joy
Does itself destroy
For a harlot coy

(E. 471, K. 168)

In an androcentric universe, everything rhymes, and 'torches' (stars) illumine the human. But this is rejected by behaviour which knows nothing of such fittingness, and subverts the idea of language as a structure adequately representing reality. Night, though silent, is active as 'quench' suggests. The first stanza simultaneously asks that night surrenders its power to attract, and evokes a deeper attraction, in a night without stars. The thousand spirits stray, betraying what they possess, the day, and sweet joys. Yet sweet joys also betray, actively, and they work with deceit and with sorrow, contrary to the last verse's 'honest joy', and the syntax allows those joys to be of the night, indeed to be the reason for the demand that is made of the night in the first verse. But the honest joy associated with the day destroys both day *and* joy in favour of the nighttime harlot. Night's joys, which may involve a thousand forms of straying, are plural, perhaps because associated with deceit and sorrow. If the question is asked why joys should be sweet when practised deceitfully, and why they should not meet with sorrow, no answer can be found because the sweet joys marked by deceit, and the honest joys coincide. There is an undoing of any idea that words can be 'honest' – representational, adequate to describe reality – when honesty's tendency is to destroy itself, by tending towards a 'harlot coy' which may also be a name for night. 'Coy' links night with the feminine, as an instance of literature siding with 'evil'. To the enlightenment rationalism of the third verse, which depends for its existence on an ideology of what is natural, nothing can be said except that sexuality shows such rationalism as ideological, and the poem shows in its breakdown of syntax, which accords with the word 'silent', erasing language, that there is nothing to defend itself against the totality of night's infection.

Night and day

There are further 'night' poems in the lyric poetry, some from the Notebook, and revised for *Songs of Experience*. Poem moves into poem, as with the poem preceding 'Silent Silent Night', 'Infant Sorrow' (E. 28, K. 166), whose title recalls 'Infant Joy' from *Songs of Innocence* (E. 16, K. 118), just as 'piping' in it recalls 'Introduction' to *Songs of Innocence*. The first two verses, which became the poem in *Songs of Experience* (E. 28, K. 217), contain material also in 'A Poison Tree'. Much other material remained unused finally. The first six stanzas are printed by Keynes (E. 28, 797, K. 166–7, 889–90), and I have given them plus his draft versions (K. 166–7):

My mother groand! my father wept.
Into the dangerous world I leapt:
Helpless, naked, piping loud,
Like a fiend hid in a cloud.   4

Struggling in my fathers hands
Striving against my swadling bands,
Bound & weary, I thought best
To sulk upon my mother's breast.   8

When I saw that rage was vain,
And to sulk would nothing gain,
[I began to so – *del.*] [Seeking many an artful wile – *del.*]
Turning many a trick & wile,
I began to sooth & smile.   12

And I [grew – *del.*] smil'd [*del.*] sooth'd day after day
Till upon the ground I stray;
And I [grew – *del.*] smil'd night after night,
Seeking only for delight.   16

[But upon the nettly ground
No delight was to be found – *del*.]
And I saw before me shine
Clusters of the wand'ring vine
[And beyond a mirtle tree – *del*.]
And many a lovely flower & tree
Stretch'd [its – *del*.] their blossoms out to me.   20

[But a – *del*.] [But many a Priest – *del*.]
My father then with holy look,
In [their – *del*.] his hands a holy book,
Pronounced curses on [his – *del*.] my head
[Who the fruit or blossoms shed – *del*.]
And bound me in a mirtle shade.   24

Phillips, 51, follows with these verses, given with Keynes's drafts:

[I beheld the Priests by night;
They embrac'd [my mirtle – *del*.] the blossoms bright:
I beheld the Priests by day;
[Where beneath my – *del*.]
Underneath the vines [he – *del*] they lay. – *del*.]   28

Like [a – *del*.] to serpents in the night,
They [*altered to* He] embrac'd [my mirtle – *del*.] the blossoms bright
Like [a – *del*.] to [serpents in the – *del*.] holy men by day
Underneath [my – *del*.] the vines [he – *del*.] they lay.   32

Keynes follows a suggestion Max Plowman made in 1926, putting the four-stanza poem, which became the separate poem 'in a mirtle shade' (E. 798, K. 169) – the first two lines deleted – after his line 24. (This existed also as a separate fragment, 'To my Mirtle' (E. 496, 852, K. 176).) Leaving out the two stanzas quoted above, which Phillips retains, Keynes's four stanzas, completing a ten-stanza poem, are with variants:

[To a lovely mirtle bound
Blossoms show'ring all around – *del*.]

O how sick & weary I
Underneath my mirtle lie,
Like to dung upon the ground
Underneath my mirtle bound.

Why should I be bound to thee,
O my lovely mirtle tree?
Love, free love, cannot be bound
To any tree that grows on ground.

Oft my mirtle sigh'd in vain
To behold my heavy chain
Oft [the priest beheld – *del*.] my father saw us sigh
And laugh'd at our simplicity.

So I smote them & [his – *del*.] their gore
Stain'd the roots my mirtle bore;
But the time of youth is fled,
And grey hairs are on my head.

Erdman (E. 798) and Stephenson (S. 151) see the whole as a cyclic poem, like 'The Mental Traveller', which would build the concept of repetition into this sense of night, but it seems there are different narratives, one, and more than one, poem. In the draft, line 8 'sulk' – aggression biding its time, as with 'A Poison Tree' – is also 'suck'. Smiling (line 12) suggests *Hamlet* (1.5. 108), while line 13 makes the speaker the poison tree with the deleted 'And I [grew – *del*.]'. 'Grew' appears in line 16, while line 14 suggests a tree spreading all over the ground like the upas. This, part of eighteenth-century Orientalist constructions of Java, was 'described' in the *London Magazine* of 1783 as a fabulous, nightmarish poison tree which would kill anything within fifteen miles.[11] The passage shows rage as powerless, as 'A Poison Tree' represses anger in favour of wiles. The 'shade' of line 24 intertwines the night, and the danger of being held within the killing darkness of the poison tree, while, through its links with the ghostly, it gives the sense of an early appearance of the spectrous: being under the tree is under the spectre's power. Night associates with attraction to 'the blossoms bright' – like the worm attracted at night to the bed of crimson joy. Brightness and colour are indiscernible at night, as the apple in 'The Poison Tree' does not shine by night; the attraction of these things becomes more perverse, more a mark of an attraction working which is heterogeneous, and non-rational because non-visual.

(Hence, earlier, the emphasis on quenching the light.) The 'serpents in the night' evoke 'The Sick Rose' and Genesis.

The poem, going from birth to grey hairs, includes marriage, if that is meant by the evergreen mirtle. It associates with Venus; in *Aeneid* 6, 442–4, in the 'Mourning Fields' of the underworld, those 'whom stern love has consumed with cruel wasting are hidden in walks withdrawn, embowered in a myrtle grove'.[12] Cowper writes of those 'who sell their laurel for a myrtle wreath' (*The Task* 2.229). But the myrtle, hiding Venus and solitary lovers, punning on 'mortal', perhaps the 'mortal part' of 'To Tirzah' (E. 30, K. 220), associates with nettles, vines, blossoms, 'and many a lovely flower & tree'. If the 'I' has become a tree, he is bound by other trees; as priests also are trees choking the blossoms, with branches as serpents, the serpents under the trees as roots. Text and tree are labyrinthine, places to be lost in, like night thoughts. There is a cumulative loss of energy, beginning in the withdrawal of the self (which is its constitution) in sulking. The last line anticipates the Notebook's 'Earth's Answer', which appears without the *Songs of Experience* 'Introduction':

> Earth rais'd up her head,
> From the darkness dread & drear.
> Her [eyes fled – *del.*] [orbs dead – *del.*] light fled:
> Stony dread!
> And her locks cover'd with grey despair.
>
> (E. 18, K. 168, 210)

(One draft reading makes Earth a dead planet; her grey hair suggests the ashes that Job put on his head.) The labyrinthine mirtle shade induces two poems, plural narratives (like *The Four Zoas*), the first with a priest, or priests, or the father, whose killing is the result of jealousy of what this figure or figures are doing. In the second, the complaint to the tree 'Why should I be bound to thee?' branches into words suggestive of 'Earth's Answer': 'Love free love cannot be bound / To any tree that grows on ground'. The words 'heavy chain' recur: the change of gender from one poem to the other while retaining the language further pluralizes narrative. The mirtle sighs and the priest laughs at the simplicity of the two, producing his death, the point at which the poems nearly coincide, with priests or singular father killed. The death of the father – weeping, binding (twice over) and cursing as though anticipating this – ends the narrative as single, and Oedipally constructed, but the death of the patriarchy ends the self constituted by the patriarchal structure.

Strains of 'Infant Sorrow' and of 'A Poison Tree' appear in *Songs of Experience*: 'The Angel':

> I Dreamt a Dream! what can it mean?
> And that I was a maiden Queen:
> Guarded by an Angel mild:
> Witless woe, was ne'er beguil'd!
>
> And I wept both night and day
> And he wip'd my tears away
> And I wept both day and night
> And hid from him my hearts delight
>
> So he took his wings and fled:
> Then the morn blush'd rosy red:
> I dried my tears & armed my fears,
> With ten thousand shields and spears.
>
> Soon my Angel came again;
> I was arm'd, he came in vain:
> [But – *del.*] For the time of youth was fled
> And grey hairs were on my head.
>
> (E. 24, K. 182, 213–14)

The subject's dream multiplies identity, perhaps changing gender. It is a fantasy of being a specially favoured single female identity, a Queen Elizabeth, sedulously guarded. 'Witless woe, was neer beguiled' implies that woe that the subject cannot know (i.e. sexuality) never tricked it; but the weeping implies guile. In the first two lines of the second stanza, 'day' seems a moment of openness, in comparison to the night, so the angel wipes the tears away, but the second half of the second stanza leads from day to night – the time of attraction for the subject – and to repression of 'heart's delight' so that the angel goes, leaving the speaker to fend for herself with armour that resists a response by the angel. Identification with night means that dawn blushes, but 'rosy red' recalls the staining of the myrtle's roots: it is a sexuality that induces fear (is there a gender-change here for the speaker?), and the angel (not separate from the dawn) comes in vain because the subject has lost energy and has arrived at despair, and is also armed against him.

The speaker leaves open the question whether this can be read critically or whether the egotism and repression of the 'I' have gone so far that the dream has no effect. In 'A Dream' (*Songs of Innocence*, or, in three copies,

Songs of Experience), the speaker is at the centre. After hearing the emmet, he says, 'pitying, I dropt a tear'. This prompts the glowworm (which contrasts with the 'invisible worm') to illumine the emmet 'while the beetle goes his round' (E. 16, K. 111–12); in the language of Collins's 'Ode to Evening': 'the beetle winds / His small but sullen horn'. The slightly comical officiousness of the glowworm, 'the watchman of the night', with his 'ineffectual fire' (*Hamlet* 1.5. 89–90) appears in 'I am set to light the ground' (E. 16, K. 112), and pairs with the beetle, enabling a gentle pun on 'beadle', like the beadles of 'Holy Thursday' (*Songs of Innocence* E. 13, K. 121); The 'dream' 'weaves a shade' like a text, like a Blakean poem; it alters the speaker's mood and changes the situation. But in 'The Angel', the spontaneous tear which evokes help is replaced by an attitude that fears the self; a melancholic response echoed by the melancholia of these grey hairs.

Death

Associations pluralize, making each lyric, fragmented or not, part of a larger text, neither whole nor singular, which cannot be accessed. No single reading can make sense of 'The Sick Rose'. If the rose is the woman, is the worm – mocking phallic male sexuality, as in Marvell's 'To his Coy Mistress' – despoiling a virginal state in the bed of crimson joy? But that bed already implies a sexual state. The poem disallows a distinction between the virginal and the sexual, unless the 'rose' symbolizes a love relationship, in which case the worm's love represents a third thing. Events in the lyrics follow certain repeated shapes, often seen in similar word-clusters. 'Silent Silent Night' ends with joy/destroy/coy, associating it with 'The Sick Rose' (joy/destroy: the reader holds 'coy' unconsciously in mind), and another Notebook poem, 'Eternity', which plays on night and death, and day:

> He who binds to himself [to – *del.*] a joy
> Does the winged life destroy
> But he who [just – *del.*] kisses the joy as it flies
> Lives in [an eternal – *del.*] eternity's sun rise.
>
> (E. 470, K. 179)

'Silent Silent Night' compares with the draft of 'My Pretty Rose-Tree' (E. 25, K. 215, draft K. 161):

A flower was offerd to me;
Such a flower as May never bore.
But I said I've a Pretty Rose-tree:
And I passed the sweet flower o'er.

Then I went to my Pretty Rose-tree;
[In the silent of the night – *del.*]
To tend her by day and by night.
But my Rose [was turned away from me – *del.*]
[was fill'd – *del.*] turnd away with jealousy:
And her thorns were my only delight.

The flower offered (on a page with three flower poems) seems not just another woman because she is outside comparison, but something else, as exceptional, perhaps, as the tyger is. The deleted phrase in 'My Pretty Rose-Tree', 'the silent of the night' links with two other Notebook poems, both drawing on *The Sick Rose*'s word, 'invisible'. The first succeeds 'My Pretty Rose-Tree' in the Notebook:

[Never [seek – *del*] pain to tell thy love
Love that never told can be;
For the gentle wind does move
Silently, invisibly – *del.*]

I told my love, I told my love,
I told her all my heart,
Trembling, cold, in ghastly fears –
Ah she doth depart.

Soon as she was gone from me
A traveller came by
Silently, invisibly –
[He took her with a sigh – *del.*]
O was no deny.

(E. 467, K. 161)

The 'silence' also compares with the poem interrogating patriarchy, 'To Nobodaddy' (that term of the Notebooks):

Why art thou silent & invisible
[Man – *del.*] Father of Jealousy
Why dost thou hide thyself in clouds
From every searching Eye

Why darkness & obscurity
In all thy words & laws
That none dare eat the fruit but from
The wily serpents jaws
Or is it because Secresy
gains [feminine – *del.*] females loud applause

(E. 471, K. 171)

Silence and invisibility intersect with the 'Silent Silent Night', while 'darkness' makes this a night-poem. Secrecy is, summing up these qualities, in 'The Sick Rose', what destroys; though the night here is not silent, because of the 'howling storm', implying the madness of the damned.[13]

In 'Never pain to tell thy love', the lover believes in secrecy, 'For the gentle wind doth move / Silently, invisibly'. He fears uncertainty, but those second two lines indicate that the wind teaches the need for secrecy. The second stanza is upstream from this conclusion, implying the desire to stabilize, where telling tolls the death-knell. Telling 'all' entails death or despair ('trembling, cold, in ghastly fears') in a movement which fears giving the self to the power of the Other (which therefore imposes secrecy as a mode of operation) or, in the repeated telling, trying to fix or possess the other (compare 'Eternity'). It is Urizenic, love's labour's lost (title of the Shakespearian opera Adrian Leverkühn writes, *Doctor Faustus* 174–5). The second stanza shows a desire to believe that the other can be possessed in words; to love means the desire to possess. The traveller, in contrast, comes by like the wind, 'silently, invisibly', and 'O was no deny' implies that the other person is taken without protest.

In *Jerusalem*, Albion, alienated from Jerusalem, thinks of his daughters' falls:

Their secret gardens were made paths to the traveller:
I knew not of their secret loves with those I hated most,
Nor that their every thought was Sin & secret appetite
Hyle sees in fear, he howls in fury over them, Hand sees
In jealous fear: in stern accusation with cruel stripes
He drives them thro' the Streets of Babylon...

(*Jerusalem* 21.25–30, E. 166, K. 644)

This is male accusation, obsessed with the idea of something 'secret' (repeated thrice), which joins in the public accusation made by 'Hand', power of the judging selfhood. Linking the lyric with these lines implies that the male desire for possession drives the woman into a secrecy which makes her the victim of the traveller, and therefore ready to be condemned for her own 'secret appetite' (Blake's 'Jane Shore' theme). It also implies that the traveller as male operates by the same lack as the speaker: he takes the woman, possessing her. Either way, she loses.

Secrecy in 'Never pain to tell thy love' shares with 'The Sick Rose' a common matrix, when Viola (*Twelfth Night*) tells the Duke 'my father had a daughter lov'd a man/As it might be perhaps were I a woman/I should your lordship' and answers 'And what's her history?' by suggesting that women have been deprived of history:

> A blank, my lord; she never told her love,
> But let concealment like a worm i' th' bud
> Feed on her damask cheek; she pin'd in thought,
> And with a green and yellow melancholy
> She sate like Patience on a monument
> Smiling at grief.
>
> (*Twelfth Night* II. iv. 110–15)

'Damask cheek' implies a damask rose. Concealment (secrecy) is the worm in the heart of the rose; the product of secrecy in the woman is Ophelia-like pining and melancholia. Viola's 'pin'd' associates with 'the youth pined away with desire' in 'Ah! Sun-flower', the poem succeeding 'My Pretty Rose Tree' in *Songs of Experience* (perhaps, then, we may hear alongside this, 'Never seek to tell thy love', its successor in the Notebook):

> Ah, Sun-flower! weary of time,
> Who countest the steps of the Sun:
> Seeking after that sweet golden clime
> Where the travellers journey is done.
>
> Where the Youth pined away with desire,
> And the pale Virgin shrouded in snow:
> Arise from their graves and aspire,
> Where my Sun-flower wishes to go.
>
> (E. 25, K. 215)

Ophelia sings in her madness, of whoever she laments, 'White his shroud as morning snow'. Perhaps it is herself, as 'Ah! Sun-flower' might imply, so she sings 'Go to thy death-bed' (IV. vi. 190). Whiteness is her obsession, for she returns to it in this last song mourning patriarchy: 'His beard was as white as snow, / All flaxen was his poll'. Yet going to the deathbed solves nothing. In 'Ah! Sun-flower', 'golden' appears for its only time in *Experience* (only twice in *Innocence*: 'The Little Girl Found' and 'The Little Black Boy', both implying an 'other' state), but the poem may recall 'Fear no more the heat o' the sun' from *Cymbeline*, whose couplet aligned opposites in: '*Golden* lads and girls all must / As chimney-sweepers, come to *dust*' (*Cymbeline* IV. ii. 262–3).[14] Blake has many chimney sweepers, but neither the youth nor the virgin are white, being out of the sun – 'chaste as unsunn'd snow' (*Cymbeline* II. v. 13). Posthumous and spectral, they still breathe, still lack.

The words in *Twelfth Night* are quoted by Clementina in Richardson's *Sir Charles Grandison* (1753–1754) driven melancholy-mad between the demands of love, patriarchal wishes, and her Catholic opposition to Grandison's Protestantism.[15] Viola's first line evokes Blake's 'Never pain to tell thy love', the second 'The Sick Rose', and the third 'Ah! Sunflower', linking all through 'concealment': female for Viola (though, since she is concealed as a male, she may make concealment a law for males), male in 'Never pain'. The woman pines in Shakespeare, the male youth in Blake, secrecy assuming different forms in male and female.[16] In Shakespeare, 'concealment' that 'fed on her damask cheek' is the worm even without 'like a worm i' th' bud' because 'damask' brings in the rose. This gives more emphasis to the 'dark' of 'his dark secret love': a dark secret implies something obscure, enigmatic. But dark follows on from 'in the night' so that the poem suggests two forms of loss of light, two nights. The invisible worm is the one that flies in the night (the character of the night is that it has that kind of worm), and its love is dark, secret. 'Earth's Answer' implied the impossibility of the plowman ploughing in darkness, but here darkness is erotic.

'Ah! sunflower' associates 'seeking', 'pined', 'desire', 'arise', and the word it becomes, 'aspire', and, finally, 'wishes'. 'Weary' produces the anaphora of 'where', as though each line was reaching for a definition. The sunflower would want to be 'where the traveller's journey is done' – which perhaps assumes the evening, after the sun has set – and that 'where' is the place of the youth and the virgin rising; but their aspiration is either 'where my Sun-flower wishes to go', meaning that they wish to be where the sunflower wishes to be, or they aspire in the place where the sunflower is, which means that they have not gone anywhere. The place of the youth and the virgin is no place. 'My Sun-flower' wishes to go, but is rooted in its grave, out of which it rises in its heliotropism.[17] It has no place to go (the possibility of a place is implied in the language of the third line to the end of the poem). The sunflower is weary of time, which can only be measured by the day, by the steps of the sun, another traveller. In that sense the poem notes the lack of night, without which its imprisonment is more felt; indeed the poem may be satirical about the day. If it moves between the sunflower and the youth and the virgin, none of them quite at the centre, one more point of reference is implied: the poem has a speaker, apparent in the possessive 'my', and that possessiveness is another form of 'rooting' the sunflower. The words 'Ah! Sun-flower' are the slightly sentimental tones of a subject who appropriates the 'flower' and suggests another reason why the flower cannot move away from the point where it/she is fixed.

Jealousy

The word 'my' introduces a moment of possible jealousy. 'Nobodaddy' seems to go one stage further back in understanding events of which all these poems seem to be shadows. The serpent tempting Eve is 'wily'. In Blake's *Paradise Lost* illustrations, Eve takes the fruit, which like the poison that the serpent vomits out, comes from his jaws; he coils round her body as though she were the (myrtle) tree. In Michelangelo's Sistine Chapel fresco, a female serpent coils round the tree. Here, the coiling is masculine and sexual; giving her the fruit is kissing her.[18] In the plate 'Raphael Warns Adam and Eve' the serpent was seen coiled round the tree, binding it, like the Priest embracing the blossoms. There is a comparison with Los's vision in *Jerusalem*:

Reasonings like vast Serpents
Infold around my limbs, bruising my minute articulations
(*Jerusalem* 15.12, 13, E. 159, K. 635)[19]

The sexuality which 'bruises' (in the spirit of Genesis 3.19) comes from a rationalistic spirit. It seems as if, in 'Infant Sorrow', the myrtle is being enjoyed sexually, but the image in *Jerusalem* means that the expression of sexuality shows rationalism taking a sexual form, in another mode of compressing/repressing the subject, like the father's gesture which left the infant 'bound and weary'.

So in 'To Nobodaddy', these wiles, aiming themselves at the feminine (note the male/feminine antithesis in the draft), respond to 'Nobodaddy' who does not wish to be seen and hides himself. To be silent and invisible is to be the father of jealousy, like the father of 'Infant Sorrow' or 'Starry Jealousy', the 'Selfish father of men / Cruel jealous selfish fear' of 'Earth's Answer' (E. 18, K. 211). If 'my Rose turn'd away with jealousy' she has learned it from this Father, and from the subject of that poem who displays it in desiring to 'tend' the rose tree in the silent of the night (time, and mode, of possessiveness, but at the moment when possession disappears). 'Tending' produces 'turning'. The 'I' thinks possessionally (the word 'my' dominates), hence he excludes the flower, not out of sexual failure, but desiring to stabilize himself through the Other in the night: a form of jealousy over what he possesses because his possessions define him. His belief in ownership produces, as a response, the concomitant of possession: jealousy. The thorns are a form of delight because they tell him that, in his self-justification, he was right to accept suffering in refusing the Other. Possessing the Other is not just a form of control but a way of securing his single identity, for the flower which May never bore is heterogeneous, making identity something which cannot be known. The masochism of the poem, imposed by the superego, starts with the narration of the poem, which records loss, and punishment accepted.[20]

For Freud, the death instincts are 'mute'.[21] The result of Nobodaddy's silence is darkness and obscurity (in 'The Poison Tree' the foe appears 'when the night had veiled the pole'). The wily serpent of 'Nobodaddy', apparently in opposition to the God who issues words and laws, is not antithetical to him, for wiles relate to the secrecy of the poem's last line, which consorts with darkness and obscurity. Out of the silence comes loud applause. The speaker in 'A Poison Tree' may be analogous to God if not God himself (making sense of the title 'Christian Forbearance') but the poem makes the foe not the serpent or the Satanic, but the person who tries to take the fruit, object of wiles in both 'A Poison Tree' and 'To Nobodaddy'.[22] It is Eve, or Adam, or even, because of 'outstretched', Christ. The illustration shows a figure supine, head towards the viewer, arms spread out, as though taken down from crucifixion. If it is Christ, the animosity of the father to the son of 'Infant Sorrow' illuminates the Father/Son relationship in the Bible, so that the 'swaddling bands' recall those in which Mary wrapped Jesus. That fits the adoration seen in the opening flower in the illustration to 'Infant Joy' and the hint, in 'Infant Sorrow' that the child who 'thought best / To sulk upon my mother's breast' recognizes the mother as stronger than the father. It seems, however, that the sexes stand between the ambiguous identity and non-identity of Nobodaddy and the serpent, who are both masculine, though it is not clear that this gender-distinction can be maintained, since the worm of 'The Sick Rose' in one draft was female.[23]

The tree growing as a form of aggression, and as the sulky, shady self, male and female together, and mutually destructive ('Infant Sorrow') invokes another poem: in the Notebooks 'The human Image'; in *Songs of Experience* 'The Human Abstract':

Pity [*written over* Mercy] would be no more
[If there was not somebody Poor]
If we did not make somebody Poor;
And mercy no more could be
If all were as happy as we;

And mutual fear brings peace;
Till the selfish loves increase.
Then Cruelty knits a snare,
And spreads his [nets – *del.*] baits with care.

He sits down with holy fears,
And waters the ground with tears;
Then Humility takes its root
Underneath his foot.

Soon spreads the dismal shade
Of Mystery over his head;
And the Caterpiller and Fly
Feed on the Mystery.

And it bears the fruit of Deceit,
Ruddy and sweet to eat;
And the Raven his nest has made
In its thickest shade.

The Gods of the earth and sea,
Sought thro' Nature to find this Tree
But their search was all in vain:
[Till they sought in the human brain]
There grows one in the Human Brain

[They said this mystery never shall cease;
The priest [loves – *del.*] promotes war & the soldier peace.

There souls of men are bought & sold,
And [cradled – *del.*] milk fed infancy [is sold – *del.*] for gold;
And youth to slaughter houses led,
And [maidens – *del.*] beauty for a bit of bread.

(E. 27, K. 217, K. 174)[24]

An earlier version had derived 'Mercy could be no more / If we did not make somebody poor' to be what a Devil says as a curse in response to an Angel singing: 'Mercy, Pity, Peace / Is the world's release'.[25] In 'The human image' there was the spreading of nets, like Urizen's 'net of religion' (E. 82, K. 235); now, baits. One bait is the apple bright, like the bed of crimson joy. Emanating from deceit, it produces deceit, as Humility has begun as a reaction to the Cruelty whose sadism appears in its use of the 'foot'.

In 'The Human Abstract' everything seems contained in the first six lines. Stanzas two to five reprise 'A Poison Tree', naming its angry spirit Cruelty, and making the last stanza comment on what has gone before. It is almost three poems, the last stanza saying that the self-love which has motivated everything is not natural, despite Pope: 'God and Nature linked the general frame / And bade self-love and social be the same' (*Essay on Man* III. 317–18) or, in a line influencing line 6: 'Self-love but serves the virtuous mind to wake' (IV. 687). In 'A Little Boy Lost' (E. 28–9, K. 218–19), the boy is confronted by the contradictory elements of eighteenth-century ideology: this Pope, and Isaac Watts's Song XXIII 'Obedience to Parents' on those who do not honour their parents. The boy's 'Thought' – which the Priest calls 'Reason' and which is a better 'Enlightenment' – opposes such 'mystery' and his death results, in a poem which is a parable like 'The Human Abstract' for the boy's parents, who conform, like others of Albion, to the logic of priestcraft.[26]

The voice speaking as 'we' in the first few lines of 'The Human Abstract', contrasting with the boy who opens his poem, is fully-fledged, sophisticated, organized, and abstract because unnamed. Allegorical qualities are named – pity, poverty, mercy, fear, peace, selfish loves, cruelty, humility, and mystery. The catterpiller and the fly, recalling 'The Sick Rose', and the raven are the least abstract. Allegorical thinking, abstraction, and melancholia go together (note 'with care' and the 'tears' that are wept); the figure in the illustration is Urizen, holding and held by ropes that keep him at the tree's foot in the mire (or dung, remembering 'To a lovely mirtle bound'). The figure gets nowhere, just as in 'The Human Abstract' the figure of Cruelty gets nowhere, except that the result of the tree – never called such, abstract again – is there in potential as the fruit of Deceit, as though it is the tree to drive people out of Paradise. But if the rationale for creating the Fall appears in the first few lines, such a fall has long since occurred in the speaker himself, in a desire either to create inequality which is then rationalized by the sense that this will enable Pity and Mercy, or in a fear that Pity and Mercy will be 'no more' unless a system is found enabling professional benevolence. Pity and Mercy are both feared and sought after, as only obtainable after cruelty. Philanthropy proves its aggressive nature; relying upon annihilating the other to prove its own complete being. 'Pity divides the soul' (*Urizen* 14.53, E. 77, K. 230) because it is a mode of declaring separateness from the Other.

The prompting behind being 'Nobodaddy' is the desire for individuation, including gender-individuation: hence the hiding the 'self' in clouds and the Hamlet-like emphasis on obscurity in words and laws. None dare eat the fruit because it is identified as his: 'he knew that it was mine'; 'my garden'. As much possessive individualism is here as is in 'My pretty Rose-Tree' – so eating must become transgressive.[27]

'The Clod & the Pebble'

Following 'Never pain to tell thy love' comes 'The Clod & the Pebble' draft (E. 793, E. 19, K. 162, K. 211). As 'deceit to secresy confin'd ... forges fetters for the mind' (E. 472, K. 175), so secrecy – male or female, for this poem avoids gender ascriptions – is here possessive:

> Love seeketh not Itself to please,
> Nor for itself hath any care;
> But for another gives its ease,
> And builds a Heaven in Hells despair.
>
> So sang a little Clod of Clay,
> Trodden with the cattles feet:
> But a Pebble of the brook,
> Warbled out these metres meet.
>
> Love seeketh only Self to please,
> To bind another to Its delight:
> Joys in anothers loss of ease,
> And builds a Hell in Heavens despite.

The love in 'The Clod & the Pebble' is presented in the clod by saying that it seeks not itself to please; it presents itself as singular and if it denies 'itself' then that presupposes its prior singular being. The 'another' is the one which love has selected to be its other, with the implications that has of claiming to be able to speak for the other who has been singled out in a form of 'possessive individualism'. The poem presents an Augustan tension between its first and second halves as if these opposed each other but 'but' is significant, for the pebble repeats what the clod has sung, having taken that articulation 'in its infernal or diabolical sense' (*Marriage of Heaven and Hell* E. 44, K. 158), not quite reversing but parodying the clod. The pebble takes away the piety of the clod's words, challenging them by showing 'love' is attached to an ideology of individualism, which necessitates its promotion as something making sense in the context of property and the individual. A slight variation of the sense shows up its secret implications: in the same way all these poems, slight variants on each other, read each other.

For the clod, love 'builds a Heaven in Hell's despair'. It is the second, and only other use of 'despair' in *Songs of Experience*, succeeding 'Earth's Answer', where Earth's locks are covered with 'grey despair'. Earth's rebuke, recalling Oothoon in *Visions of the Daughters of Albion*, is analogous to the curse of the 'youthful harlot' in 'London' (which virtually succeeds the poem in the Notebook version) and like hers, its scope is intragenerational. The clod however, unlike Oothoon, but like the youthful harlot, offers no political way forward. Love becomes an attempt to reconcile the self to hell's despair, but the pebble, rationalistic, underwater like Newton in the colour print of 1795, annihilates this as a hope with 'And builds a Hell in Heaven's despite'.

'Despite' means the feeling of looking down, or despising something. Love builds a hell in the face of the contempt of a superior heaven or builds a hell to defy (to spite) heaven; defies its contempt, spites its despite. If love joys in another's loss of ease, heaven becomes contemptuous, but love goes on to build a hell. The clod had sung that love builds a heaven in hell's despair, making despair normative for hell, or meaning that hell despairs at love's ability to transcend it. But heaven is in virtual despair (called despite) when it sees love's ability to create a hell. The clod finishes with heaven, the pebble with hell, but the phrasing of the last lines of both implies that it is because of the other that the creation of heaven or hell takes place. But all depends on the viewpoint, and if the pebble corrects the clod, then its heaven is the pebble's hell.

Break of day

Wordsworth speaks of earth's 'diurnal course' ('A Slumber Did My Spirit Seal'): diurnality appears in *Songs of Innocence*, in 'The Ecchoing Green', 'The Chimney Sweeper', 'Cradle Song', and 'Night'. Throughout the poems discussed, the same antithesis has appeared. There is 'night and morning' and 'day and night' in 'A Poison Tree', 'Silent Night' and 'Day' in 'Silent Silent Night', 'And I sooth'd day after day...And I smil'd night after night' in 'Infant Sorrow' (E. 28, K. 166), with its variants: priests by night / priests by day; serpents in the night / holy men by day; serpents in the day underneath the vines, and serpents in the night, who 'embraced my mirtle bright'. Night and day, day and night are integral to 'The Angel' and 'My Pretty Rose-Tree'. Perhaps they are implied in 'The Clod & the Pebble'. Day and night appears in the two 'Nurse's Songs' and in 'A Little Girl Lost' where 'the curtains of the night' – perhaps seen in the illustration to 'Infant Sorrow' (*Songs of Experience*) – contrast with 'rising day'. In *Songs of Experience*, night is the deeper, only state possible for 'A Poison Tree' or 'The Sick Rose'. It is the moment antici-pated in 'My pretty Rose Tree', locking together sexual strife, jealousy, possession, and acceptance of suffering, all confirming the ego. It seems, too, the moment that cannot be escaped from. There is *no* day/night antithesis: in so many of these poems, the values of the night are trans-ferred to the day, which is night in a different form.

There seems an antithesis of night and break of day in 'Introduction' to *Songs of Experience*, set amongst 'the ancient trees'. The poem contains the yearning 'That might control / The starry pole / And fallen, fallen light renew!' The repetitions, italicized, carry over into the next stanzas:

> *O Earth O Earth return!*
> *Arise* from out the dewy grass;
> Night is worn,
> And the morn
> *Rise*s from the slumberous mass.

> *Turn away* no more:
> Why wilt thou *turn away*
> The *starry* floor
> The *watry* shore
> Is giv'n thee till the break of day.
>
> (E. 18, K. 210)

The repetitions imply that the shorter lines may be duplicating each other; that a worn night is no more than the morn, and that the starry floor (an inversion plus an impossibility, giving no floor at all) is the same as the watery shore (making the land the water, also no floor: perhaps this is why Newton is underwater). 'Starry' and 'watry' resonate, too, as in 'The Tyger', 'When the stars threw down their spears / And watered Heaven with their tears'. Geoffrey Hartman reads those lines as a periphrasis for dawn, so if dawn and tears associate, so do morning and mourning.[28] If mourning, then night-colours must be put on: night is worn. Whatever mo(u)rn arises from the slumberous mass – OED relates the noun 'mourn' to 'murmur' and 'moan' – it will not arise as 'Albion rose', for a sick rose gives no morning of Enlightenment, rather a mourning of Enlightenment. Though Earth's answer refuses the night – her protest identifying her gaoler with 'Starry Jealousy' so that if stars have been thrown down, it is by a figure akin to them – there seems a weakness observable in the plangency of the 'Introduction', to be glossed by the statement of *A Vision of the Last Judgment*: 'Creation was an act of Mercy' (E. 563, K. 614). Earth's hatred of the night may be too absolute, especially if her words are read in the light of 'Infant Sorrow'. The 'break of day' compares with 'break this heavy chain': for day to come will break the night, the chain, but will break creation, if that is the night, breaking the day, if the day is night. The 'given' comes in the interval between a worn out night and a morn that rises from the slumberous mass, as if struggling for differentiation. It is the opposite of the moment of 'Nurse's Song' in *Songs of Experience*, where the given is the moment between the sun gone down and the light fading away. Here, it is equivocal: both the starry floor (light disintegrated) and the 'wat'ry shore', recalling the 'dewy grass'. Since 'the dews of night arise' in both 'Nurse's Songs', the dew making up the 'watry shore' may also imply self-absorption, based on memory and on being absorbed in the sexual (kept, as 'Earth's Answer' implies, by jealousy), from which the self is asked, vainly, to free itself and to 'turn'. The state is 'night thoughts', the heavy chain.

It seems impossible to go further, especially when 'night is worn' is the time of 'the evening dew' – night giving way to evening, and to more fragmentation. 'Night is worn' compares with the sunflower 'weary of time'. As in 'The Ecchoing Green' 'the little ones weary / No more can be merry' so the daytime wearies or wears out the sunflower; and the night is worn out. 'Starry Jealousy' becomes feebler and may not – unlike Milton's God or Pope's Zeus – control the 'starry pole' (*Paradise Lost* 4.724, Pope's *Iliad* 8.472–3). The pole might be a form of guidance revealed at night in Shakespeare (*Hamlet* I. i. 36, 37), but not in Blake. In the other use of 'pole' in *Songs of Experience*, 'the night had veil'd the pole' ('A Poison Tree'). The pole may be the tree, whose poison the night conceals, or the starry pole, which is therefore controlled by something uncontrollable, as formless and unknowable as night which takes away distinction.[29]

If there can be no 'break of day', what is the morning of the end of 'A Poison Tree'? A fantasy of enlightenment? The morning is still under the sign of night. If the foe is outstretched, it is another example of the sense of a fall which runs through this 'Introduction'. If the foe is Adam, there is an equivalence between the weeping and calling of the lapsed soul in the 'evening' dew – when the sun has gone down, which wearied the sunflower – and 'In the morning, glad I see/My foe outstretch'd beneath the tree'. The repeated 'arise' is heard again, in 'Arise from their graves and *aspire*'. 'Fallen light' has not been renewed; everything of light lies upon the floor, shattered or 'fled'. Knowing this means seeing the impossibility of renewing, or of thinking that 'starry jealousy' can be a figure of completeness: the fall that means night is also irreversible.

3
Young and 'Weary Night'

Only by accepting the physical presence of night have we
come to accept it morally. O Night Thoughts of Young, many
is the headache you have caused me![1]

Young's *Nights* are Surrealist from one end to the other; unfor-
tunately it is a priest who is speaking, a bad priest no doubt,
but a priest nonetheless.[2]

But when everything has disappeared in the night, 'everything
has disappeared' appears. This is the *other* night. Night is this
apparition: 'everything has disappeared'. It is what we sense
when dreams replace sleep, when the dead pass into the deep
of the night, when night's deep appears in those who have
disappeared. Apparitions, phantoms and dreams are an allusion
to this empty night. It is the night of Young, where the dark
does not seem dark enough, or death ever dead enough.[3]

'Does the Eagle know what is in the pit? Or wilt thou go ask the Mole'[4]

In the nineteenth century, it required a long essay from George Eliot to
disavow Young's impact on her realism, for *Night Thoughts*, the subject
of this chapter, was immensely influential.[5] Karl Philipp Moritz (1756–
1793) in *Anton Reiser* (1785–1790) shows the Pietistic, melancholic, young
autobiographical subject letting his physical pain 'put his soul in a mood
where Young's *Night Thoughts*, which he happened to acquire at that
time, was a most welcome book – he fancied that here he recognized
all his previous ideas about the emptiness of life and the vanity of all
earthly things'. He writes that 'his complaints acquired more nobility

than ever... [when] Shakespeare supplanted even Young's *Night Thoughts'*. Shakespeare, of course, had influenced Young. Anton Reiser thinks of writing of 'a confrontation between the worlding, whose hopes end with this life, and the Christian, who has a joyous prospect of the future beyond the grave'.[6] The contrast recalls Young's ninth night, which offers Christian consolation, though contradictorily expressed in the last line's expectation: 'MIDNIGHT, *Universal* Midnight! reigns' (9.2434).

Another Pietistic work, Novalis's *Hymnen an die Nacht*, begun in 1797, comprises six pieces, the first contrasting day and night, indicated via the grave:

Away I turn to the holy, the unspeakable, the secretive Night. Down over there, far, lies the world – sunken in a deep vault – its place waste and empty.

[Abwärts wend ich mich zu der heiligen, unaussprechlichen, geheimnisvollen Nacht. Fernab liegt die Welt – in eine tiefe Gruft versenkt – wüst und einsam ist ihre Stelle.][7]

Night is associated with sorrow [Wehmut] and memory, but also with the power of the sedative – opium, and with the power of feelings that make the Light superficial. The second hymn, also prose, praises sleep, which is not only seen as accompanying Night, but felt 'in the grapes' golden flood – in almond trees' wonder oil – in poppies' brown juice' [der goldnen Flut der Trauben – in des Mandelbaums Wunderöl, und dem braunen Safte des Mohns]. Night and sleep are associated with sex, drugs, and suicide, and the values of the *poète maudit*.

The third Hymn dates from 1797, after the death of Sophie von Kühn aged seventeen. The bereaved figure stands 'at the barren mound which hid the figure of my life in its narrow, dark space' [am dürren Hügel, der in engen, dunklen Raum die Gestalt meines Leben barg] and feeling suddenly a 'twilight shiver' [ein Dämmerungsschauer] which snaps his bond to his birth, 'Light's chains' as he calls it [des Lichtes Fessel]. Night is the moment of removal from the sense of the natural. In the fourth prose section, he speaks of an impossible knowledge: of the 'final morning' when the Light will no longer frighten away the Night – in a reversal of the opening verses of Genesis. The prose is followed by a poetry desiring death.

The fifth text, written in 1799, gives a narrative of the world of the Greeks dominated by Apollo and light. This first Enlightenment, however, was unable to deal with death, and had to personify it on the tomb by a youth extinguishing the light. The narrative of Greece is succeeded by the birth of Christ, who is seen by a Greek singer coming to Palestine – a figure of Novalis – as the embodiment of the youth figured on the sarcophagus; Christ is already, then, a figure of resurrection, the fulfilment of sleep and of death. The poem, which the section becomes, prefigures life beyond the grave, to which it looks and evokes, and is followed by a last poem, the only one named, 'Longing for Death' [Sehnsucht nach dem Tode]. The tension in *Hymns to the Night* is between the Enlightenment Day and the Night, with its introspection and intuition, and its alliance of the erotic, the Dionysiac and death. The question is asked in the fourth piece, 'Doesn't all that inspires us bear the colour of the Night?' [Trägt nicht alles, was uns begesitert, die Farbe der Nacht?].

In the essay 'The Outside, the Night', in *The Space of Literature* (1955), Blanchot considers the night in two ways: one as the complement or opposite of the day, and associated, for Blanchot, with Novalis. The other night neutralizes concepts and abolishes the meaning that the writer could think of establishing, and Blanchot links Young's *Night Thoughts* with it. Here, writing 'desires the night, the first or pure night of Novalis's hymns, but discovers only the *impossibility* of the night'.[8] Hence, wakefulness, vigilance, the state of the opening of Proust, like the opening of Young. In *The Writing of the Disaster* (1980) Blanchot takes night as 'the extreme shuddering of no thoughts' – time of the abolition of what can be conceptualized.[9] 'The Outside, the Night' begins with night as 'white, sleepless night – such is the disaster: the night lacking darkness, but brightened by no light' (2). If it was dark then that would imply a break with the day, but the formlessness, the neutrality, and the sense of non-relation of this night is different. In the first night, it is possible to think of inspiration, and of the subject writing. In the second night, marked by worklessness (*désouvrement*), by what Blanchot calls 'the neuter', the subject is outside, taken away by death (66), and if he writes to avoid madness, like Kafka, he knows that writing is madness (43).

The strangeness ghosting *Night Thoughts*, more than Young knew in his social world, is of Blanchot's 'other night'. Blake told Samuel Palmer that they were one century behind the civilization that would enable them to appreciate Fuseli (*SP* 105). This was right: Fuseli, whose work relates to Young, was, like him, taken up by Surrealism; his 'Nightmare' (1782), evoking 'night thoughts'.[10] And, following Lautréamont, surrealism, as, for Breton (p. 26), 'the actual function of thought. Dictated by thought, in the absence of any control exercised by reason' responds to the wanderings of Young's thought. These wanderings are accompanied by

Blake's illustrations (1795–1797) to Young, and we will map both.[11] Here and in Chapter 4 are considered two other post-Youngian texts. One is the emblem-pictures, *For Children: The Gates of Paradise* (1793, E. 32, K. 209), revised as *For the Sexes: The Gates of Paradise* (1818, E. 259, K. 760), adding a Prologue, and after the sixteen engravings, 'The Keys to the Gates' (lines of rhyming couplets), and the 'Epilogue'. The other text is *The Four Zoas*, Blake's 'dream of nine nights', which has Young as a palimpsest since part of it was written on Blake's version of Young's manuscript.

The Grave

Graves associate with night. Blake drew tombs in Westminster Abbey for James Basire, then working for the Society of Antiquaries, while 'The House of Death' (1795) for *Paradise Lost* (11.477–93) puns in its title on the grave: Adam sees a 'lazar house' of all forms of sickness. Blind Death hovers above with darts and the scrolls of the law in his outstretched hands. Despair, with a knife, stands to the right. A literary history centred on the graveyard includes Thomas Parnell (1679–1718), manic-depressive author of 'A Night Piece on Death', James Thomson (1700–1748), and Thomas Chatterton (1752–1770).[12] The Calvinist James Hervey (1714–1758) published an essay on it amongst others in two volumes of *Meditations and Contemplations* (1746–1747), and that Blake has no distance from Hervey is apparent when he is made one of the guards of the 'Four-fold Gate / Towards Beulah' (*Jerusalem* 72.49–50, E. 227, K. 712). As part of a newer cultural revaluation of Evangelicalism, he is there with Whitfield. In *An Island in the Moon* (c. 1784), Steelyard the Lawgiver – perhaps John Flaxman (1755–1826) – sits at his table 'taking extracts from Hervey's Meditations among the tombs & Young's Night thoughts' (E. 456, K. 52). And the year 1820 saw the production of the watercolour 'Epitome of Hervey's "Meditations Among the Tombs"'.

Blair's poem *The Grave* (1743), full of reminiscences of *Hamlet*, appeared through the offices of the non-conformists Isaac Watts (1674–1748) and Philip Doddridge (1702–1751). Blake's illustrations for *The Grave* (1805) came from a commission from Robert Hartley Cromek to produce some forty for a new edition. They ended as twelve, engraved by the more fashionable Louis Schiavonetti, Cromek virtually cancelling Blake's commission.[13] With Schiavonetti, *The Grave* (1808) had for title-page design an angel descending, blowing a trumpet and reviving a skeleton. It is a design similar to the opening of *Night Thoughts* 2 (no. 38), save that here the genitals of the angel are revealed, not the case with the Young design, re-used in *The Four Zoas* (p. 109). There is nothing of the neuter in resurrection, rather, the triumph of masculinity; giving the 'appearance of libidinousness', according to *The Examiner* (*BR* 197).

The engravings follow a narrative, partly independent of Blair. The first design is 'Christ descending into the Grave' holding the keys of death and hell in either hand. Behind him is an open door; before him the grave, with flames leaping forth. It is followed by 'The Descent of Man into the Vale of Death', where all generations are entering and exploring the caverns of death, as though this was the activity of life, and as though the entrance into the grave was entrance into the mother's womb. Entering life through birth and being interred in the grave through death are equivalent. It is followed by 'Death's Door': as in *The Gates of Paradise* no. 15, and *America* plate 14 (D. 64–5), an old man enters the doorway. Below the title, another legend:

> 'Tis but a Night, a long and moonless Night,
> We make the Grave our Bed and then are gone.
>
> (762–3)

A nude male, like Michelangelo's Adam, emerges above the doorway, from a stony grave-mound (the sense of petrification is strong in the picture), the sun's rays behind him. Old man and the youth link in a composite image, the relation between the two parts remaining uncertain, as in allegory, which allows the emblem to be seen as either the victory of the day, or the triumph of the night. Old man and youth are unaware of each other; they exist in different spaces. The youth derives from *The Marriage of Heaven and Hell* plate 21 (EEV, pp. 138–9), and reappears in *America* plate 8, with arms back, as though just raising himself up, his masculinity displayed (not the case in the Blair). A skull is beside him, for as 'the morning comes, the night decays' (E. 53, K. 198). He may also inspire the revolutionary youth of plate 12 (D. pp. 57–8, 62–3).

'The Death of the Strong Wicked Man' (who is young) comes next, and 'The Death of the Good Old Man' follows. In both, the soul flies out of the window, in the latter, accompanied by two angels. The death of the old man is succeeded by 'The Soul Hovering Over the Body' as it dies, in a position like that of *Gates* no. 13, with Blair's words:

> How wishfully she looks
> On all she's leaving, now no longer here!
>
> (357–8)

'The Soul Exploring the Recesses of the Grave' follows: the body, a young man, searches for the female soul, who with a candle is entering into the cavern of the grave, where fires burn and a corpse is to be seen. A set of medieval, Gothic tombs appear in 'The Counsellor, King, Warrior, Mother and Child in the Tomb'. The final illustrations are post-apocalypse. 'The Reunion of the Soul and the Body' takes place as the flames consume the grave, as a female soul swoops down to embrace the male body; there are seven souls, all dressed, seen in 'The meeting of a Family in Heaven' and 'The Day of Judgment'.

Young and Gray

Blair's work is contemporary with Young, whose first Nights (1) 'Of Life, Death, and Immortality' (dedicated to Arthur Onslow, Speaker of the House of Commons) (2) 'On Time, Death and Friendship' (for the Earl of Wilmington, Sir Spenser Compton, Speaker and Prime Minister), and (3) 'Narcissa' (perhaps deriving from Young's step-daughter Elizabeth Temple's death, and written for the Duchess of Portland, Mary Cavendish Harley, an acquaintance of Young's wife) all appeared in 1742.[14] The husband of the real-life Narcissa, Henry Temple, who had died in 1740, may serve as the dead good man Philander, though the allegorical name is ambiguous; 'the Temple of my Theme' (2.628) is the grave. Nights (4) 'The Christian Triumph: Containing our Only Cure for the Fear of death; and Proper Sentiments of Heart on that Inestimable Blessing', dedicated to the son of the Lord Chancellor, Philip Yorke, and (5) 'The Relapse' for George Henry Lee, the Earl of Lichfield, nephew of Young's wife, followed in 1743. Night (6) 'The Infidel Reclaimed: Containing the Nature, Proof and Importance of Immortality' (1744) was directed to Henry Pelham, a Walpole appointee, Chancellor of the Exchequer. It referred to Lucia, by whom Young said later he intended his wife, who had died in 1741. Night (7) 'Being the Second Part of the Infidel Reclaimed', which includes a record of the death of Pope, was the first produced by Samuel Richardson, who shows the influence of Young, to be when his despairing rake, Sir Hargrave Pollefen, writes in *Sir Charles Grandison*:

At Twenty-eight, I am on the very brink of the grave. It appears to me as ready dug: It yawns for me: I am neither fit to die nor to live. My days are dreadful: My nights are worse: My bed is a bed of nettles, and not of down...[15]

Night (8) 'Virtue's Apology, Or, the Man of the World Answered. In Which are Considered, The Love of this Life, The Ambition and Pleasure, with the Wit and Wisdom of the World' appeared in March 1745. Night (9) 'And Last' – 'The Consolation, Containing, among other Things, I. A Moral Survey of the National Heavens, II. A Night-Address to the Deity' (1745) completes these names amongst which Young wished to be enrolled, being for the Duke of Newcastle, Thomas Pelham-Holles.

The dedicatees' names recalls how all of Edward Young's career involved looking for patronage. Ordained in 1727 and, on the death of George I the following year, a chaplain to George II, but never the bishop he wished to be, his collusion with culture opposes his work to Gray's 'Elegy in a Country Churchyard' (1751), written in his and Blair's shadow and drafted four years after the death of Gray's friend Richard West in 1742.[16] 'The Curfew tolls the Knell of parting Day' makes it a poem of mourning, perhaps for the West whose path has followed the sun. Gravestones are the chronicle of Gray's death fore-told, for he must 'fade' following the line 'Now fades the glimm'ring Landscape on the Sight' (5). 'Fade', making the landscape like writing, carries into Blake and describes disappearance many times, as in 'Nurse's Song' from *Songs of Innocence*: 'Well well go & play till the light fades away' (E. 15, K. 121).[17]

Blake, illustrating Gray, shows the poet contemplative, separate from what he sees, his back turned to the viewer.[18] He looks up to a woman with a black veil who floats towards him from above, Night, and Milton's Melancholy:

> Come, pensive Nun, devout and pure,
> Sober, steadfast and demure,
> All in a robe of darkest grain,
> Flowing with majestic train,
> And sable stole of cypress lawn
> Over thy decent shoulders drawn ...
>
> (*Il Penseroso* 31–6)[19]

Night so appears in Blake's no. 81 to *Night Thoughts* (3.11–29), where a naked woman, her hair adrift and a fetter round her ankle, is about to be covered up by a swathed figure above her, illustrating:

> Where *Sense* runs Savage, broke from *Reason's* chain,
> And sings false peace, till smother'd by the Pall.
>
> (3.25–6)

The Pall – a shroud, or veil – is Blake's night: it reappears in 'London' in verb-form.

Gray's melancholia relates to a homoeroticism leaving the subject feeling uniquely unable to speak, and relating night to sexuality and the poems to the loss of male friendship.[20] The 'despondency and madness' that Wordsworth in 'Resolution and Independence' makes endemic to poets, records anxieties that react from the rationalism of the Augustans. T.S. Eliot wrote that the idiom of the Augustans could not last, 'but so positive was the culture of that age, that for many years the ablest writer were still naturally in sympathy with it; and it crushed a number of smaller men who felt differently but did not dare to face the fact'.[21] *Night Thoughts* affirms and denies that crushing, rational culture. It addresses Lorenzo, the social man, the rationalist, the libertine, the unbeliever; perhaps Young's son Frederick, or Philip, Duke of Wharton, whose father had been a patron of Young's father. Young's lines on male friendship (2.503–618) imply knowledge of the erotic ('the Wafture of a Golden lure; / Or Fascination of a high-born Smile' (2.545–6)) as he speaks to Lorenzo, while the lines on male friendship become a *Lycidas*-like evocation of his dead friend Philander: 'Am I too warm? Too warm I cannot be, / I loved him much, but now I love him more' (2.595–6): death lifting the power of repression.

The text's difference from its social culture is in drawing Lorenzo away from the day and the social:

> *Night*, sable Goddess! from her *Ebon* throne,
> In rayless Majesty, now stretches forth
> Her leaden Scepter o'er a slumbering world:
> Silence, how dead? and Darkness, how profound?
>
> (1.18–21)

The passage recalls Chaos, and, 'with him enthroned/Sat sable-vested Night, eldest of things' (*Paradise Lost* 2.961–2), and Pope's 'She comes! she comes! the sable Throne behold / Of *Night* Primaeval and of *Chaos* old' (*Dunciad* 4.629–30). Milton's night is 'eternal', 'unoriginal' (*PL* 3.18, 10.476), and 'the wide womb of uncreated night' (2.150) makes it female, like Michelangelo's Night on the Medici tomb, which, because derived from his Leda, makes the night the mother. The telescope had shown night to be not the shadow of light (light, not the condition of darkness), but the very condition of the heavens, while Milton's adjectives may make night older than God.[22] Here Milton anticipates Blanchot's sense of night, just as with Hegel. The philosopher H.S. Harris argues (a) for the primacy of night in Hegel: 'The Absolute is the night and the light is younger than it' and (b) for its negating power over 'the distinctions that daylight reveals'. The Absolute is 'the night in which . . . all cows are black'.[23] What distinction night has is the strange non-figural power of the mother, the 'faceless figure' who for Derrida 'gives rise to all the figures by losing herself in the background of the scene like an anonymous persona. Everything comes back to her. beginning with life; everything addresses and continues itself to her. She survives on the condition of remaining at bottom'.[24]

Night Thoughts: Book 1

Night Thoughts is moved by fear of the night which is nothing, is attracted by it, and tries to recuperate it for meaning and even for optimism. It begins with lines on 'Tir'd nature's sweet Restorer, balmy *Sleep*' (1.1) which in Blake (no. 8) appears as a bent, winged, naked youth, touching with his rod the flock of sleeping sheep, while the poet, a vine above his head, stretches out awake at the foot of the page. He sees what he is separated from, having woken at one in the morning 'from short (as usual) and disturb'd Repose' (1.6) and repeating 'I wake':

> I wake, emerging from a sea of Dreams
> Tumultuous; where my wreck'd, desponding Thought
> From wave to wave of *fancy'd* Misery,
> At random drove, her helm of Reason lost;
> Tho' now restor'd, 'tis only Change of pain,
> A bitter change; severer for severe:
> The *Day* too short for my Distress! and *Night*
> Even in the *Zenith* of her dark Domain
> Is Sun-shine, to the colour of my Fate.
>
> (1.9–17)

There is no origin: disturbed sleep is displaced by change of pain. Dreams are seen as the sphere of Thought without Reason, and Thought, which is feminine ('her helm'), as inherently 'desponding'. The restoration of reason is only productive of pain. The lines, echoing Hamlet, resolve into a preference for Night, which imposes a 'pause' of Nature, which is 'prophetic of her End' (1.25): Blake (no. 10) shows a female winged figure allegorizing silence, since she has her right finger on her lips, while Thought rises from the muffled figure of Night. The muses to assist Young are '*Silence*, and *Darkness*! solemn Sisters' (1.28) – figures of absence who cannot authorize an origin.

The self is marked by self-contradictions:

> I tremble at myself, /
> And in myself am lost! At home a Stranger,
> Thought wanders up and down, surpriz'd, aghast'.

(1.80–2)

Dreams are another, consoling life:

> While o'er my limbs *Sleep*'s soft dominion spread,
> What, tho' my soul phantastic measures trod,
> O'er Fairy Fields; or mourn'd along the gloom
> Of pathless Woods; or down the craggy Steep
> Hurl'd headlong, swam with pain the mantled Pool;
> Or scal'd the Cliff; or danc'd on hollow Winds,
> With antic Shapes, wild Natives of the Brain?
> Her ceaseless Flight, tho' devious, speaks her Nature,
> Of subtler Essence than the trodden Clod;
> Active, aerial, tow'ring, unconfin'd,
> Unfetter'd with her gross Companion's fall,
> E'en silent Night proclaims my soul immortal....

(1.91–102)

Young's 'flights' are followed by a line with an Augustan qualification, 'Her ceaseless flight, tho' devious, speaks her Nature'. Blake (no. 14) shows the poet asleep over his book, while above and around are six dream episodes, celebrations of vitality, including, above his head, a naked male dream-sleeper entering the space between dead trees, which leads to another world. (The Dantean illustration for no. 311, 'Why in this thorny *Wilderness* so long' (7.778), recalls no. 14.) On the top of the cartouche formed by the inset printed poem, a figure dances with a yellow-clad woman. No. 14 is used for page 107 of *The Four Zoas*, where the poet asleep figures the 'petrific hardness' of Urizen, and the 'stony stupor' of Tharmas and Urthona, which is also called 'a living death' (107, 8.449, 467, 481, E. 382–3, K. 352–3) – an intensification of Young's sense. For Young, dreams' wildness and madness (note 'antic' and 'ceaseless') appears in the verbs of motion, which Blake's art reproduces. They mark the figures of *The Four Zoas*.

A comparison appears with *The Gates of Paradise*, which is part of the 'school of morbid contemplation, dominated by Young, Blair and Hervey ... [where it] continued to be seen as the condition of mind inherited from the Fall and manifested as a kind of spiritual starvation or even demonic possession'.[25] Blake's revised title, *For the Sexes: The Gates of Paradise*, foregrounds sexuality, a word OED credits to Cowper in 1800 (for the sexing of plants), and reads life in relation to what it calls 'the Sexual strife'. This runs through Blake's night thoughts much more than in Blair or Young. In Young, discussing friendship, 'True Love strikes root in *Reason*; Passion's Foe' (2.524). Blake illustrates male friendship with images of male pairs: runners, angels clasping hands, the Good Samaritan in no. 68 (used in *The Four Zoas* p. 129), two Bacchic figures touching glasses in no. 69, and two Urizens embracing (nos 66–70). Passions, which may take the form of wrestling with heaven, are sexualized in Blake in the male wrestling of no. 45, of Jacob and the angel (Young 4.627–8, *The Four Zoas* p. 137) but not in Young, despite the homosociality. 'Passion is Reason' (4.640) and passion appears in the line following Young's tribute to Pope:

> *Man* too he sung: *Immortal* man I sing;
> Oft bursts my song beyond the bonds of life
>
> (1.452–3)

Blake's no. 34, used in *The Four Zoas* no. 91, shows the poet Young, indeed young, in a white gown, reading on the grass, his left ankle chained with a manacle, wrapped in briar vines with leaves. There are tiny fairy women on and around him of whom he is unaware, and above the cartouche is a lark. Young confesses that he reads, rather than writes: 'I roll their Raptures but not catch their flame' (1.447). Reading, as a melancholic act, escapes from passion, ignoring the 'emanations' which Blake inserts. The soul, who was reading, oblivious to the female fairy, when leaping up with its harp, finds it is chained at the ankle, or solitary.[26]

Young speaks of 'a golden net of Providence' (9.1430) which, as Blake illustrates (no. 488) shows two disciples, one on either side of the cartouche, in a boat, catching souls like fish in the net: Christ is above the cartouche. Young's phrase which recalls the 'Golden Lure' (2.545) echoes in 'How sweet I roam'd' (*Poetical Sketches* E. 412, K. 6), and appears as the title of a poem 'The Golden Net' (E. 483, K. 424) which asks for morning to arise to free the subject from entrapment in the net, comprising 'burning Fires' and 'ungratified desires'. In the same Pickering manuscript, 'The Crystal Cabinet', 'the Maiden', like the Prince of Love, catches the 'I', and he says 'put me into her Cabinet' with its golden key. The attempt to break out when another maiden, like the former, is seen in the cabinet, reduces the subject to a 'weeping babe' again in the wild (E. 488, K. 429), associating melancholia, again, with sexuality.

The Frontispiece of the *Gates* shows a relation to Young: the child is a chrysalis on a leaf, a caterpillar on another leaf, while in no. 6, a winged child breaks out of a shell. This design recurs in Blake's *Night Thoughts* no. 13, illustrating '*Helpless* Immortal! Insect *infinite*' (1.79) – a line which sums up something of the *Gates* – by showing a child with butterfly wings breaking out of an egg-like sphere. Above the cartouche lies a dead 'frail child of dust', like the dead child in the illustration to 'Holy Thursday' (*Songs of Experience*). Coming out of death, and life as death, evokes the tomb in Young, which Blake illustrates (no. 15) by showing 'a rather epicene person, decently clad'[27] praying over an open grave:

> Strong Death alone can heave the massy Bar,
> This gross impediment of Clay remove,
> And make us Embryos of Existence free.
> From *real* life, but little more remote
> Is *He*, not yet a candidate for Light,
> The *future* Embryo, slumbering in his Sire.
> Embryos we must be, till we burst the Shell,
> Yon ambient, azure shell, and spring to Life . . .
>
> (1.127–32)

Blake's no. 16 illustrates this with a broken eggshell and a female spirit with flowing hair, arms upraised, rising into the air free from it. Above the cartouche, a cocoon sleeps under an oakleaf. The grave of no. 15 has become the eggshell. Arising as the female spirit, in relation to the figure kneeling before 'strong death' (death as castration), gives a gender-contrast. Is Death the 'Sire', in which case the birth is a parthenogenesis?

Young's non-sexualism relates to a conservatism aligning Fancy with the deceptions of daytime dreams:

> How was my Heart encrusted by the World?
> O how self-fetter'd was my groveling soul?
> How, like a Worm, was I wrapt round and round
> In silken thought, which *reptile* Fancy spun
> Till darken'd Reason lay quite clouded o'er
> With soft conceit of endless Comfort *here*
> Nor yet put forth her Wings to reach the skies?

> Night-visions may befriend (as sung above)
> Our waking Dreams are fatal: how I dreamt
> Of things Impossible? (could Sleep do more?)
> Of joys perpetual in perpetual Change?
> Of stable pleasures in the Storms of life?
> How richly were my noon-tide Trances hung
> With gorgeous Tapestries of pictur'd joys?
> Joy behind joy, in endless Perspective?
> Till at Death's Toll, whose restless Iron tongue
> Calls daily for his Millions at a meal,
> Starting I woke, and found myself undone?
>
>   (1.155–73)

In Blake's no. 17, evoking the opening lines of this, an aged human-torsoed green caterpillar, Reason, with a long beard and a bald head looks at himself in a mirror held by his left hand; there is no reflection in it, however. He is in a sphere which is surrounded by a chain, and the chain appears on the other side of the cartouche, linked to another sphere. Above, and to the left of the lower sphere appears another, perhaps, female figure looking on helplessly. Perhaps it is the poet, in which case Blake has introduced the sexual difference that Young represses. Blake's image shows Urizen: whereas for Young, 'darken'd *Reason* lay quite clouded o'er' because of Fancy, Blake expands 'darken'd' by showing Reason to be the agent of self-destruction, since it is looking at itself in a mirror. It cannot see that it is held by a chain which fetters it. Reason is made reptilian and Fancy aligns with the female figure of the poet.

   In no. 18, used later in *Four Zoas* plate 53, illustrating the last lines of the quotation, the sleeper wakes in fear to be aware of Death, as a Urizenic figure with a white beard and with a bell in his left hand and a dart in his right. Death becomes a form of rationalism, oppressive of the self. (Blake's bell follows Young's punning on Death's 'tongue', but not the pun on 'counting', as well as 'ringing', in 'toll'.) Behind and to the side of Death are an hourglass, a pen, a lamp and an open book: perhaps the lamp indicates that Blake thought of this as another night-scene, aligning Death and Urizen.

Night Thoughts: Book 5

Book 5, 'The Relapse' – the term appears at line 279, and refers to a temporary fall from wisdom – directs attention towards the poem's contents:

...solemn *Counsels,* Images of awe,
Truths, which Eternity lets fall on Man
With double Weight, through these revolving Spheres,
This Death-deep Silence and incumbent Shade.
Thoughts, such as shall revisit your last Hour;
Visit uncall'd, and live when Life expires;
And thy dark Pencil, *Midnight!* darker still
In Melancholy dipt, embrowns the whole.

(5.72–9)

Blake's no. 166 shows a feminine, closed-eyed Eternity, a book in her lower right hand and a pencil in her left, handing the book down to the wide-awake soul lying on his bed, who is about to receive it with his left hand. The illustration shows the night, and night's spheres. Midnight and melancholia (Greek: black choler) combine, associating with 'death-deep silence' and 'shade' and the sense of darkening in the last two lines. Night as Dürer's *Melencolia* also seems relevant in no. 103, illustrating Night 3.430–2.[28] Young says of Life:

Compare it to the Moon;
Dark in herself, and Indigent; but Rich
In borrow'd Lustre from a higher Sphere.

A woman with long hair and in the posture of the figure of Melancholia looks at two spheres, the smaller bright and the larger dark. The visual image is complex: is the woman the moon? Or night? Or life? And why is the smaller sphere – which should be the moon – bright, while the larger sphere, which should be the sun, remains dark? (It is placed lower, not higher, on the page.) Young's lines imply that life is absence, and dark – night indeed – and feminine in having no identity. If Blake's illustration makes the moon to draw its light from a dark sphere, it implies that there is nothing outside the night.

Yet Young's verse is also social, as the next quotation from Book 5 indicates, for example in the near-rhyme of the third and fourth lines, where the tone veers towards Pope, though asserting the need to be separate from the 'throng' (a word repeated). The sociality of the verse is apparent in the urbanity of the reference to American Indians and their headdresses. For those who think in the night, the stars are a guide, and Blake's no. 168 for the first line of the quotation shows a man, his back turned, walking towards the starry sky:

> By *them* best lighted are the Paths of *Thought*;
> *Nights* are their *Days*, their most illumin'd Hours.
> By *Day*, the Soul o'erborne by Life's Career,
> Stunn'd by the Din, and giddy with the Glare,
> Reels far from Reason, jostled by the Throng.
> By *Day*, the Soul is passive, all her Thoughts
> Impos'd, precarious, broken ere mature.
> By *Night*, from Objects free, from Passion cool,
> Thoughts uncontroul'd, and unimpress'd, the Births
> Of pure Election, arbitrary range,
> Not to the Limits of one World confin'd;
> But from *Etherial* travels light on *Earth*,
> As Voyagers drop Anchor, for Repose.
> Let *Indians*, and the gay, like *Indians*, fond
> Of feather'd Fopperies, the Sun adore:
> *Darkness* has more Divinity for me;
> It strikes Thought inward; it drives back the Soul
> To settle on Herself, our Point supreme!
> There lies the Theatre; there sits our Judge.
> *Darkness* the Curtain drops o'er Life's dull Scene;
> 'Tis the kind Hand of Providence stretcht out
> 'Twixt Man, and Vanity; 'tis *Reason*'s reign,
> And *Virtue*'s, too; these Tutelary Shades
> Are Man's Asylum from the tainted Throng.
> Night is the good Man's *Friend*, and *Guardian* too;
> It no less rescues Virtue, than *inspires*.
>
> (5.112–38)

Night, feminine with flowing hair, holds out her right hand to support the walking traveller, in Blake's illustration (no. 169) to line 137. Stephen Cornford says that 'the aim of *Night Thoughts* is, simply and absolutely, to make us conscious'[29] – making night the moment when Lockean daytime passivity is broken and thoughts wander unlimited.

> This sacred Shade, and Solitude, what is it?
> 'Tis the felt Presence of the Deity.
> Few are the Faults we flatter when alone,
> *Vice* sinks in her Allurements, is ungilt,
> And looks like other Objects, black by Night.
> By Night an Atheist half-believes a God.
>
> (5.171–6)

'Shade' means 'darkness' and 'shadow'; 'solitude' is solitary and doubled by something uncanny, a 'Presence' which is 'felt'; noticeably the passage suspends reference to what is seen, replacing the visual with other senses.

The link between night and death comes in Night 5, which declares its subject:

> 'Th' Importance of Contemplating the Tomb,
> *Why* Men decline it, *Suicide's* foul Birth;
> The various *Kinds of Grief;* the *Faults of Age;*
> And *Death's dread Character....*
>
> (5.294–8)

It recalls Narcissa's tombstone, her 'moral Stone' (5.319). Blake's no. 178 illustrates the lines about the man who takes his 'favourite Walk / Beneath *Death's* gloomy, silent, Cypress Shades' (5.312–13), by showing a man walking past graves and being startled by one open tomb. Night the Fifth makes the grave prescribe the only cure for life as 'the Thought of Death' (5.376) – ignored in the illustration (no. 181), which shows a youth attempting to catch butterflies on a tombstone using his hat. This aspect of the design is repeated in *For the Sexes*, no. 7, 'What are these? Alas! the female Martyr, Is She also the Divine Image?' (In 1793, this was simply 'Alas'.) It shows a youth trapping a female or male joy in his cap which he uses as a net; another, female, lies dead in front of him. Hence: 'One Dies! Alas! the Living & Dead, / One is slain & one is fled'. Repeated, the 'Thought' becomes 'the Machine...that heaves us from the Dust / And rears us into Men' (5.684–6). To forget death may be 'Life's chief *End*' but the hour of death is 'the chief *Aim* in Life' (5.382) and the poem fights neglect of that, as 'O *Britain*, infamous for Suicide' (5.443) also attacks (and glamourizes) what the poem's nationalism calls 'Britannia's Shame' (5.436). In 1744, George Cheyne published *The English Malady – A Treatise of Nervous Diseases of All Kinds*, a study which said that depression was 'a Reproach *universally* thrown on this Island by Foreigners, and all our neighbours on the* Continent, *by whom* ... Spleen, Vapours, *and* Lowness of Spirits *are in Derision, call'd the* ENGLISH MALADY'.[30] Suicide is 'the Madness of the *Heart*' (5.486), while Blake's no. 186 dramatizes madness by showing a crazed Michelangelesque soul at the castle window about to plunge into 'fathomless destruction', a black moat. He is menaced by demons alternately pushing and pulling him, while the iron clasp round his ankle is the one of the 'Chains of Providence' he is bursting.

Young's text contests 'the melancholy Face of human Life' (8.175) by another melancholia attached to the night, which it accepts as making it an 'enthusiastic' (6.603) text. In contrast, the text asks Lorenzo if he has ever 'weigh'd a *Sigh*' – which Blake illustrates with an angel, reminiscent of *Melencolia I* in holding scales – in the lighter, a king, in the heavier, a sigh, again; and telling him to study 'the Philosophy of *Tears*' (5.516–17). Discussion of tears follows, centring on the death of Narcissa, declared '*Young, Gay* and *Fortunate*' (5.592). Each adjective suggests a rhetoric and yields a theme, expanded on in lessons taught for the rest of the Night. But it seems that the two forms of melancholia – one depressive, one enthusiastic – cannot be easily distinguished, for both are of the night (it would be an act of the day to separate them).

Omnipotence of thought

In Night the Sixth, the soul is associated with Imagination in being able to hear at the same moment both the beginning ('Fiat lux') and, in the trumpet call to the Last Judgement, the end of all creation. In this passage, repeating 'What *wealth*', a phrase heard in the preceding section, verbs of motion will again be noted. They give the soul the amplitude of the whole universe to explore, as a pastoral walk takes the traveller on Creation's 'outside', showing a world bound by neither time nor space:

> What *Wealth* in souls that soar, dive, range around,
> Disdaining limit, or from space or time;
> And hear at once, in thought extensive, hear
> The almighty *Fiat*, and the *Trumpet's sound*!
> Bold, on Creation's Outside walk, and view
> What was, and is, and *more* than e'er shall be;
> Commanding with omnipotence of Thought
> Creations new in Fancy's field to rise!
> Souls, that can grasp whate'er th'Almighty made,
> And wander wild thro' Things impossible!
> What *Wealth*, in *Faculties* of endless growth,
> In quenchless *Passions* violently to crave,
> In *Liberty* to chuse, in *Power* to reach,
> And in *Duration* (how thy Riches rise?)
> Duration to perpetuate – boundless Bliss?

> (6.462–75)

The soul is 'active' (1.100) and the 'omnipotence of thought' – a phrase which may be glossed by Freud on the 'oceanic feeling' and the narcissism of 'the ego's old wishes for omnipotence' – goes beyond Fancy, now seen as positive, in contrast to 1.158.[31] (Night thoughts produce contradictions.) Blake's no. 246 shows, Butlin says, 'the power of omnipotence of thought', as a lion and a horse, and a tiger, the most clearly delineated of the three animals, bow down, their muzzles to the ground, before a naked male seen frontally beneath a sky pouring down brightness. The picture, reversing 'The Tyger', points up a fantasy of complete identity possessed in the night.

Night thoughts give the 'unconfined' (1.99), and freedom ('*Freethinking*' – 7.1222), which is outside the spatial and temporal. Blake shows it (no. 332) when an angel starting up from behind the poet's head points upwards with both hands. He makes the melancholic Lorenzo, whose right elbow leans on his book (in a posture again derived from Dürer), so confining him from 'curious Travel', to turn and point upwards with his left arm, following the angel's gesture. The contrary states of the arms gives the sense of the split subject: no. 333 follows, containing the quotation below. Here, an aghast Michelangelesque Moses stands on the right, the fragmented Ten Commandments at his feet, and an armed sceptic crouching contrite to the left. The text affirms that God 'not in *Fragments* writes to Human Race' (7.1240) but the illustration belies this: night thoughts *are* fragments, and they fragment. In implicit contrast to the book, which would impose authority:

> *This, this* is *Thinking-free*, a Thought that grasps
> Beyond a Grain, and looks beyond an Hour.
> Turn up thine Eye, survey this Midnight Scene;
> What are Earth's Kingdoms, to yon boundless Orbs,
> Of human Souls, one Day, the destined Range?
> And what yon boundless Orbs, to Godlike Man?
> Those num'rous Worlds that throng the Firmament,
> And ask more Space in Heavn, can rowl at large
> In Man's capacious Thought, and still leave Room
> For ampler Orbs, for new Creations, There.
>
> (7.1242–51)

To go 'beyond a grain' may suggest going beyond a grain of sand in an hourglass; the point is that such visions, going beyond the indicators of personal time and making thought infinite, are of the 'midnight scene'.[32] 'Thinking free' is compared with 'Freethinking' which is, relatively speaking, rejected in favour of the former, just as Young uses the night to assert certainties. But this is a perverse strategy because, as with melancholy, it is not obvious that the text can impose a difference because of all the other senses of night; it becomes especially problematic that there can be any certainty when Blake fragments the divine commandments.

There are images of confinement:

> Our Freedom chain'd; quite wingless our Desire;
> In Sense dark-prison'd....
>
> (2.342–3)

> When mount we? when these shackles cast? when quit
> This Cell of the Creation? this small Nest...
>
> (6.137–8)

Blake (no. 229) illustrates the latter passage with a soul on clouds mounting to heights where Virtue sits, brought into that sphere by a crowned and winged figure of Reason (6.134–5). The confined is associated with day and with rhyming couplets.

For a last emphasis, night thoughts fasten on Time – the theme of Book 2 – and it is said that 'Time's a God' – 'to stand blank *Neuter* he disdains' (2.194, 197). The 'neuter' is what night thoughts give when suspending time, while they also question what is 'experience':

> *Time* passes like a Post: we nothing send
> But poor *Bellerophon*'s express: our Doom.
> 'Tis greatly wise to talk with our past Hours;
> And ask them, what report they bore to Heaven;
> And how they might have born more welcome News.
> Their Answers form what men *Experience* call,
> If *Wisdom*'s Friend, her best; if not, worst Foe.
> O reconcile them; kind *Experience* crys,
> 'There's nothing here, but what as nothing weighs;
> 'The more our joy, the more we know it Vain;
> 'And by Success are tutor'd to Despair'.
> Not *is* it only thus, but *must* be so:
> Who knows not this, tho' Grey, is still a Child.
> Loose then from Earth the Grasp of fond Desire,
> Weigh Anchor, and some happier Clime explore.
>
> (2.387–401)

In Blake's no. 58, adopted in page 125 of *The Four Zoas*, for the line: "'Tis greatly wise', the young man in white, seated, receives a scroll from a female Hour, who reaches as far as his knee. Another five Hours circle round him, ascending to the clouds and descending, each with a paper scroll which they are eager to show. There is no melancholia in the Hours, only in the pensive earnestness of the young man; perhaps the more so because Experience is Lockean, confined to memory, and is not, as in Blake, an intuitional state (see ME 91–2). Yet Blake's following illustration (no. 59) goes with the line from the quotation: 'Loose then from Earth'. Here is an older, bearded man, his hair 'grey' rides in a boat down a dark stream with trees behind him, pulling on a rope which is presumably attached to an anchor. Another smaller rope on the boat appears attached to a tree. The message here is conservative, but Young's following two lines 'Art thou so moor'd thou canst not disengage / Nor give thy Thoughts a ply to future Scenes?' (2.402–3) actually call for more Experience, and since the 'Thoughts' are 'Night Thoughts', they contain adventure.

At the end of Night the Eighth, Young tells his 'minute, Devoted *Page*' to go forth into the world, expecting that it will not rest 'when thou [i.e. the poem] art Dead' since it will be 'in *Stygian* Shades arraign'd / By LUCIFER, as Traitor to his Throne' (8.1295–6, 1300–1). Blake's illustration (no. 415) shows an angry Satan tearing a book with NIGHT written on it. Lucifer is of the day, not of the night: night disrupts the power of the 'Throne' he enjoys possessing. Lucifer is part of a binary system of power that night as a third force takes away, and whether or not Young sees these implications, it is part of what he gives to Blake.

The passage concludes with the power of the will, which returns him to the power of Satan:

> .... The noblest *Intellect*, a Fool without it,
> *World-Wisdom* Much has done, and More may do,
> In Arts and Sciences, in Wars and Peace;
> But Arts and Sciences, like thy Wealth, will leave thee,
> And make thee twice a Beggar at thy Death.
> *This* is the *most* Indulgence can afford,
> Thy Wisdom All can do, but – make thee Wise.
> Nor think this Censure is severe on Thee:
> Thy Master, *Satan*, I dare call a Dunce.
>
> (8.1309–17)

Blake's no. 416 shows the first temptation of Christ, positioned to the left, under a tree, while Satan kneeling at his foot, a contrast to the previous picture, looks a figure of desperation, holding up the stones – empty oyster shells – to be made bread. In this abject state, he contrasts with his earlier naked but reactive energy, which in the previous picture tears the book. It is as if Satan too knows the emptiness of 'world wisdom' but cannot move away from it; certainly, cannot embrace the night, which would be a form of wisdom. Perhaps the definition of the dunce (a Medieval Schoolman, like Duns Scotus, so, perhaps, a rationalist) is that he has no time for night thoughts: these, which escape the materiality of wealth with which Satan tempts Christ, make the poem's addressee wise. Blake shows his agreement with Young in using Christ's temptation as the choice of illustration.

The mother: *For the Sexes*

To the Accuser who is the God of This World:

> Truly my Satan thou art but a Dunce
> And dost not know the Garment from the Man
> Every Harlot was a Virgin once
> Nor canst thou ever change Kate into Nan

> Tho thou art Worshipd by the Names Divine
> Of Jesus & Jehovah: thou art still
> The Son of Morn in weary Nights decline,
> The lost Travellers Dream under the Hill

(E. 269, K. 771)

The first line of the Epilogue to *For the Sexes* shows Blake using Young almost twenty years after illustrating *Night Thoughts*; something strange in it makes it impossible to lay aside. Agreeing with Young about Satan, though being more assertive, taking the limitation further, into the sphere of gender, he asks, who is the Accuser? His double identity appears in the Prologue:

> Mutual Forgiveness of each Vice
> Such are the Gates of Paradise
> Against the Accuser's chief desire
> Who walkd among the Stones of Fire,
> Jehovahs fingers [later: Finger] Wrote the Law:

Then Wept! Then rose in Zeal & Awe,
And in the midst of Sinais heat
Hid it beneath his Mercy Seat.
[And the dead Corpse from Sinai's heat
Buried beneath his Mercy Seat. – later]
O Christians, Christians! tell me Why
You rear it on your Altars high.

The Prologue begins with words from the Notebook (c. 1818), *The Everlasting Gospel*, 'The Christian trumpets loud proclaim / Thro' all the World in Jesus' name / Mutual forgiveness of each Vice, / And oped the Gates of Paradise' ('Supplementary Passages' 2.24–7, E. 876, K. 758–9). The Accuser, walking among the stones of fire, in the sphere of an energy which he accuses – the split nature of Milton's Satan – attracts Jehovah's negative writing of the law to counter his desire. Jehovah, writing and weeping and then marked by 'Zeal & Awe', properties associated with wrath not weeping, is also split when he hides the law (first, the dead soul, overwhelmed by Sinai's heat) beneath his mercy seat. He is not split in Young who refers to Sinai 'whose Cloud-cover'd Height, / And shaken Basis own'd the present GOD' (8. 1109–10), which Blake illustrates (no. 327) with a Michelangelesque God identifiable with Moses, wielding a rod over a fallen monarch. His head, visible only, represents Egyptian forces drowned in the Red Sea. Nor is he split for the eighteenth century when, as part of the triumph of Urizenic Christianity, every church put a tablet with the Ten Commandments accusatorily on it above the altar, perpetuating Jehovah as the Accuser.

Beneath the Epilogue appears a picture of Satan with black wings, in flight, over a sleeping man, his staff by his side. Addressing 'my Satan' the subject perhaps addresses his own superego, his own accuser, the priest inside himself, since, in the words of Revelation 12.10, 'that old serpent, called the Devil and Satan' is 'the accuser of our brethren... which accused them before God day and night'. He is the 'God of this world' who has 'blinded the minds of them which believe not' (2 Corinthians 4.4). Not knowing the garment from the man – which makes him a dunce, and implies, as in Young, an inability to distinguish the superficially worldly-wise from the essential – relates to lines from 'The Keys of the Gates':

I rent the Veil where the dead dwell
When weary Man enters his Cave
He meets his Saviour in the Grave

> Some find a Female Garment there
> And some a Male, woven with care
> Lest the Sexual Garments sweet
> Should grow a devouring Winding sheet...
>
> (18–24)

Entering the cave is entering the grave. Nelson Hilton shows how Blake puns on the grave, grave (as adjective) and on graving, quoting Robert F. Gleckner: 'Blake's general symbol of experience is the grave'[33] – the sphere for night thoughts, even if 'The Grave is Heaven's Golden Gate' (E. 480, K. 442). The grave also means experience for Wordsworth, as with the end of 'The Boy of Winander' from *The Prelude* Book 5 (364–97, 1850 edn) and with the Lucy of 'She dwelt among the untrodden ways' who 'is in her grave, and oh, / The difference to me'. But Gleckner's example, in Blake's case, is Thel entering into the realm of death through the 'northern bar' (the 'massy bar' of *Night Thoughts*) and coming to her own grave plot (*The Book of Thel* 6.1, 9, E. 130, K. 130). The voice speaking from there comments on what her 'mortal part' comprises; or it speaks negatively from the standpoint of what her life will have proved to be. Christ's graveclothes were left separated (John 20: 6, 7): here, the graveclothes separate – which means they also construct – gender, which itself has on it the mark of death. Incarnation condemns the self to the 'Sexual Garments sweet', which become 'a devouring Winding sheet' (the worm is already inside: the body is the sarcophagus). Identity has nothing to do with assignment to gender: the inverse of Foucault's argument in *The History of Sexuality*, which shows a process – exacted through accusation and confession – whereby the subject is constituted as sexual in specific ways which construct identity. In *Jerusalem*, a voice consoles:

> Man in the Resurrection changes his Sexual Garments at will
> Every Harlot was once a Virgin: every Criminal an Infant Love!
>
> (*Jerusalem* 61.51–2, E. 212, K. 694)

If every Harlot was a Virgin once, every sexual state is contingent. They are both names, as Kate and Nan are generic, interchangeable names (three women affecting Blake were called Catherine Blake). Names can be changed as garments, but Satan cannot change the identity these names purport to describe. In *Jerusalem* 92.13, Los anticipates the time when 'sexes must vanish and cease to be' and he associates with their existence 'Accusations of sin' (92.15, E. 252, K. 739). For the 'Accuser' works by fixing gender and sexuality, when it is once constructed, fixed in place, becomes what is accused. If 'the Sexes sprung from Shame & Pride' ('To Tirzah', E. 30, K. 220), this points to divided emotions in the accuser which are projected, through the creation of gender, onto the gendered subject.

The first stanza makes Satan a dunce, lacking discrimination, the second, unaware of his own identity. Misnamed as Jesus or Jehovah, he is the Son of Morn (Isaiah 14.12) at the end of the 'weary' night when the Morning Star (Christ – Revelation 22.16) appears. Yet he cannot appear as this other: he is held by weary night, where 'weary', recalling 'when weary Man enters his Cave', puns with wearing garments (morning will reverse the necessity for sexual garments: identity will no longer be so measured). Night goes downhill like a weary traveller, declining like the sun. A decline is a downward slope, a place 'under the hill'. As for Gray, 'The ploughman homeward plods his weary way', so night is weary of being night, like Michelangelo's Night. Melancholic, characterized by vigilance, it has had to watch, for 'Wakefulness is anonymous. It is not that there is *my* vigilance in the night: in insomnia it is the night itself that watches.'[34] 'Weary night's decline' recalls 'Night is worn', giving the fear that there is nothing other than the anonymous *il y a*. There is the gap between night as a discrete entity and morn as another, but that gap is indeterminate and day may never come.

The 'lost Travellers dream under the Hill' endures through the night. Night thoughts mean inability to 'read' accusation critically, rather than accepting it as authoritative. The traveller is 'under' the hill which is both Sinai and its accusatory law, just as in 'Death's Door' in *America* plate 14 (whose landscape shows that the man is the traveller), and, to a lesser extent also in the Blair illustration, the grave is under the hill. He has always been lost, as he has always been dead, sleeping like the sleeping chrysalis of the *Gates* plate 1. 'The lost Traveller's dream under the hill' may name Satan as the dream-creation of the traveller, perhaps producing him in a nocturnal emission, another 'night thought'.[35] He is the dream of a traveller already lost, the false consciousness of a false consciousness. 'Lost' invites comparison with 'The Little Boy Lost' (*Songs of Innocence* E. 11, K. 120), also travelling, in a nightshirt, as if in a dream: 'The night was dark, no father was there'.[36] In weeping: 'And away the vapour flew', vapour corresponding to Satan fading in *For the Sexes*, his back concealing his hermaphroditism.

Young's Satan despised night thoughts, making himself a dunce: this text observes his limitation and that of the traveller. The accusatory power, named the God of this world called 'Jesus & Jehovah' and the

'Son of Morn', unable to give way to anything else is contained within a series indicating that there is no reality to the accuser. Yet in saying 'my Satan', the speaker is not outside Satan's reality: both part of the night, and under the power of weariness.

The initial couplet of the 'Keys', 'My Eternal Man set in Repose / The Female from his darkness rose' associates weary night with the negative power of the woman. The couplet commented on plate 1, where a woman collects mandrakes: 'I found him beneath a Tree', as if he was a windfall. The sun, the 'Eternal Man' – the implications of the phrase wait for the next chapter – has set, giving way to the female, rising as the moon in the darkness, hiding a child in her veil. She is the mother, for 'The Caterpiller on the Leaf / Reminds thee of thy Mother's Grief', and her dominance makes the male 'I' hermaphrodite. He appears against images of water disintegrated into tears (the mother's grief), made melancholic. He sits under a tree as he was found under one; trees give shade in at least five pictures here. He is prison-bound in 'Earth's Melancholy', like the mole, the creature of night thoughts; anxious in no. 4, exposed in air. In no. 5:

> Blind in Fire with shield & spear,
> Two Horn'd Reasoning, Cloven Fiction,
> In Doubt, which is Self contradiction,
> A dark Hermaphrodite I [*later*: We] stood,
> Rational Truth Root of Evil & Good.
> Round me flew the Flaming Sword
> Round her snowy Whirlwinds roard,
> Freezing her Veil the Mundane Shell.

> (5–17)

The horns do not establish masculinity, nor the javelin (re-used in no. 8). He is blind (like the mole of no. 3), caught by the ideology of single, 'Rational Truth', as an Adam and Eve (called 'We'). Around him, as the hermaphrodite, is the flaming sword (which 'turned each way', Genesis 3.24). Around the sword (which may be feminine, see 'her'), is the whirlwind's coldness, and, around that, the feminine 'veil' of matter, the Youngian and Platonic 'Mundane Shell'. No. 6 begins a new series, where the male asserts himself against the woman, and is Oedipally aggressive. In no. 9, 'I want, I want', his narcissism means that he climbs through 'nights highest noon', as though it was all open to him. Perhaps this mocks something within Young's own confidence in his 'night thoughts'. He is plunged into the sea, calling 'Help, Help!' in an engulfment like the night. In no. 11, 'Aged Ignorance', 'holy & cold', he stretches out a boy's golden wing while his shears cuts through the other. In no. 12 (Ugolino and his sons), as the revengeful spectre, he creates melancholic, cold spectrous, separated prisoners.

No. 13 starts something else – an intuition of the 'Immortal' as opposed to the 'Eternal' 'Man':

> But when once I did descry
> The Immortal Man that cannot Die,
> Thro evening shades I haste away
> To close the Labours of my Day.
> The Door of Death I open found
> And the Worm Weaving in the Ground:
> Thou'rt my Mother from the Womb,
> Wife, Sister, Daughter to the Tomb,
> Weaving to Dreams the Sexual strife
> And weeping over the Web of Life.
>
> (39–48)

The 'traveller' looks like the figure with broad-brimmed hat and staff knocking at a Gothic door opened to him by Urizen or Death in *Night Thoughts* 61 which illustrates the lines:

> Life speeds away
> From point to point, tho' seeming to stand still
> The cunning Fugitive is swift by stealth.
>
> (2.422–4)

Life is the traveller, as Death is at his door in no. 15. No. 16 returns to the mother seated amongst the roots of the trees, identified with the worm and death: 'I have said to corruption, Thou art my father: to the worm, thou art my mother, and my sister' – Job 17.14.[37] This woman in white, different from anything in Young, holds the traveller's staff: Death (female) has claimed life (male). She is writing, which like weaving is textual. Weaving – weaving dreams ('A Dream' in *Songs of Innocence*) – entraps the subject in the sexual strife, making life an imprisoning 'Web', identified with death, as nos 14 and 15 are mutually inter-changeable figures of death and life. 'The Keys' make the female the destructive principle, contrasting with the Epilogue, addressed to the Accuser, but beneath the fear of her is woman not as the night of the moon (the first night), but as the 'void profound / Of unessential

Night' (*Paradise Lost* 2.438–9) that which is outside. 'Void' is Milton's coinage (*OED* void 4a), and in Blake it is associated with Urizen, who falls into the dismal void when exploring his dens (*The Four Zoas* 71.6.147–56, E. 348, K. 315). But this is the sphere of the mother as night, as the void. Everything in 'The Keys' stands in uncanny relation to this night, her weariness and her melancholy.

4
Night Dreams: *The Four Zoas*

'The Bible of hell, in nocturnal visions collected – Vol. 1. Lambeth'[1]

To begin with the title. The first, *VALA, The Death and Judgment of the Ancient Man a Dream of Nine Nights by William Blake 1797* was crossed through, with, written above: 'The Four Zoas: The Torments of Love & Jealousy in *The Death and Judgment of* Albion *the Ancient Man'*. This was followed by the next page, 'Rest before labour' with a pencil-drawing of a male nude, and on page 3, a Biblical quotation (Ephesians 6.12), and the title, 'VALA: Night the First' with the text beneath. Below that comes a picture of a sexually provocative Vala, reclining in a posture analogous to Michelangelo's awakening Adam, which she parodies.[2] The idea of the dream, a night thought, remains as a palimpsest, while 'night' appears some hundred times, in a work called neither a book, or a prophecy; and because not engraved, remaining incomplete, non-centred renderings of thoughts whose lack of organization and incompleteness point to the melancholia in 'torments of love & jealousy'.[3] The term recalls Theotormon in *Visions of the Daughters of Albion*. *The Four Zoas* combines two things impossible to unite: narrative, which implies consistency of space and time, and night thoughts, moments in 'an awful pause' which brings narrative to an end or else makes it exfoliate irreconcilably.

Torments of love and jealousy (like energy and reason) violently change or annihilate the self, but the subject is division within 'Man' – the 'Four Mighty Ones' – Urthona, named Los, in his state of loss of Eden, Tharmas, Luvah, and Urizen. Tharmas is, in one beginning, 'Parent power, darkning in the West' (4, 4.6, E. 301, K. 264): he is father of Los. 'Dark'ning' has associations of the loss of the day, and Tharmas sinking into the sea evokes the west, the evening (the German *Abendland*), and so night and night thoughts. However many accounts of the fall appear, the concept of a fall is already apparent in the name 'Urthona', for possessing the earth as owner initiates jealousy since jealousy implies possession (in two senses of that word). Urizen's name first appears, in *Visions of the Daughters of Albion* 5.3 (E. 48, K. 192), with the qualifier, 'Father of Jealousy' (7.12, E. 50, K. 194). 'Jealous' compares with its cognate, 'zeal', as with 'In trembling zeal he siez'd his hair' (the Priest in 'A Little Boy Lost', E. 28, K. 218). Jehovah shows 'zeal' in *For the Sexes*; a text which also supplies the term: 'Self Jealous', for the man under the tree of whom the emblem says, 'Thou Waterest him with Tears': the *tear*s being *Tirzah's*, who appears in Night the Eighth.

Jealousy in Young, in the context of male friendship, is controllable:

> since Friends grow not thick on ev'ry bough,
> Nor every Friend unrotten at the core,
> First, on thy Friend, deliberate with thyself:
> Pause, ponder, sift; not eager in the Choice,
> Nor Jealous of the chosen. . . .
>
> (2.581–5)

In Blake, jealousy, implying possession, and the fear of losing that, with its feeling of identity-loss, cannot be so moved away from. 'Jealous' and 'jealousy' appear some twenty-six times in the text, the first a deleted 'jealous despair' (1.27, E. 819, K. 264). Whenever jealousy appears, as in Blake's noticing it in his patron William Hayley (who will be, Blake writes, 'no further My friend than he is compelld by circumstances... As a poet he is frightend at me & as a Painter his views & mine are opposite' (letter of 30 January 1803, E. 725, K. 819)), it seems Urizenic.

Gender splittings in the text are part of wider splittings which make it impossible to trace *The Four Zoas* through its several re-writings. I shall not attempt to follow what is now called 'the genetic text' as opposed to the 'reading text' but to read it as it currently stands, though a unified text put together chronologically in terms of actions or in terms of writing, is an impossible dream, and nothing can be made to depend on arguing for acceptance of one order of events. Night thoughts presuppose splittings within the text, which argue not for an originary psychic split, but that there can be nothing but a split state to start with.

do not Exist they are Allegories & dissimulations' (E. 563, K. 614). Allegory makes absolute, reifies, moral virtues such as Mercy, Pity, Peace, and Love. This point may apply to the 'Human form Divine' in *Innocence*, in which case it joins with another term which has also become an abstract allegorical dissimulation: Man. There is, then, a problem in the concept of the divine image but, returning to Night the First, if Urizen refuses to centre himself via the divine image then that is the emergence of madness.

Night the First shows no unity between Los and Enitharmon, who moves the dispute onto a different plane when she invokes Urizen, descending as a serpent in Blake's page 12. The First Night gives a triumph of Urizen in an invitation to social oppression and to war; he dominates by asking if Los is 'a visionary of Jesus, the soft delusion of Eternity' and contends that 'The Spectre is the Man the rest is only delusion & fancy' (12, 1.337, 341, E. 307, K. 273). The choice is, then, between two abstractions, the spectre and the divine image, the second being a dream of a unity which can only be an abstraction. And 'delusion' is a key to the text, appearing some seven times, being sexual and of the night. So we read of 'the sweet delusions of Vala' and Enitharmon's spirit is called 'O lovely/Delusion' (82, 84, 7.229–30, 306–07, E. 358, 360, K. 326, 327). Urizen, sceptical of delusion, is caught by 'the female death', a 'deadly dull delusion' (106, 8.418, E. 381, K. 352). 'Delusive' appears thirteen times, and some of its occurences will be marked (pp. 78–79).

The Night ends with Enion's lament, and Urizen's proposed division to Luvah:

> do thou alone depart
> Into thy wished Kingdom where in Majesty & Power
> We may erect a throne. deep in the North I place my lot
> Thou in the South ...
>
> (21, 1.489–92, E. 311, K. 277)

This will give Urizen his chance to remain 'in porches of the brain' (497). Luvah brings in war, which is 'energy Enslav'd' but Urizen represents 'religion, / The first author of this war ... a deciet so detestable'.

> (120, 9.152–5, E. 390, K. 361)

Night the second

Page 23, opening the Second Night, shows Albion, possessing Urizen's attributes. He has also lost the divine vision, and is 'weary', a word associated with 'weariness' and – in this text only – 'wearier and wearier' (8, 1.212, E. 304, K. 270). 'Weariness' appearing over twenty times implies the impossibility of the dawn, the deepening of night thoughts. Albion comments on Enion's voice that has sounded in his ears and which he rejects; he speaks in the first eight lines as afflicted by Luvah and tells Urizen to rule. Urizen as the 'great Work master' builds the Mundane Shell, as a new form of centring activity, in a passage implying the power of industrial control.[4] The building of the city, as a new thing, follows:

> Petrifying all the Human Imagination into rock & sand
> Groans ran along Tyburns brook and along the River of Oxford
> Among the Druid Temples. Albion groand on Tyburns brook....
> (25, 2.38–40, E. 314, K. 281)

The city is Urizen's, hence it is stone. In one way, the passage implies that the power of brick is being used to build London as the modern Babel (compare Genesis 11.3) and that the city is a crass materialization and degradation, one of whose manifestations is the spoiling of rivers: Tyburn, associated with hangings, and the Thames, which is the river of Oxford, also manifest here as Oxford street, through which the Tyburn flowed. Later in the same Night, Vala as a shadow is seen by Urizen 'among the Brick kilns compelld / To labour night & day among the fires' (31, 2.215–16, E. 320, K. 285), her lament being heard at night.[5]

Urizen also casts Luvah into the furnaces of affliction, Vala being complicit, so that male sexuality is punished by the female. Luvah's complaint against the woman, who became a scaled serpent then a Dragon, is illustrated by the extraordinary grotesque polymorphic, polysexual monsters of page 26, night-thought productions.[6] Luvah mourns his own 'delusion' to free people from 'the Human form' (27, 2.107–8, E. 318, K. 282): the illustration on page 27 showing a male and female form not fully separated from each other, while the eroticism associated with the female continues over the following pages, 32 and 35 especially. The Night closes with two songs, Enitharmon's (34, 2.343–78, E. 323–4, K. 289–90) and Enion's, speaking in bondage (35–6, 2.387–418, E. 324–5, K. 290–1) separated from Tharmas. Enitharmon suffers from 'strong vibrations of fierce jealousy' (34, 2.331, see also 338, E. 323, K. 289), considering Los her own, 'created for my will, my slave'. She joys in the death of the man 'who dies for love of her / In torments of fierce jealousy & pangs of adoration' (34, 2.349–50, E. 324, K. 289). Jealousy originates both in Urizen and in the woman; it is produced in the subject male, causing his death, but, not the less for that, it inheres in the woman too, who makes the man die of jealousy because of hers. Yet the prelapsarian tones of a world under the power of the moon cannot be ignored: Enitharmon thinks she has the power of the first night (as Blanchot would call it), as indeed she has. However, her song is 'delusive' as it must be if it ignores the other night (34, 2.379, E. 324, K. 290). In contrast, Enion begins by acknowledging her share in bringing about postlapsarian conditions, that is, city existence, but continues with the necessity of this state:

> What is the price of Experience do men buy it for a song
> Or wisdom for a dance in the street? No it is bought with the price
> Of all that a man hath his house his wife his children
> Wisdom is sold in the desolate market where none come to buy
> And in the witherd field where the farmer plows for bread in vain
> (35, 2.397–401, E. 325, K. 290)

Experience and wisdom are within the realm of the 'heterogeneous', to use the term of Georges Bataille; they fit no 'restricted economy' based on exchange, and control of what is given and what received. If, for Bataille, eroticism is 'assenting to life up to the point of death', so too experience, which cannot be had by measure or through prudentialism.[7] Enion says it is easy 'to speak the laws of prudence to the houseless wanderer' (35, 2.405, E. 325, K. 290), which shows what she thinks of it. The desire for experience, like that for innocence, is for the heterogeneous: it is not bourgeois or utilitarian.

Urizen's night

Ahania hears Enion's lamentation (one emanation responds to another), and in Night the Third is thrown out, but not before Urizen has given her warning of his fear of the rising of Orc (38, 3.14–23, E. 326, K. 292) which leads to her telling him to 'resume thy fields of Light':

> Why didst thou listen to the voice of Luvah that dread morn
> To give the immortal steeds of light to his deceitful hands
> No longer now obedient to thy will thou art compell'd
> To forge the curbs of iron & brass to build the iron mangers
> To feed them with intoxication from the wine presses of Luvah
> Till the Divine Vision & Fruition is quite obliterated

They call thy lions to the field of blood, they rowze thy tygers
Out of the halls of justice, till these dens thy wisdom framd
Golden & beautiful but O how unlike those sweet fields of bliss
Where liberty was justice & eternal science was mercy
Then O my dear lord listen to Ahania, listen to the vision
The vision of Ahania in the slumbers of Urizen
When Urizen slept in the porch & the Ancient Man was smitten
                                            (39, 3.26–43, E. 326, K. 292)

Urizen, building curbs of iron and brass for the horses, and iron mangers, has been made paranoid by fear of the future. 'Why wilt thou look upon futurity, darkning present joy' she asks (37, 3.11, cp. 3.30, E. 326, K. 291), again with that significant word 'dark'ning'. The story she tells of the past implies collusion between Urizen and Luvah, but that Luvah has tricked Urizen and that Urizen gave him the horses (50, 4.113, E. 334, K. 300), a point repeated when Tharmas says that 'foul ambition' seized Urizen, the Prince of Light, and Luvah, the Prince of Love.

Ahania tells Urizen how 'the Ancient Man' was smitten when, 'dark'ning', Vala walked with him 'in dreams of soft deluding slumber' till the Man became victim of 'A sweet entrancing self delusion, a wat'ry vision of man / Soft exulting in existence, all the Man absorbing' (40, 3.44, 45, 52–3, E. 327, K. 292–3). The delusion is considering the shadow – extension of his split self – as a God, and himself as a guilty Adam, which produces his fall and the dismissal of Luvah and Vala together, making them go off 'in jealous fears' (42, 3.96, E. 328, K. 294).

Ahania's complaint does her no good. Urizen takes over the language of the shadow by assuming that he is God, and shows how paranoia and masculinity interrelate, opposing 'night thoughts' associated with femininity. Male paranoia, also reason, must defend itself against the night and its intermittences which speak of death. Blake makes reason sexually passionate, and Urizen's paranoia is a concomitant of his reason, which is also jealousy, which is, indeed, almost a definition of reason. The drawings for this section (pp. 38–42) have startling portrayals of the phallic and the vaginal, as the return of what reason has repressed. Page 43 begins to use the proof pages for *Night Thoughts*. Here, a Urizenic figure illustrates Young's 'Death, the great Counsellor, who Man inspires' (*Night Thoughts* 3.512, G. 108). Death, reclining but wide-awake, suggests an ornamental personification above a door in classical architecture: he resembles one of the figures in Michelangelo's Medici tombs, sculptural forms visible in the rapidly building city. Young's death-figure not only counsels but rejects:

> Art thou also become like Vala. thus I cast thee out
> Shall the feminine indolent bliss. the indulgent self of weariness
> The passive idle sleep the enormous night & darkness of Death
> Set herself up to give her laws to the active masculine virtue
> (43, 3.113–16, E. 328–9, K. 295)[8]

Blake's *Night Thoughts* no. 246 ironized 'The active masculine virtue', when the tiger bowed down to the man. Failing to distinguish, Urizen sees Ahania as if like the shadow that menaced the Fallen Man, as threatening his identity, and doing so sexually:

> And thou hast risen with thy moist locks into a watry image
> Reflecting all my indolence my weakness & my death
> To weigh me down beneath the grave into non Entity ...
> (43, 3.125–7, E. 329, K. 295)

Ahania is cast out and ends the Night 'repelld on the margin of Non Entity' (46, 3.211, E. 331, K. 297), a word deriving from *Visions of the Daughters of Albion* (7.14, 15, E. 36, K. 194). Oothoon's fate resembles Ahania's: the male prefers the woman not to be and, associating all women with Vala in a hatred of 'delusion' itself problematic because of its ascetic overtones, casts her out into Non Entity (44, 3.144, 211, E. 329, K. 295). Perhaps Urizen thinks of Tharmas here, associated with water, the more so as he loses his form after his identity has come under attack from the accusation of sin.[9]

Urizen's question to Ahania puts indolence and weariness against active masculinity, but then shows his own indolence, after he says he has been wearied (line 123).[10] Weariness – the state of night thoughts – threatens because it seems feminine indolence; the male must be active and doing in a fear of feminine night thoughts, fearing to become what the woman – who also prevents the dawn – represents. Trying to dissociate his weariness from her indolence, this eventuates, later, in the aggressive gospel of work, whose militarism enforces volunteers for the army, while it makes workers an army of labour:

> Then left the Sons of Urizen the plow & harrow the loom
> The hammer & the Chisel & the rule & compasses
> They forgd the sword the Chariot of war the battle ax
> The trumpet fitted to the battle & the flute of summer
> And all the arts of life they changd into the arts of death
> The hour glass contemnd because its simple workmanship

Was as the workmanship of the plowman & the water wheel
That raises water into Cisterns broken & burnd in fire
Because its workmanship was like the workmanship of the Shepherd
And in their stead intricate wheels invented Wheel without wheel
To perplex youth in their outgoings & to bind to labours
Of day & night the myriads of Eternity. that they might file
And polish brass & iron hour after hour laborious workmanship
Kept ignorant of the use that they might spend the days of wisdom
In sorrowful drudgery to obtain a scanty pittance of bread
In ignorance to view a small portion & think that All
And call it Demonstration blind to all the simple rules of life
(92, 7b.170–86, E. 364, K. 337)[11]

The intensified militarism destroys the values of *Songs of Innocence*, whose flute and shepherd, evoked, are lost, the flute of summer (associated with the day) made as relevant to war as the trumpet. The repetitions of 'simple', 'workmanship', and 'ignorant' (implying the loss of 'art') show agrarian skills dismissed by a new technologizing, which is military / industrial together, wheel outside wheel; but with no life – no Zoas – within the wheels (Ezekiel 1.20). Workers gain no sense of the use of their labour (repeated in 'laborious workmanship', the fifth time for that substantive), when getting only the 'scanty pittance of bread'. Industrial time, urban time, demands obliteration of the distinction between 'day & night'. This homogenizing of experience threatens a state of indifference, different forms of mental existence collapsing into each other, and being neutralized, making 'night thoughts' impossible, and it comes from a fear of these, fear of being identified with indolence and delusion.

Urizen's accusations against Ahania return with the Eternal Man in Night the Ninth, when he calls up Urizen, and asks:

When shall the Man of future times become as in days of old
O weary life why sit I here & give up all my powers
To indolence to the night of death when indolence & mourning
Sit hovring over my dark threshold.
(120, 9.115–18, E. 389, K. 360)

What the Eternal Man fears is expressed in similar terms to Urizen. *The Four Zoas* ends in the morning, which is what Blake's poetry seeks, while being fascinated by the night. For Oothhon, fear of the feminine only teaches masturbation: she asks why the 'Father of Jealousy' has taught Theotormon 'this accursed thing' – masturbation being read as a triumph of rationality, the avoidance of eroticism – and masturbation as she describes it belongs to the night (*VDA* 7.6–13, E. 36, K. 194). But could Oothoon speak so negatively of masturbation if she and the text were not so complicit with the day?

Ahania is lost, like Enion, but so is Urizen, 'dash'd in pieces from his precipitant fall' (44, 3.159, E. 330, K. 296). Throwing out Ahania makes him only a shadow. Night 3 concludes by bringing about a return of Tharmas and Enion and showing their separation from each other, and mutual loss.

Night the fourth

In Night the Fourth, Tharmas speaks as alienated, a figure of emotional self-contradiction – 'Are love and rage the same passion? they are the same in me' (47, 4.18, E. 331, K. 298). Page 47 (G. 87, Young, 3.120–7) shows the poet supporting his dying daughter Narcissa, while the sun, unheeding, charioted by Apollo, races on ahead. Blake contrasts two forms of poetry, Young's and the Apollonian: feminine and masculine; these find expression in Tharmas's divided state. An alienated figure of 'dark despair' (47, 4.22, E. 331, K. 298), he asks Los to build 'a Universe of Death and Decay', the phrase deriving from *Paradise Lost* 2.622. Los, as alienated as he is, recalls that Urthona was his name but that now he is all-powerful Los, and Urthona, once 'keeper of the gates of heaven', is but his shadow (48, 4.43, E. 332, K. 298). Enitharmon resists the intrusion of Tharmas into a world associated with Urizen's architecture, and Tharmas, jealous, takes her from Los, leaving Los to 'howl', mad like Tharmas, 'become a Rage' (49, 4.81, E. 333, K. 299).

There appears the Spectre of Urthona, perhaps figured in the Laocoon-like figure enwrapped by a serpent (the power of jealous masculinity) in the illustration (plate 47, G. 49, Young, 1.314–30: the design recurs on page 77).[12] There is a moment of mutuality between him and Tharmas, who then shows his self-division, for which he blames Luvah and Urizen. In telling Los he beholds 'Eternal Death', (no. 51 shows the fatal writing on the wall at Belshazzar's feast, G. 60, Young, 2.212–30), he urges him to rebuild the furnaces. The work that begins is the binding of Urizen (53–6, 4.199–295, E. 336–8, K. 302–5).

This binding derives from *The First Book of Urizen* where Urizen is an abstraction, no other reality than a shadow, a form of darkness, which is the absence of light. The Eternals try to expel this by giving him a place in the north; Los's actions are to give a body and shape to Urizen, which marks out Urizen's 'changes' and runs through seven ages. Giving form to absence means rejecting night thoughts. Theseus in *A Midsummer Night's Dream* (5, 1.21, 22) rationalizes away the capacity of imagination – 'in the night, imagining some fear / How easy is a bush supposed a bear' – but his wife Hippolyta's succeeding line stresses the validity of 'the story of the night' that she has heard from the lovers.[13] Giving form to Urizen means rationalizing night thoughts which have no empirical existence, but which comprise, as Hippolyta would say, 'more than fancy's images'. Los's actions are therefore negative, shown in that he becomes divided, producing Enitharmon, the first female. Urizen's single identity comes from a rationalism that fears the night. As much as the disorganized – the night – is dreaded in Blake, so is the organized. The action of binding – 'He [Los] watch'd in shudd'ring fear / The dark changes, & bound every change / With rivets of iron & brass' (plate 8, 9–11, E. 81, K. 227) is like the action of the priests in 'The Garden of Love': an attempt to confine, limit, and name.

This is also the case with the binding that, following Freud in *Beyond the Pleasure Principle* (Chapter 5), the conservative 'pleasure principle' performs on mobile excitations within the body. Derrida reads that binding, which he puns on as the 'double bind', taking the term from Gregory Bateson to say that, though Freud does not notice this, binding must be dual, not singular, since the primary processes come from within and without. In Bateson the schizoid-inducing 'double bind' operates when the subject is constricted by two opposite and contrary parental demands, from which it cannot separate itself.[14] The effort to bind primary processes is the drive towards constructing a single 'proper' identity for the self, which is the death drive, where the self anticipates its proper death. It is sadistic: for Derrida it is productive of schizophrenia.[15]

In *The Four Zoas*, binding comes later in the history of Urizen than it did in *The First Book of Urizen*. Los binds Urizen, who had collapsed at the end of Night the Third, in revenge upon him, after the binding of Enitharmon, for Urizen's intrusion into the pairing of Los and Enitharmon (Night the First). But Los 'became what he beheld' in the action of binding (53, 4.203, E. 336, K. 302), an act productive of his own madness, his 'pulsative furor' (52, 57, 4.178, 182, 5.1, E. 335, 338, K. 302, 305). The one who binds is bound. Forming and being formed are alike, dangerous. Night 5 (p. 57) is illustrated by 'Death that mighty Hunter' (G. 117, Young, 4.96). Here Orc, born from Los and Enitharmon and identified also as Luvah, gives form to Los's self-division. He starts to build Golgonooza, while allowing jealousy of the 'ruddy' boy to induce self-binding:

'Grief rose upon his ruddy brow: a tightening girdle grew / Around his bosom like a bloody cord': 'the chain of Jealousy', while, in the 'torments of jealousy', Los is attended by a 'spectre dark' (60, 5.76, 83, 84, 94, 95, E. 340–1, K. 307). Orc's binding follows, and when Los repents, it is too late, for the boy has grown into his chains, and is equally the subject of jealousy (62, 63, 5.157, 161, 182, E. 342, K. 309). Page 63 (G. 44, Young, 2.107–25) shows the birth of the boy, with the Father, a classical figure, kneeling over the child measuring his length as if spanning it, his hand in the shape of the dividers in the hand of the Ancient of Days.

Urizen and melancholy

Urizen as the 'King' – like George III, mad in 1801 – hears the voice of Orc in terror, and utters his Woes:

My songs are turned into cries of Lamentation
Heard on my Mountains & deep sighs under my palace roofs,
Because the Steeds of Urizen, once swifter than the light,
Were kept back from my Lord & from his chariot of mercies.

O did I keep the horses of the day in silver pastures!
O I refus'd the lord of day the horses of his prince!
O did I close my treasuries with roofs of solid stone
And darken all my Palace walls with envyings & hate!

Objectifying himself, referring to the 'Steeds of Urizen', and dropping into the passive in the next line, these verses evoke the politics of 'London' (*Songs of Experience*) as though this was a penitential king recognizing the limits of his authority and, in the last quoted line, seeing that the Palace focuses city-passions which it arouses and which find expression on its external walls. But the questions raised, which turn on memory and on that as a memory of a stable self, repeat the textual repression that informs the language of primal unity, and therefore leave ambiguous whether he refused himself something, or refused Luvah. Night thoughts, resisting linear time, make narrative based on identity impossible. It is also apparent that he recognizes that he has no identity apart from that of the one who called him into existence from the 'deep' as an allegorical expression of light:

O Fool! to think that I could hide from his all piercing eyes
The gold & silver & costly stones, his holy workmanship!

O Fool! could I forget the light that filled my bright spheres
Was a reflection of his face who call'd me from the deep!

I well remember, for I heard the mild & holy voice
Saying, 'O light, spring up & shine', & I sprang up from the deep.
He gave to me a silver scepter, & crown'd me with a golden crown
Go forth & guide my son who wanders on the ocean.

I went not forth: I hid myself in black clouds of my wrath;
I call'd the stars around my feet in the night of councils dark;
The stars threw down their spears & fled naked away.
We fell. I siez'd thee, dark Urthona. In my left hand falling

I siez'd thee, beauteous Luvah; thou art faded like a flower
And like a lilly is thy wife Vala wither'd by winds.

The response to mildness and holiness is to have come out of the deep into black clouds, into wrath, expressed not as burning but in this night-form, and into the night of councils *dark* (my emphasis), a phrase echoing King Lear's 'darker purpose' (*King Lear* 1.35). Like Lear, Urizen dominates and centres himself (note 'around my feet'), until the stars throw down their spears, fleeing naked away, like the youth of Mark 14.52 slinking out of the night of Gethsemane. Their fall includes Urizen (so that Urizen is in 'The Tyger' – to be discussed in Chapter 6 – with the stars who threw down their spears). Associating Urizen with stars recalls the Father's name, 'Starry Jealousy' ('Earth's Answer', E. 18, K. 211), and may be visualized in no. 4 of *For the Sexes* (E. 261, K. 763) with the crouched, melancholic figure sitting 'On Cloudy Doubts & Reasoning Cares' with stars behind him. Reason, which tried to repress, fails when trying to overthrow energy, and Urizen takes with him Urthona (who is also Los), 'beauteous' Luvah, and Vala. (There is no reference to Ahania.) But 'we fell', like the Fall of Lucifer, is not an original fall because Urizen is already fallen, or because there is no state not already fallen, only a series of memories of falls, partial repetitions of an event re-created and put in the past.

Urizen laments to Luvah that he (Luvah) too has been bowed down with him, and then appears his confession, where he now says he gave the steeds that earlier he said he had not given, which Ahania said Luvah had been deceitful to get and which Vala had said Luvah had taken. In Urizen's narrative, nothing further emerges because Luvah and Urizen are the same, both taking, both denying, both figures of the day and so of light. The wine and the steeds are also equivalents, both stolen. And Luvah too is Orc (80, 7.151, E. 356, K. 324). Further, Urizen's fall is Luvah's:

Because thou gavest Urizen the wine of the Almighty
For steeds of Light that they might run in thy golden chariot of pride
I gave to thee the Steeds I pourd the stolen wine
And drunken with the immortal draught fell from my throne sublime

I will arise Explore these dens & find that deep pulsation
That shakes my cavern with strong shudders. perhaps this is the night
Of Prophecy & Luvah hath burst his way from Enitharmon
When Thought is closd in Caves. Then Love shall shew its root in
    deepest Hell.

                                              (64, 65, 5.208–41, E. 344, K. 311)

The last line shows his split state: thought is closed in caves, but he hopes that love – that deep pulsation, visualized in a dark figure of energy (65, Blake, 133, Young, 4.397) – might show its power. The night of councils dark gives way to more historically locatable material, implied already in the building of London, and to the 'night of Prophecy', which makes the Prophetic Books 'night thoughts'.

Page 67, opening Night the Sixth, shows a Gothic door, pointed to by Sense and Reason who in Young are pointing to death. Blake makes these two Eve and Adam, and so connects Urizen's 'den' – the word means a prison when it appears at the beginning of *The Pilgrim's Progress* – with death, and a church (G. 119, Young, 4.136). Urizen, 'cold demon', confronts his world: the illustration to p. 69 portrays a cold Justice (G. 151, 'Reason' in Young, 4.753). He sees dull matter and industrialized 'fiery cities' placed on a war-footing ('castles built of burning steel' [69, 6.115, E. 347, K. 314]), and workers in industrial systems, 'dishumanizd men' (6.116). He knows that 'they were his Children ruind in his ruind world' (6.130). The melancholia of loss, which makes him like Narcissa surrounded by the Ouroboros (73, G. 78, title-page for Young's Night the Third), makes him assert a 'New dominion' in a 'selfish lamentation' (6.238). Luvah's place is empty: he sees in the south the cave of Orc, where – as Prince of Light, the midday sun – he should be; in the west, his own cave; in the north, the Pole Star, Urthona's throne, 'shut up in stifling obstruction, rooted in dumb despair' (73, 6.269, E. 351, K. 318); the East (for Luvah) is void.

> But in Eternal times the Seat of Urizen is in the South
> Urthona in the North Luvah in East Tharmas in West
>
> (74, 6.279–80, E. 351, K. 319)

Urizen has desired the North, which seems to be equated with the
brain, and has offered Luvah the South (21, 1.491–7, E. 311, K. 278).
These are London's, and psychic, boundaries. Appropriately, the last
illustration for the Night (p. 75, G. 125), gives midnight veiling the
face of the sun (Young, 4.250).

The Tree of Mystery: seventh nights

In the first 'Night the Seventh' appears the Tree of Mystery (it was
pictured on page 72 and hinted at in the pose of the woman on page
68), and the spirit of Orc, who is seen as an angelic figure reaching
down (79, G. 96, Young, 3.299). Urizen becomes envious trying to
reach Orc, his envy meaning that under his heel the root shoots
upwards to produce the tree of mystery whose branches are 'intricate
labyrinths' (78, 7.35, E. 353, K. 321). The chain of jealousy, the tree of
mystery and the prison, and, if labyrinths imply city-streets, then the
city, all fuse, and this was anticipated in Enion's lament that her decep-
tiveness has brought forth 'a poison tree' (35, 2.398, E. 325, K. 290). The
labyrinth, like Blake's London, also the Tree of Mystery, is mental and
geographical, and public and private, for Tharmas, in a cancelled
passage, tells Enion 'I will build thee a Labyrinth [where we may remain
for ever alone – *del.*] also' (4, 1.28, E. 301, K. 265). Similarly, Los leads
Enitharmon 'down into the deeps & into his labyrinth' (61, 5.111, E. 341,
K. 308): places of repression (like Minos concealing the Minotaur), like
the grave, in Blake's illustration for Blair of the soul searching its
caverns. It is the space of the dream, of night thoughts. Urizen's books
derive from 'the dismal shade' of the labyrinth and the tree. He speaks
to Orc like Zeus to Prometheus; Orc shows contempt for Urizen's books
which, however, Urizen reads from, advising his daughters to use the
language of 'Moral Duty' with a view to destroy Los. Drawing out a
tendency in Young who calls Christ 'thou great *Philanthropist*' (4.604:
G. 143; the illustration appears for page 55), Urizen speaks like the
Unitarian Malthus, of the *Essay on Population* (1798).[16] His language
typifies those defining Dickens's figures of official charity or hypocrisy –
Bumble, Pecksniff, Scrooge, Mrs Pardiggle and Chadband, and
Gradgrind – those who patronize the 'little vagabond' of the *Songs of
Experience*. It is the energy of the new urban type (it was significant that

Blake dated his book from Lambeth), whose comic mode disguises the intensity of the Benthamite:

Compell the poor to live upon a Crust of bread, by soft mild arts
Smile when they frown frown when they smile & when a man looks pale
With labour & abstinence say he looks healthy & happy
And when his children sicken let them die there are enough
Born even too many & our Earth will be overrun
Without these arts If you would make the poor live with temper
With pomp give every crust of bread you give with gracious cunning
Magnify small gifts reduce the man to want a gift & then give with pomp
Say he smiles if you hear him sigh If pale say he is ruddy
Preach temperance say he is overgorgd & drowns his wit
In strong drink tho you know that bread & water are all
He can afford Flatter his wife pity his children till we can
Reduce all to our will as spaniels are taught with art
                                             (80, 7.117–29, E. 355, K. 323)

The production of this repressive, jealous, and sanctimonious economy stifles the body while producing desire, for the next lines speak of the woman as an incentive towards male 'ambitious fury': indeed, Urizen sounds like Enitharmon in *Europe*. It leads to the reduction of Orc, losing his revolutionary potential in the face of the 'Grey obscure' (80, 7.150, E. 356, K. 324) and becoming ambiguously reactionary, a serpent within the shade of the tree. It is illustrated by Young's sun plucked out of its sphere by death (81, G. 20, Young, 1.206, re-used for page 133). Los and Enitharmon are also held within this tree's penumbra. It produces the 'jealous lamentation' (81, 7a.183, E. 357, K. 324) of Los, feeling his separation from Enitharmon, illustrated by the 'vale of death' (83, G. 94, Young, 3.259).

In a section reminiscent of 'A Poison Tree', the Shadow of Enitharmon meets the Spectre of Urthona beneath the Tree of Mystery and prepares 'the poison of sweet Love' (82, 7a.219, E. 358, K. 325). In this Eden-parody, under this changed version of Milton's 'fruit / Of that forbidden tree' (*Paradise Lost* 1.1, 2) she narrates the Fall. The Eternal Man was captivated by Vala: they brought forth Urizen. But then a 'double form Vala' appears, comprising Luvah as a male form of Vala, and Vala herself, and Luvah confers with Urizen 'in darksom night' 'to bind the father & enslave the brethren' (83, 7a.255, 256, E. 358, K. 326). These conferrings of a feminized Luvah and a masculine Urizen are night thoughts. The Spectre of Urthona follows with another narrative of how 'the manhood was divided' (84, 7a.279, E. 359, K. 327), producing, so the Spectre of Urthona says, himself, born as a 'masculine spirit' from Enion's brain, and returning to Enion for the birth of Enitharmon and Los: 'Ah, jealousy and woe!' (84, 7a.295, E. 359, K. 327). A double-form Vala – male and female as both female, making Luvah not quite male – and a 'divided' manhood point to a crisis in the text in reading gender, while Urizen embodies, through part of the text, desire for a masculinity which disdains the feminine out of fear, illustrated in page 85 (G. 153), showing the disdainful and superior male.

The Spectre of Urthona and the shadow of Enitharmon converse and embrace, engendering the shadowy female, with further oppression resulting, including the rising of the Spectres of the dead, 'male forms without female counterparts, or emanations': a male without a counterpart being declared to be 'without a concentering vision' (85, 87, 7a.329, 402, E. 360, 369, K. 328, 330). Definition follows later:

> Man divided from his Emanation is a dark Spectre
> His Emanation is an ever-weeping melancholy Shadow
> > (*Jerusalem* 53.25,26, E. 203, K. 684)

The Spectre is the 'reasoning power in every man' (*Jerusalem* 54.7, E. 203, K. 685).

This excess of masculinity, to which both versions of Book the Seventh tend, alters when Los embraces the Spectre, who tells him 'I am thy real self, / Tho' thus divided from thee & the slave of Every passion / Of thy fierce Soul' (85, 7a.345–7, E. 368, K. 328). Embraced by Los, there is a slow movement towards reconciliation, first towards Enitharmon, whose 'jealousy & fear & terror' (87, 7a.421, E. 369, K. 330) are spoken to, and then in Los towards Urizen.

The second version also shows destructive masculinity, emanating from 'beneath the Roots of Mystery in darkest night / Where Urizen sat on his rock' (95, E. 360, K. 333 in the first line reads 'rock' then 'tree'). Roots, rock, and tree associate. Urizen launches 'Trades & Commerce ships & armed vessels' (95, 7b.12, E. 360, K. 333). Orc is glimpsed, as in the opening of *America*, as the flaming youth of revolution dominated by Vala who is controlled by Urizen; so that Orc knows that 'the arts of Urizen were Pity and Meek affection / And that by these arts the Serpent form exuded from his limbs'. It makes him 'Silent as despairing love & strong as Jealousy / Jealous that she was Vala, now become Urizens harlot...' (91, 7b.134–7, E. 363, K. 336). The passage preludes a war, destined to produce desolation: 'this is no warbling brook, nor Shadow of a Myrtle tree' (93, 7b.204, E. 365, K. 338). The phrases recall 'The Clod & the Pebble' and the Notebook 'Infant Sorrow': torments of love and jealousy under the shade of the myrtle are the innocent pastoral this rejects. Certainly, 7b continues with Tharmas's lament over Enion to Vala, and Vala's lament over Los, Tharmas's wrath against Vala who, recalling 'The Sick Rose' but reversing the gender there, returns 'swift as a blight upon the infant bud' and is called a 'howling melancholy' in which form she appears on page 94, dominant over Orc, called 'the Demon' (94, 7b.261, 280, 286, 287, E.366, 367, K. 339, 340).

Night the Eighth

Pierce divides Night the Eighth into three, the first showing war between Urizen and Los, and the apparent victory of the Shadowy Female, who demands the restoration of Luvah, 'source of every joy that this mysterious tree / Unfolds in Allegoric fruit' (103, 8.168, 169, E. 375, K. 345). The allegoric substitutes as an abstraction for the real. The section introduces another figure, for the first time in Blake, but foreshadowed, in a fragment not re-worked nor placeable in the main text, by a 'demon', who is 'male formd', but 'the parts / To love devoted. female' (E. 845, K. 380). S/he seems to be Tharmas.[17] Like the Spectre, the hermaphrodite – the man/woman, like the 'double form Vala' of 7a.246 – raises issues deepening in later prophecies, especially in *Jerusalem.* 'Hermaphrodite' characterizes the battle and Satan within it, 'black & opake' and 'hiding the Male' (101, 8.103, 105, E. 374, K. 343),[18] emphasizing that the war is gender-inspired.

The middle of the three parts of the Night from 8.182 (103, E. 376, K. 345) to 8.340 (106, E. 379, K. 349), moves away from night thoughts, to something more deliberate, by adopting figures from Christianity: Rahab, Tirzah, the Lamb of God, and Satan. Here, the 'hermaphroditic' returns to describe the war, and it throws up Satan, 'dishumanizd monstrous / A male without a female counterpart.... / Yet hiding the shadowy female Vala as in an ark & Curtains (104, 8.248, 251–6, E. 377, K. 347). Tirzah appears from the 'fruit of Urizen's tree' and her song is heard as the triumph of the 'false Female' and the castrating mother who presses 'the girdle of strong brass...around the loins of this expanding cruelty' (105, 8.287–321, E. 378–9, K. 348–9).[19] The Lamb is nailed to the Tree of Mystery: its baleful influence has constructed Christianity (Christ is the victim of Christianity, and of the values of the tree). The Night reaches the limits of Urizen's reign, identifying him with Satan.[20] In this third section, Los's attempt to limit Urizen's rule differentiates between 'States and Individuals of those States' (115, 8.380, E. 380, K. 351), a distinction recurring in *Milton*:

> Distinguish therefore States from Individuals in those States.
> States Change: but Individual Identities never change nor ccase.
>
> (*Milton* 32.22–3, E. 132, K. 521)

The argument reappears in *Jerusalem*:

> Satan is the State of Death, & not a Human existence:
> But Luvah is named Satan, because he has enterd that State...
> Learn therefore O Sisters to distinguish the Eternal Human
> That walks about among the stones of fire in bliss & woe
> Alternate! from those States or Worlds in which the Spirit travels:
> This is the only means to Forgiveness of Enemies.
>
> (*Jerusalem* 49.67–75, E. 199, K. 680)

The work of forgiveness must name a state (which means its creation, *Jerusalem* 25.13, E. 170, K. 648) to separate the individual from it. In Night the Eighth, it is the state of Urizen that causes the most disturbance (106–7, 8.415–66, E. 381, K. 352). But the nameless shadow binds all things in a living death (107, 8.481, E. 383, K. 353), producing, against Urizen, whose being and thoughts are identifiable with 'the caverns of the grave', Ahania's protest against graveyard poetry, with the 'mouldering churchyard' and 'the jaws of the hungry grave' (108, 8.481, 492–6, E. 383, K. 355–6). Urizen has lost power to the 'shadowy female' but at the end, perhaps identified with the Tree of Mystery, she is burned to form another, which becomes 'Deism / And natural religion' (111, 8.618–19, E. 386, K. 357), the triumph of abstraction and of Vala: a pattern where ongoing narrative turns out to be repetition.

'Night the Ninth, Being The Last Judgment' gives the lament of the Eternal Man and the change in Urizen, who now wishes to reassume the human from his scaly form and wishes he had never 'cast his view into [the past – *del.*] futurity'. Once Urizen is changed, the poem becomes a night-dream of the morning, and Blake deletes the last words 'End of the Dream' – which might imply *A Midsummer Night's Dream* – as if in a rationalism, indicating that the poem is not of the night, not a night desire for the morning, but of the morning, and that the poem has made a difference in bringing about a morning. The drive is that the Zoas 'their disorganizd functions / Again reorganize' (126, 9.371–2, E. 395, K. 366) rather than staying with the lack of identity within the night. Andrew Lincoln (p. 96) thinks Blake used the title page of Young's poem on the verso of the last leaf of *The Four Zoas* manuscript 'to indicate the oppositional relationship between his narrative and Young's poem'. It is not necessary to be so definite but if so, it might indicate the desire to get away from Young's fear that all is 'unresolveable' (*NT* 7.602). In any case, the end of the dream may imply no more than that: knowledge that dreams do not necessarily resolve themselves.

Sexuality and night thoughts

As *The Four Zoas* absorbs material found or developed in later prophecies, it becomes impossible to separate it from other constructions of gender in Blake's 'night thoughts', including those in *For the Sexes: The Gates of Paradise*. Its 'torments of love & jealousy' continue from the lyric poetry, but the place of the woman is more questionable, since all four Zoas are masculine. Their splitting from the Universal Man presupposes another exclusion of women, apparent in the names the 'Universal Brotherhood of Eden' and 'The Universal Man'. This threatens the text from the beginning with a repression lifted in the line drawings, for in considering the illustrations for *The Four Zoas* – those taken from Blake's *Night Thoughts*, and the drawings which supplement these – one generalization may be ventured. Those for Young are primarily masculine, and that may relate to something in *Night Thoughts*, while the drawings are more often of the feminine, and this difference shows the textual unconscious – night thoughts – which bring back the excluded woman. The text, visually, marks its paranoia and attraction to what it fears. The moments, too, within the text of overcoming are necessarily of disunifying male unity, while also threatening a new madness within the text of infinite pluralizing of all states.

The Four Zoas gives the Emanation, the Hermaphrodite, and the Spectre, as figures within Blake's sense of 'sexual strife'. In *The Four Zoas*, 'Man' is primary, and 'feminine' and 'masculine' are both his emanations. In *Jerusalem* 90: 1, 2, 'The Feminine separates from the Masculine & both from Man, / Ceasing to be his Emanations' (E. 389, K. 359). For Andrew Efelbein, 'Emanations are the fallen, female portions of beings who, in an unfallen state, supposedly have no sex, although Blake usually refers to them as male even before they fall.'[21] That underlines the problem: the unfallen creature is male before sexual division, which creates femininity. *The Four Zoas* shows horror at males without emanations, which are virtually always feminine, except for Shiloh, 'the Masculine Emanation among the Flowers of Beulah' (*Jerusalem* 49.47, E. 199, K. 680); flagged as male, he appears with non-Utilitarian, non-masculine flowers. A masculine emanation is allowed, for in *Jerusalem* 90: 1, 2, 'The Feminine separates from the Masculine, & both from Man, / Ceasing to be His Emanations'.

Must *The Four Zoas* be read as torments within masculinity, its females derivations of men? If so, it responds to Young, who, addressing Lorenzo and going no further than poetry about male friendship, implicitly denied night thought to women, unlike Milton (*Paradise Lost* 4.799–809). Yet in Milton, Eve was the emanation of Adam, 'a rib / Crooked by nature, bent, as now appears, / More to the part sinister from me drawn' as Adam says (*Paradise Lost* 10. 884–6). As his emanation, the woman exists only as an expression of something in the male. In the following quotation, giving advice to Lorenzo, Young puts male sexuality into the sphere of night thoughts, requiring it to be part of the night, making sex the subject of shame:

> Why should the Joy most poignant *Sense* affords,
> Burn us with Blushes and rebuke our Pride?
> Those Heav'n-born Blushes tell us Man *descends*,
> Ev'n in the Zenith of his earthly Bliss:
> Should Reason take her infidel Repose,
> This honest *Instinct* speaks our Lineage high;
> This Instinct calls on Darkness to conceal
> Our rapturous Relation to the Stalls.
> Our Glory covers us with noble Shame,
> And he that's unconfounded, is unman'd.
> The man that Blushes is not quite a Brute.
>
> (7.486–96)

Blushing both evokes the erection and its loss: a lost erection confirms that 'man descends' in orgasm, while not to suffer this loss of manly pride 'unmans' the man. The morning blushing, as in 'The Angel', makes it 'Heav'n-born', licenses sexuality and embarrassment as a 'proper' response to it: day thoughts are modest, embarrassed, like Eve, of whom Adam says 'to the nuptial bower / I led her blushing like the morn' (*Paradise Lost* 8.510–11). This bower of bliss is like the myrtle shade.

Blake illustrates Young first with no. 296, a female snake coiled round the tree and trying to tempt, not Eve but an angel, as though following Young in excluding the woman, and in no. 297 (containing the quotation given above), with Adam and Eve ashamed and hiding themselves and their nakedness.

Young writes differently about the woman, saying that 'our [male] passions':

> When *Reason* moderates the Rein aright,
> Shall reascend, remount their former Sphere,
> Where, once, they soar'd illustrious; ere seduced
> By wanton *Eve*'s Debauch, to strole on Earth,
> And set the sublunary World on Fire.
>
> (7.540–4)

Eve, as a generic name for the 'wanton' woman, is set in opposition to Reason.

In contrast to Young, making the woman the seducer, Blake's 'Satan Exulting Over Eve' (1795, B. cat. 292) coils the serpent round Eve, supine, her eyes closed, the fruit under her right hand. Flames rise from behind her, while he, naked and perhaps not fully masculine, flies over her, as if covering her body in a rape-like sequence, spreading his wings over her in flight, as though cutting off the light, making this a night thought – hers, or the viewer's. Blake addresses what Young will not, while being unable to affirm female difference that the woman is not the emanation. So, in *A Vision of the Last Judgment* (1810), 'In Eternity Woman is the Emanation of Man she has No Will of her own There is no such thing in Eternity as a Female Will' (E. 562, K. 613).

In *Jerusalem*, 'Man is adjoind to Man by his Emanative portion' (*Jerusalem* 39.38–40, E. 187, K. 675): the emanation being the opposite of the abstract. The abstract reasoning power, the Spectre, male, disallows such contact and makes the emanation become its own shadow. The emanation is feminine but not an actual woman, though in some passages, she must be. The man / man links are affirmed by Los:

> When in Eternity Man converses with Man they enter
> Into each others Bosom (which are Universes of delight)
> In mutual interchange. and first their Emanations meet
> Surrounded by their Children. if they embrace & comingle
> The Human Four-fold Forms mingle also in thunders of Intellect
> But if the Emanations mingle not; with storms & agitations
> Of earthquakes & consuming fires they roll apart in fear
> For Man cannot unite with Man but by their Emanations
> Which stand both Male & Female at the Gates of each Humanity.
> How then can I ever again be united as Man with Man
> While thou my Emanation refusest my Fibres of dominion.

> When Souls mingle & join thro all the Fibres of Brotherhood
> Can there be any secret joy on Earth greater than this?
>
> (*Jerusalem* 88.3–11, E. 246, K. 733)

Is this a homoeroticism or male friendship which excludes women, or is the exclusion of women the refusal to mark male/female gender difference? That still leaves unacknowledged the specificity of women.

The woman creates the hermaphrodite of *The Four Zoas*, and elsewhere. *For the Sexes: The Gates of Paradise* showed the male becoming a 'dark Hermaphrodite'. The phrase recurs in *Jerusalem* 64.31 (E. 215, K. 699) when Vala asserts her dominance, telling Los: 'Thou, O Male! Thou art / Thyself female' because his social roles in life are in relation to the woman. She says the 'Human Divine is Woman's Shadow' and calls the Spectre a 'Male Harlot' (64.11–15, E. 215, K. 699). Los replies:

> All Quarrels arise from Reasoning. the secret Murder, and
> The violent Man-slaughter. these are the Spectres double Cave,
> The Sexual Death living on accusation of Sin & Judgment...
>
> (64.20–2, E. 215, K. 699)

Sexual relationships are 'sexual death' for which Los blames the power of reasoning, which is of the Spectre, who responds by linking himself further with Vala, weeping 'in self-contradicting agony' till 'A dark Hermaphrodite they stood frowning upon London's River', threatening the city.

In *Jerusalem* 90, set in London, 'the Valleys of Middlesex', between Highgate's heights and Brockley hills, Los cries that 'no Individual' should appropriate to themselves any of the 'Universal Characteristics' of specific names; they would be 'Blasphemous Selfhoods'. Further, 'A Vegetated Christ & a Virgin Eve are the Hermaphroditic Blasphemy' (90.28–35, E. 250, K. 736). A vegetated Christ means one not male, or Christ in his incarnation resulting from a non-sexual union. Natural religion, which vegetates the divine vision (and which Night the Eighth ended by associating with the woman), relates to a non-sexual (non-male) Christ. For Los:

> When the Individual appropriates Universality
> He divides into Male & Female: & when the Male & Female,
> Appropriate Individuality, they become an Eternal Death.
> Hermaphroditic worshippers of a God of cruelty and law...'
>
> (90.52–6, E. 250, K. 737)

Appropriating Universality means appropriating a single 'state' of being as the complete one: at that point the individual makes an invidious gender-choice of one: male or female. When the male or female assumes that this is the complete state (individuality), they become both an 'eternal death', a recurrent phrase in Blake and in *The Four Zoas,* and a hermaphrodite (these things may not be different), driven by a female force, either because they desire femaleness (the God of cruelty and law being a castrating figure) or because they have already been feminized. The God of cruelty and law is either female-inspired, or female-created, or in collusion with the female.[22]

In response to the union of men in Eternity, Enitharmon reacts scornfully, saying this is 'Woman's World' and that she needs no spectre to defend her from man (the spectre's function being to increase feelings of male guilt). She speaks with 'scorn & jealousy, alternate torments' (*Jerusalem* 88.22, E. 247, K. 733 compare *The Four Zoas* 9, 1.237, E. 305, K. 270). Sitting 'on Sussex shore' – making the passage relate to the time of writing *The Four Zoas,* Felpham (Sussex) being the Blakes' home from 1801 to 1803 – she thinks she has been triumphant. Nonetheless, the Spectre knows that he is the 'author of their divisions & shrinkings'. A split between men produced by opposition from the feminine or from the female – Enitharmon – while it seems productive of a woman's world, has actually come about through the (already feminine) masculine, who warns:

> The Man who respects Woman shall be despised by Woman
> And deadly cunning & mean abjectness only, shall enjoy them
> For I will make their places of joy & love, excrementitious.
> Continually building, continually destroying in Family feuds
> While you are under the dominion of a jealous Female
> Unpermanent for ever because of love & jealousy.
> You shall want all the Minute Particulars of Life
>
> (88.38–43, E. 247, K. 734)

The 'love & jealousy' of *The Four Zoas* have been applied to heterosexual relationships. The jealous Spectre constructs women as jealous. Sexual enjoyment (not a sexual relation) only exists in conditions presupposing cunning and mean abjectness. This goes beyond Young, and implies the social conditions and bourgeois types of nineteenth-century London, to which I will turn in the next chapter. The Spectre's rationality reacts, nauseated, from sexuality, as if jealousy or reason conceals an abject state, horror at what sullies the self's boundaries.[23] If sexuality is identified with the excremental, this implies that the Spectre supports the reign of decency, while his words are misogynistic. That was apparent when Urizen cast out Ahania, feeling that he was being accused by the feminine, like Young, fearing being unmanned.

5
'I see London, blind...'

Midnight thoughts

Blake's 'London' (*Songs of Experience*) ends nocturnally in 'midnight streets'. Night thoughts in midnight streets make the night the true Enlightenment, by questioning daytime identity. So does the American Djuna Barnes's novel *Nightwood* (1936, originally *Bow Down: An Anatomy of Night*), which also has *Night Thoughts* behind it.[1] *Nightwood* starts with Hedvig Volkbein, a Viennese, giving birth to Felix, a posthumous child. During the 1880s, Vienna was close to the racism where it was dangerous to be Jewish, like Felix's father; so Hedvig had no wish for the son. Felix grows up obsessed with 'Old Europe' (p. 22) – self-hating, guarding a racial purity that excludes him. He also involves himself with the circus, which brings him into contact with the Irish/American homosexual Dr Matthew O'Connor, and the American Norah Flood. Felix would like to be a Gentile, and O'Connor would like to be heterosexual or a woman. O'Connor is seen later in his home in Paris and Felix meets the American Robin Vote, 'a tall girl with the body of a boy' (71). Felix marries Robin to have a son (desiring to perpetuate the official past), and Chapter 2 describes her giving birth to a boy, and rejecting maternality. She leaves Felix and becomes Nora's lover.

Robin stays with Nora and Barnes writes: 'two spirits were working in her, love and anonymity. Yet they were so "haunted" of each other that separation was impossible' (84). The 'they' refers to the lovers or to the two spirits, love and a desire for anonymous sex. Robin seems to want a mother (O'Connor says that Nora 'should have had a thousand children, and Robin...should have been all of them' [145]); Robin continues to be a somnambule: while Nora watches, she walks in the night in Paris streets, looking for women. As Nora says later: 'sometimes Robin seemed to return to me...for sleep and safety, but...she always went out again' (197), so posing the question of what night's attraction may be, while, whatever that attraction, it compels Nora to keep on going out looking for her. In Chapter 4, Nora finds another woman and returns to America, and the desolate Nora, in Chapter 5 'Watchman, what of the Night', finds O'Connor at three in the morning to say: 'Doctor, I have come to ask you to tell me everything you know about the night' (97).

The subject is what night is and does, bringing about love (desire) and anonymity (loss of identity). O'Connor (dressed as a woman) says 'Every thought is meditated upon and calculated, but the night is not premeditated' (118). Nora says, 'Now I see that the night does something to a person's identity, even when asleep' (119). For the doctor, in the night 'distress is wild (mad) and anonymous' – the will has been suspended and a person's identity 'is no longer his own'. Speaking of 'the fury of the night' (125), and of it as the time when 'thousands unbidden come to his bed', he speaks of it as the time when he cruises for anonymous lovers in lavatories, so that night becomes a time of desire and profound identity-uncertainty, incarnated in making love to identities concealed in the dark, for 'the face is what anglers catch in the daylight, but the sea is the night' (135). At such a time, when sexuality overcomes knowledge of identity, night's liminal identity taking away daytime identity, he says of lesbians: 'these can never again live the life of the day. When one meets them at high noon they give off, as it were a protective emanation, something dark and muted. The light does not become them any longer. They begin to have an unrecorded look' (137). Blake's 'midnight streets' relate to these Parisian ones, making the city part of the 'other night', which is not part of the passage from day to day, but 'always the other, and he who senses it becomes the other'. For, as Blanchot says, there is 'no exact moment at which one would pass from night to the *other* night, no limit at which to stop and come back in the other direction. Midnight never falls at midnight.'[2]

If the city so deranges identity, it is more complex that *The Four Zoas* ends with Urizen's wish that he had never constructed:

arches high & cities turrets & towers & domes
Whose smoke destroyd the pleasant gardens & whose running Kennels
Chokd the bright rivers burdning with my Ships the angry deep...

(*FZ* 9.167–9, E. 390, K. 361)

'Kennels' are open sewers draining eighteenth-century streets. Urizen, paranoid, maddened and maddening at once, in building the city destroys it, for he builds in his own image, ruining the city. Lewis Mumford, a historian of cities, is aware of them as paranoid structures, while also having utopian possibilities. He relates their growth to militarism; the city has served 'as a container of organized violence and a transmitter of war'. He adds about city walls, which give features of both protection and aggression:

> Not only did the walled city give a permanent collective structure to the paranoid claims and delusions of kingship, augmenting suspicion, hostility, non-co-operation, but the division of labour and castes, pushed to the extreme, normalized schizophrenia, while the compulsive repetitious labour imposed on a large part of the urban population under slavery, reproduced the structure of a compulsion neurosis. Thus the ancient city, in its very constitution, tended to transmit a collective personality structure, whose more extreme manifestations are now recognised in individuals as pathological.[3]

In *Jerusalem* plate 10, the 'sons of Albion', who are sons of Urizen, reduce the contraries, which are in every substance, to 'Good & Evil', and they make an 'Abstract' called 'the Reasoning Power / An Abstract objecting power, that Negatives every thing (10.13–14, E. 153, K. 629). After the creation of this organization:

> Therefore Los stands in London building Golgonooza . . .
>   (*Jerusalem* 10.8–17, E. 153, K. 629)

Golgonooza implies transforming London from the abstract state implied in 'refusing all Definite Form' (*Milton* 3.9, E. 97, K. 482).[4] That suggests the spoiling effects of sprawling urbanization; but Dostoyevsky called centrally planned St Petersburg 'the most abstract and intentional city in the whole round world'.[5] Abstract because producing suburban and industrial waste, or because formed to model an imperial idea, the city as abstract is Urizen's work. In *Milton*, Ololon comments on the 'dreadful Loom of Death' that she sees at work in Ulro, here identifiable as London:

> O piteous Female forms compelld
> To weave the Woof of Death, On Camberwell Tirzahs Courts
> Malahs on Blackheath, Rahab & Noah. dwell on Windsors heights
> Where once the Cherubs of Jerusalem spread to Lambeths Vale
> Milcahs Pillars shine from Harrow to Hampstead where Hoglah

> On Highgates heights magnificent Weaves over trembling Thames
> To Shooters Hill and thence to Blackheath the dark Woof!
>
> (*Milton* 35.6–13, E. 135, K. 525)

The women are the 'cruelties of Ulro' (*Milton* 17.9–11), and their weaving criss-crosses London, linking it as a web. The passage names eight sub-urban places, whose height makes them 'clouded hills'. They ring low-lying London ('Lambeths Vale' and 'trembling Thames'), a valley enclosed by a veil whose cruelty is inseparable from its inhibition of vision.

The passage indicates the power of increasing urbanization, both enclosing and extending London. In 1600, London's population was 200,000. By 1801, date of the first census, ordered by Parliament for enrolling men for the wars, the population of London, comprising some 200 parishes and called 'the Metropolis of England, at once the Seat of Government and the greatest Emporium in the known world', was 900,000.[6] It had touched a million by 1811, and 1,379,000 by the census of 1821. By the mid-century census of 1851, confirming Britain as primarily urban, it was 2.7 million.

John Stow's (1525–1605) *Survey of London* (1598) mapped the city. Eighteenth-century markers include Pope making London 'Augusta' in *Windsor Forest* (1713), John Gay's *Trivia, Or The Art of Walking the Streets of London* (1716), Samuel Johnson's imitation of Juvenal, 'London' (1738), and John Rocque's mapping of London in 1745 as the 'Plan of the Cities of London and Westminster and Borough of Southwark'. Rocque's map confirms the sense that the separate jurisdictions of the City of London, Southwark, Westminster and Middlesex had been constructed as a single place.[7] In 1799, Richard Horwood produced another map. The period 1800–1840 has been seen as the moment when London became, incontestably, a world city, since foreign visitors visited it to write about it.[8] It becomes the subject of fiction, as with Pierce Egan's *Life in London or, The Day and Night Scenes of Jerry Hawthorne, Esq. and his Elegant Friend Corinthian Tom in their Rambles and Sprees through the Metropolis* (1821), recording the adventures of Jerry, the cousin from the country who comes to visit Tom, the Regency buck, in London, in order to see, in a manner reminiscent of Hogarth, high and low life together, the usual division in Regency art.[9] London had by then lost its medieval houses on London Bridge (1759) and its city gates (1760). A Paving Act of 1762 began a significant 'improvement' of the streets.[10] The capital underwent planning through George IV and Blake's contemporary, John Nash (1752–1835), and modernization through John

Rennie (1761–1821). Building increased rapidly after Waterloo, in Blake's last decade, with new Thames bridges (Westminster, 1750, Blackfriars, 1769; Vauxhall, crossing from Lambeth to Millbank, which was begun as Regent's Bridge in 1811 and finished in 1816; Rennie's Waterloo bridge, called the Strand in 1811 and finished in 1817, its new name creating a new area; Southwark, the first iron bridge, 1819; Hammersmith, 1827). Rennie's rebuilt London Bridge, begun in 1823, was opened by William IV in 1831. There were 38 'Waterloo' churches and Rennie's West India dock in the Isle of Dogs (1802), the London dock (1805), the East India dock (1806) for the East India Company which, to cope with its expansion, had rebuilt its premises in Leadenhall Street (1796–1799), the Surrey docks and the Surrey canal (1807), the Regent's canal (1812–1820), St Katherine dock (1828), and the opening up of the Shadwell basin (1831). Two years after Blake's death came the first horse-drawn omnibus, from Paddington to the City (1829), and in 1836 a railway ran from Deptford to Bermondsey.

The city: the *Songs*

Night thoughts produce the city in different forms in the lyric poetry and the prophecies. A first view appears in 'Holy Thursday', a poem Blake could begin but not so easily finish, which may indicate why it reads so ambiguously for one of the *Songs of Innocence*[11]:

[Upon] 'Twas on a Holy Thursday their innocent faces clean
The children walking two & two in [grey] red & blue & green
Grey headed beadles walkd before with wands as white as snow
Till into the high dome of Pauls they like Thames waters flow

O what a multitude they seemd these flowers of London town
Seated in companies they sit with radiance all their own
The hum of multitudes [were] was there but multitudes of lambs
[And all in order sit waiting the chief chanter's commands – *del*.]
Thousands of little boys & girls raising their innocent hands

[Then like a mighty wind they raise to heav'n the voice of song
Or like harmonious thunderings the seats of heav'n among
When the whole multitude of innocents their voices raise
Like angels on the throne of heav'n, raising the voice of praise – *del*.]

[Let Cherubim & Seraphim now raise their voices high – *del*.]
[Then] Now like a mighty wind they raise to heaven the voice of song

Or like harmonious thunderings the seats of heaven among
Beneath them sit the [reverend men, the] aged men wise guardians of
   the poor
Then cherish pity, lest you drive an angel from your door

(E. 13, K. 121–2)

This poem maps London, named only here in the *Songs of Innocence*,
making St Paul's dome a globular centre. In relation to the city, the
children are flowers, then lambs, and they are associated with the
river. The poem reads the city in terms of the separate schools which
have come together in a ceremony installed after 1782, when 6000
uniformed children from charity schools were brought together to
attend a service at St Paul's on Ascension Day. The poem, placing the
guardians beneath children, perhaps redeems those 'grey headed
beadles', giving them not staves, but 'wands' like magicians. 'Innocent'
appears only in these two places in the whole of *Songs of Innocence* (the
draft gives a third occurrence: 'the whole multitude of innocents'). It
appears first with relation to the faces, which are 'clean' – only here in
Songs of Innocence – and is ironic (evoking what will become Victorian
virtues of cleanliness, as in Kingsley's *The Water Babies*) and non-
ironic, like the washing in the river in 'The Chimney Sweeper'. 'Innocent'
is then used about the hands, which the gesture shows to be clean, but
since 'clean' is not used, emphasis is thrown onto the children's
defenceless appeal.

The poem associates innocence with 'Thames waters' and 'London
town', making the London children 'flowers', a word gaining meaning
from 'flow' (a significant word in 'London', for the power of continuous
river-life resisting restraint). 'Flowers' also gains from the word 'multitude',
which, appearing here at least three times, along with 'thousands',
counters a Utilitarian attitude that sees flowers as valueless. Though the
moon is like a flower in 'Night' (E. 13, K. 118), 'flowers' appears in only
other place in *Songs of Innocence* ('The Little Black Boy', E. 9, K. 125),
while something of flowers' signifying value emerges when 'The Garden
of Love' marks their loss. Since there can be no one questioning the
children's innocence, as opposed to that of the wise guardians of the
poor, its statement becomes rhetorical, part of the appeal that is made
in the last two verses, which is to individuals who must learn innocence,
learning that 'Pity' and 'the angel' are both names for the poor London
child who must be cherished in the singular, and who, part of London,
solicits attention.[12]

If 'Holy Thursday' has London as its context, then despite its pastoral illustration, the same applies to the equivalent in *Songs of Experience*, commenting on the same act of charity:

> Is this a holy thing to see,
> In a rich and fruitful land,
> Babes reducd to misery,
> Fed with cold and usurous hand?
>
> Is that trembling cry a song?
> Can it be a song of joy?
> And [so great a number] so many children poor?
> [Tis] It is a land of poverty!
>
> And their sun does never shine.
> And their fields are bleak & bare.
> And their ways are fill'd with thorns.
> [Tis] It is eternal winter there.
>
> [But] For where-e'er the sun does shine,
> And where-e'er the rain does fall:
> Babe can never hunger there,
> Nor poverty the mind appall.
>
> (E. 19–20, K. 211–12)

The irony is that it *is* a holy thing to see because that quasi-Malthusianism defines city holiness. The contradiction is that this must be a land of eternal winter (which it is not), to account for hunger's presence. Explanation comes in the last verse. The mind appalled (turned pale) by the thought, or the presence of poverty, produces not the drive to remove it but the cold hand that reduces to misery and feeds in a usurious way (the hand contrasts with the children's innocent hands). Nothing accounts for the official meanness save a subject already appalled, so rendered deficient, or abstracted.[13] So, in *The Four Zoas*, Urizen, about to build the Mundane Shell, is described repeatedly as pale (*FZ* 2.9–25, E. 313–14, K. 280).

The appalled mind of the officials (their lack of sun which would further appall, and their bleak fields and their thorns) and the city as eternal winter also work as images in the drafts of 'London':

> I wander through each dirty / charter'd street
> Near where the dirty / charter'd Thames does flow

And see / mark in every face I meet
Marks of weakness, marks of woe.

In every cry of every man
In every voice of every child / every infant's cry of fear
In every voice, in every ban
The german / mind-forg'd links I hear / manacles I hear.

But most / How the chimney sweeper's cry
Blackens o'er the churches' walls / Every black'ning church appalls,
And the hapless soldier's sigh
Runs in blood down palace walls.

[But most the midnight harlot's curse
From every dismal street I hear,
Weaves around the marriage hearse
And blasts the new born infant's tear.]

But most [from every] thro' wintry streets I hear
How the midnight harlot's curse
Blasts the new born infant's tear,
And hangs / smites with plagues the marriage hearse.

But most the shrieks of youth I hear
But most thro' midnight &
How the youthful . . .

(K. 170)

But most thro' midnight streets I hear
How the youthful Harlots curse
Blasts the newborn / new-born Infants tear
And smites / blights with plagues the marriage / Marriage hearse.

(E. 27, K. 216)

'Wintry' in one draft recalls 'Earth's Answer', where 'cruel jealous selfish fear' began as 'wintry' for 'jealous' (E. 18, K. 169). If jealousy is unconsciously in the drafts of 'London' then that adds a further reading to the manacles and the bans, including marriage banns. 'Appalls' puns on St Paul's, whose dome ('Holy Thursday') was Urizen's responsibility. Wren as Urizen pairs with Newton and Locke.[14] In *Visions of the Daughters of Albion* Oothoon speaks of the parson surrounding himself:

With *cold* floods of abstraction, and with forests of solitude,
To build him castles and high spires. where kings & priests may dwell
(5.19, 20, E. 49, K. 193, my emphasis)

In Blake's *Night Thoughts* 233, illustrating *'Ambition, Avarice,* the two *Demons'* (6.221), these figures are a bishop and a king: here they are suggested through the metonymies of St Paul's and the Palace. 'Appalls' also permits a pun on 'pall', so that the blackening church (blackening the children's character: saying that as they are sinful, they should be put to work as they are) stays black and dead, home of night thoughts. But the pun implies the complex reaction of those who people the blackening church (the phrase compares with 'the darkening green'). They are made pale, in shock, like the Nurse whose face grows green and pale, so that everything for them becomes reaction. They are deadened as with the power of the grave. 'An ancient Proverb' (Notebook of 1793) may have been a draft last verse for 'London':

Remove away that blackning church
Remove away that marriage hearse
Remove away that [place – *del.*] man of blood
['Twill – *del.*] Youll quite remove the ancient curse
(E. 475, K. 176)[15]

If the 'man of blood' evokes 2 Samuel 16.7, it invokes George III, memorialized in the 'german forged links'. Removal of the ancient curse, echoing Genesis 3.18, may take away the 'thorns' that 'Holy Thursday' sees as produced by the mindset of the inhabitants of the churches.

Edward the Third celebrated 'golden London / And her silver Thames, throng'd with shining spires' (sc. 2. l 10–11, E. 425, K. 19), the commercial centre, as Thompson in 'Rule Britannia' (1740), recorded 'the charter of the land':

> To thee belongs the rural reign,
> Thy cities shall with commerce shine.
> All thine shall be the subject main
> And every shore it circles thine.[16]

The play invokes 'Liberty, the charter'd right of Englishmen' (1.9, E. 424, K. 18), while the enemy 'fight in chains, invisible chains, but heavy; / Their minds are fetter'd; then how can they be free' (1.9.13, 14). In

'London', streets are chartered, like the Thames, still 'flowing' rebelliously, by the shipping of the chartered East India Company. We recall Tom Paine: 'It is a perversion of terms to say that a charter gives rights. It operates by a contrary effect, that of taking rights away. Rights are inherently in all the inhabitants, but charters, by annulling these rights in majority, leave the right by exclusion in the hands of a few.'[17] 'Charter'd' implies freedom for some and not for others: the river, not a common source of life; and streets not public spaces.

The 'I' of 'London' sees a distinctive city-type; the signs are detectable in marks, signs to be interpreted, but not in one way only. The 'I' who would interpret singly is also distinctive: we can compare Isaac Watts's child in 'Praise for Mercies Spiritual and Temporal', who, a product of a London Independent Meeting, says:

> When'er I take my walks abroad,
> How many poor I see,
> What shall I render to my God
> For all his gifts to me?
>
> Not more than others I deserve,
> Yet God hath given me more;
> For I have food while others starve,
> Or beg from door to door.
>
> How many children in the street
> Half naked I behold!
> While I am clothed from head to feet,
> And covered from the cold.
>
> While some poor wretches scarce can tell
> Where they may lay their head,
> I have a home wherein to dwell,
> And rest upon my bed.
>
> While others early learn to swear,
> And curse, and lye, and steal;
> Lord, I am taught thy name to fear,
> And do thy holy will.
>
> Are these thy favours, day by day,
> To me above the rest?
> Then let me love thee more than they,
> And try to serve thee best.[18]

There are similarities in the observation of children, and in their swearing and cursing, and their misery. Watts's poem, accepting urban poverty as a fact, works by antithesis, noting the poor and the contrast with himself, though the poverty of the wretches in stanza 4 brings them close to Christ (Matthew 8.20) in a reversal that, like the acknowledgement that the others of the second verse are deserving, he deserves not more but has been given more, cracks open the poem's antitheses. These exist between the subject who walks abroad because he has a home, and those who walk from door to door; and between the child, in a contrast of 'learn' versus 'taught', who swears against the Father's Name, and the child who does the Father's holy will. In 'London' the 'I' 'marks' (notes, writes) pre-existent marks in the face (which the poem re-marks), and on the church and the sigh which he remarks as being blood on the palace walls. Marks form by setting bounds, which include limits set in the face. Bodies, presented in abstracting metonymies, minds, and spaces, are locked up. Weaknesses narrate past 'woe'. While marking continues the oppression already written on people's faces, even accusingly, in the second half, the 'I' is drawn into a position where his identity is what he sees because perceiving wounds the self, writing marks on the paper scar the subject. The third verse focuses on physical pain, and the fourth on gender. The chimney sweeper's cry, 'weep weep weep weep', was heard in *Songs of Innocence* (E. 10, K. 117) and again in *Songs of Experience*: 'A little black thing among the snow: / Crying weep, weep, in notes of woe!' (E. 22, K. 212). The illustration to that poem emphasizes the winter where the child is outside the houses. In 'London', second, third, and fourth stanzas listen to the 'cry', and hear oppressiveness and oppression in the voice which is equated with the 'ban'.[19] The acrostic in the third stanza echoes the last word of the second stanza and is repeated in the rhyme-word of the fourth stanza.

The critique intensifies from the 'charter' and the 'ban', and the 'mind-forg'd manacles' (forged for the mind, forged by the mind). In a revolutionary moment in London's politics in *Europe*, the Palace of Westminster is disturbed:

Above the rest the howl was heard from Westminster louder & louder:
The Guardian of the secret codes forsook his ancient mansion,
Driven out by the flames of Orc; his furr'd robes & false locks
Adhered and grew one with his flesh, and nerves & veins shot thro'
    them
With dismal torment sick hanging upon the wind: he fled

Groveling along Great George Street thro' the Park gate; all the soldiers
Fled from his sight; he drag'd his torments to the wilderness.

(*Europe* 12.14, E. 64, K. 242)

The judge judged was Thurlow (1731–1830), Lord High Chancellor,
dismissed by Pitt in June 1792, and unnamed, unlike the street which
symbolizes the Hanoverians. Thurlow's path takes him from the Palace
of Westminster across St James's Park to St James's Palace, to resign his
seals.[20] He is like the Urizen-become-Nebuchadnezzar in the wilderness,
but the wilderness is London, not outside it.

Finishing with night and, in one draft, with winter situates this
poem within a tradition of the four stages of the day – morning, noon,
evening, night – related to the four seasons. Hogarth's 'The Four Times
of the Day' (1736–1738) presents Night amongst the bordellos near
Charing Cross, with fires, an overturned coach, prostitution, and a sense
of drunkenness and madness.[21] In urban space, prostitution exists as
'a nocturnal animal'.[22] 'The studious hours of deep midnight' ('I saw a
Monk', E. 489, K. 419) lift daytime repression, making the male street
walker aware of, though not seeing, the female 'street walker'. She is
part of night thoughts. Blake's historical artwork had already produced,
in his art of the history of England, 'The Penance of Jane Shore', a drawing prior to 1779 (E. 550, K. 585), set outside old Saint Paul's Church.[23]
The cry, sigh, curse, and tear are marks (as with a tear, the sound and the
mark are identical). The black'ning church and the blood witness to the
pre-existence of the cry or sigh, while the youthful harlot's curse is not
seen, and not heard, if it is the blasting power of syphilis. Yet audible or
inaudible, the curse *is* for hearing, for 'Hear' opens *Songs of Experience* –
'Hear the voice of the Bard . . . Whose ears have heard, / The Holy Word'
(E. 18, K. 210).[24] The marriage hearse (not bed) – compare with 'the
marriage chain' in *The Four Zoas* (5.33, E. 339, K. 306) – will evoke more
weeping. Night thoughts, inseparable from the sexual, create a narrative
in this last verse, enforcing connections between the youthful harlot and
middle-class marriage that class-perceptions of the previous stanzas cannot
quite make.[25] 'Hearse', containing as an inaudible mark 'hear' and the
'har' of 'harlot', directs night thoughts to the interior, invisible within
marriage. The terms recall 'The Sick Rose'. The *youthful* harlot ghosts the
marriage *hearse* as the newborn infant is repressed in the marriage.
'Plagues' resonates from Blake's watercolour 'Pestilence' (c. 1780, Butlin
185), illustrating the Plague of 1665. One scene in *Europe* plate 13 (10)
shows a bellman passing a door with 'Lord have mercy upon us' written
on it, a visible 'mark'. In 'London', the marks which suggest sickness

culminate in 'Plagues', which, like *Nightwood* imply a sick eros. The term re-arranges, or deranges the terms of 'The Sick Rose' as that title enigmatizes 'Every harlot was a virgin once'.

Place names

'London' is the only place name of *Songs of Innocence and Experience*, but the city is full of other place names, repeated over and over in the Prophetic Books, indicating that the city exists in the form of discourse. Its boundaries as given in *Milton* have been quoted. Place names especially mark borders or boundaries disappearing because of early suburbanization. An example of naming appears in *Jerusalem* 21.32, 33 (E. 166, K. 644), when Battersea and Chelsea are paired, as on opposite sides of the river, upstream of the city.[26] In Battersea Church Road, in the rebuilt St Mary's Church, Blake married Catherine Boucher in 1782. She had been christened in the old church in 1762; her family were market-gardeners in marshy agricultural land. The name conceals a history. Chelsea reappears in a reference to 'Ranelagh & Strumbolo, . . . Cromwells gardens & Chelsea / The place of wounded soldiers' (*Jerusalem* 8.2–3, E. 151, K. 627). Ranelagh, adjacent to Wren's Chelsea Hospital for veteran soldiers (1689), opened as pleasure gardens in 1742 and closed in 1804.[27] Strombolo and Cromwell gardens were tea gardens of 1762; the latter, which closed in 1797, was called 'Florida gardens' after 1781, a name Blake ignores, perhaps in admiration for the Republican it memorializes. Strombolo decayed more slowly, but these islands of pleasure or of relief were threatened by a movement towards nineteenth-century respectability which the Utilitarian Francis Place saluted in his autobiography.[28] In *Jerusalem* 21, Hackney and Holloway, to be discussed below, appear in the line following Battersea and Chelsea as complements to them.

 The Prophetic Books, more than 'London', articulate the metropolis in 'minute particulars', recognizing so many local histories and recalling that spatial awareness must also be temporal. For 'not one Moment / Of Time is lost, nor one Event of Space unpermanent / But all remain' (*Milton* 22.18–20, E. 117, K. 505). Dickens, to be compared with Blake in Chapter 7, marks London as modern in its concentration upon the present, but 'Shops and their Tenants' (1834), an essay in *Sketches By Boz*, begins: 'What inexhaustible food for speculation do the streets of London afford' (80) because it shows that an unsuccessful shop remains unsuccessful no matter how many times it is opened by different shop-keepers selling different goods. His 'Sketch' following 'Scotland Yard'

(1836), treating of a piece of London appropriated by Peel for the police force, portrays the 'lusty coal-heavers' in a public house on the site over a period of years talking about the Thames in ancient days before the building of the Patent Shot Manufactory in Lambeth (1789) and Waterloo Bridge. Rumours of a bridge to replace old London Bridge (the plans began in 1799) follow. So do new Hungerford market (1833), the Police Commissioners' premises (after 1829), and the Reformed House of Commons (1832) (88). And the sketch ends with the point that the old Scotland-yard has now become quite other amidst 'change and restlessness and innovation' (89):

> A few years hence, and the antiquary of another generation looking into some mouldy record of the strife and passions that agitated the world in these times, may glance his eye over the pages we have just filled: and on all his knowledge of the history of the past, not all his black-letter lore, or his skill in book-collecting, not all the dry studies of a long life, or the dusty volumes that have cost him a fortune, may help him to the whereabouts, either of Scotland-yard, or of any of the landmarks we have mentioned in describing it.
>
> (90)

The challenge in writing London is that the present-day city is situated upon other scenes, other places, which had other topographies. The future will produce the 'antiquary', a late-comer to a site which has been invested in before with other significances. Dickens, and Blake, already an antiquary in his interest in the gothic, hold on to place names, as markers of what is not abstract, but has a history, even if uprooted, taking with it a person's identity. Place names help to hold on to a past so wholly swept away as to seem never to have existed. To write the city through these names is to build it: it is the work of Golgonooza.

In *Jerusalem* plate 27, a lyric presentation of London as 'Jerusalem' links its growth – its fall – with the spectre and with Urizen. Its first part recalls the fields of the area north of the present Marylebone road (New Road, 1757), linking Marylebone with Islington, which became 'the first City suburb to be truly built up'.[29] Marylebone, south of the New Road and north of Oxford Street, had been under development through the second half of the eighteenth century. Building the Regent's Park estate on open farmland, once Henry VIII's hunting ground, began in 1811, joining Marylebone to Primrose Hill and Saint John's Wood.[30] John Nash's Grecian terraces contrast with Jerusalem's pillars:

The fields from Islington to Marybone
To Primrose Hill and Saint Johns Wood,
Were builded over with pillars of gold,
And there Jerusalems pillars stood.

Her Little-ones ran on the fields,
The Lamb of God among them seen,
And fair Jerusalem his Bride,
Among the little meadows green.

Pancrass and Kentish-town repose
Among her golden pillars high,
Among her golden arches which
Shine upon the starry sky.

The Jew's harp-house & the Green Man,
The Ponds where Boys to bathe delight:
The fields of Cows by Willans farm.
Shine in Jerusalems pleasant sight.

She walks upon our meadows green:
The Lamb of God walks by her side,
And every English child is seen
Children of Jesus & his Bride.

Forbidding trespasses and sins
Lest Babylon with cruel Og,
With Moral & Self-righteous Law
Should Crucify in Satans Synagogue!

What are those golden Builders doing
Near mournful ever-weeping Paddington,
Standing above that mighty Ruin
Where Satan the first victory won,

When Albion slept beneath the Fatal Tree,
And the Druids golden Knife
Rioted in human gore
In Offerings of Human Life?

They groan'd aloud on London Stone,
They groan'd aloud on Tyburns Brook,
Albion gave his deadly groan,
And all the Atlantic Mountains shook.

> Albions Spectre from his Loins
> Tore forth in all the pomp of War!
> Satan his name: in flames of fire
> He stretch'd his Druid Pillars far.
>
> Jerusalem fell from Lambeth's Vale,
> Down thro Poplar & Old Bow,
> Thro Malden & acros the Sea,
> In War & howling, death & woe.
>
> (E. 171, K. 649)[31]

'Gold' and 'green' (including 'The Green Man') minimize the contrast between the secular – the Jew's Harp House, the Green Man, Willan's Farm – and the religious. (The Jew's Harp House is both.) Fields, appearing twice, meadows, primroses, and wood are associated.[32] 'Little' appears twice as a daring choice of word to put into comparison with overgrown London. Pancrass and Kentish-town, two names for one medieval place, appear for what they had been, and just suffering from a building boom: Kentish Town was a village on the way to Highgate. In *Jerusalem* 37.7, Islington and Pancrass, and Marybone and Tyburn's River reappear related to 'black melancholy' which is a 'net'. The 'bone' was the Tyburn; Marybone makes the river Mary's, like the bright heliotropic Marygold of Leutha's vale (E. 45, K. 189), while, spelled Marylebone, associating the bourne from which no traveler returns with the bone (death) of 'Tyburn's Brook'. The depressive aspects of London appear there, and Jerusalem cannot escape to the west of London, but must go south to 'Lambeth's mild Vale' and to the Surrey Hills (37.9–12, E. 183, K. 668), to be discussed below.

Lamentation begins at the seventh verse, with the changed meaning of 'golden'. Paddington, a small village with a new church built in 1791, was full of poverty-stricken Irish labourers, digging the Grand Junction Canal (1795–1801) which was later to be connected to the Regent's Canal (1820), creating a canal system from the Thames to the Midlands, and is 'weeping' because of the presence of the gallows at Tyburn (removed, with the turnpike gate, in 1825). Druid pillars, perhaps the gallows, oppose the golden pillars of Nash's architecture. The language recalls the building of Golgonooza in *Jerusalem* 12.25–30 (E. 155, K. 623), where stones are pity and bricks are well-wrought affections, and accuses the spirit of Old Testament punishment which hangs people and which is allied with offerings of human life in soldiers being sent to war, where imperialism is the display of masculinity, since Albion's spectre tears forth in 'pomp of war' from his loins. The names in the last verse quoted go 'far' afield, following soldiers marching through Lambeth, punning on 'Lamb', and then to the East End. Poplar, its name changed much more than Cowper allows for in his poem about rural loss 'The Poplar-Field' – 'The Poplars are fell'd' (1785), had expanded from the development of the East and West India Docks, and from the East India Dock Road and the Commercial Road which opened up in the first ten years of the nineteenth century, and it became a parish separate from Stepney in 1817. Bow, on the London side of the river Lea (which divides London from Essex), at the beginning of the century, half Poplar's size (2000 people) and adjacent to it, was also engulfed. Further out, the Essex coast, including Maldon, reached through a Roman road out of London through Poplar and old Bow, becomes a place to export war to Europe.[33]

This lyric mode seems created by the prophetic. At the end of Chapter 1, Albion lamented that Jerusalem is a lost vision. What is built now is Babylon (24.30), which as a name for London (London becoming Babylon, one identity lost in another) becomes a common trope of the 1820s (as in *Don Juan* XI. xxiii).[34] Following the lyric, Los searches 'the interiors of Albion's bosom', entering 'the caves / Of despair & death to search the tempters out, walking among / Albion's rocks & precipices, caves of solitude & dark despair'. 'Despair' occurs three times in the survey that Los makes (2–28), while the picture of Los illustrating this – the Frontispiece to *Jerusalem* – shows him holding his 'globe of fire', so that he is going into the night of the grave from a particular high gate:

He came down from Highgate thro Hackney & Holloway towards
   London
Till he came to old Stratford & thence to Stepney & the Isle
Of Leuthas Dogs, thence tho the narrows of the Rivers side
And saw every minute particular, the jewels of Albion, running down
The kennels of the streets & lanes as if they were abhorrd.
Every Universal Form, was become barren mountains of Moral
Virtue: and every Minute Particular hardend into grains of sand:
And all the tendernesses of the soul cast forth as filth & mire,
Among the winding places of deep contemplation intricate
To where the Tower of London frownd dreadful over Jerusalem:
A building of Luvah builded in Jerusalems eastern gate to be
His secluded Court: thence to Bethlehem where was builded
Dens of despair in the house of bread: enquiring in vain
Of stones and rocks he took his way, for human form was none . . .

                    (45.14–27, E. 194, K. 656)

Some of these place names have been mapped before. Los goes south-eastwards to Hackney, at the limits of London, on the river Lea, its industrialism marked in its growth of population from 12,730 in 1801 to 22,494 in 1821. Holloway, between Highgate and Islington, came into prominence as a suburb when the Archway road opened in 1813, driven through a cutting in Highgate hill to improve the Great North Road, and with a toll which formed the northern gateway to the city. Old Stratford, on the far side of the river Lea, with Bow on the nearer side, was already industrial; Los retraces his steps to Stepney, the area east–west from the city to the Lea, and north–south from Hackney to the Thames. The Isle of Dogs, place of the 'Dogs of Leutha' (83.82), puns with the 'kennels' which the children (jewels) of Albion run down, sloping down to the river's side. The unstated pun on docks and dogs implies the degradation of dock-workers, even if, in bourgeois ideology, industrial work is presented in ideal terms, as if done for the country as the Feminine (Leutha). 'Narrows', water-courses, or narrow streets – Narrow Street runs westward along the shore through Limehouse from the Isle of Dogs – imply 'narrowed perceptions' (*Jerusalem* 49.21, E. 198, K. 679), and 'narrow' is a significant word in Blake. 'Barren mountains' and the 'grains of sand' may suggest buildings, such as chapels, monuments to 'Moral / Virtue' (the enjambement enables a double emphasis on the abstract qualities) made of sand (brick), but they make London a desert. By a displacement, the 'filth & mire' that are everywhere in this valley are not just actual filth; they represent emotions which are held to be valueless by the builders of this London, which are 'cast forth' as though they were the abject which the subject must eliminate to secure its identity, like the masculine paranoid Urizen casting out Ahania. The line 'And all the tendernesses of the soul cast forth as filth and mire', an image of abstracting, relates back to the jewels running down the kennels like waste water 'as if they were abhorr'd' (with a pun on ab-whored, emanations of the child harlot). The 'winding places of deep contemplation intricate' is an 'example of Blake conflating two images: the intricate and confusing alleys of London's poorer districts with the hidden places where the unknowable decisions are taken which produce and sanction such poverty in the first place'.[35] Los's survey of London counterpoints the Tower in the east (prison and armaments centre) with Bedlam (madhouse: home to despair, its product, and producing it). Los seems to stay north of the river, his Bedlam being Moorfields. The new Bedlam in Lambeth, south London, was built in 1815, not coincidental with Blake's residence in the area.[36] The building of Luvah shows the translation of love, a specific tenderness of the soul,

into militarism, while building the 'house of bread' – the meaning of
Bethlehem – as a den of despair shows another translation. While 'London's towers' are seen in an Utopian moment in the lyric in *Jerusalem*
77.10 (E. 232, K. 718), for the present, the reality is of 'Londons dark-frowning towers' (*Milton* 1.19.39, E. 113, K. 501).

Los's survey convinces him that he could do nothing, for vengeance
would only 'punish the already punish'd' if he could find the 'Criminals'
who have degraded the 'minute particulars' of city-life. The phrase, which
contrasts with the sense of the city as abstract, recurs four times, and
associates with the 'articulations of a mans soul' (45.10) which are
destroyed in brickmaking, and with another term the 'minutia' from
which Los is closed off: however he tries, he is alienated from the
conditions he sees.

> So spoke Los, travelling thro darkness & horrid solitude:
> And he beheld Jerusalem in Westminster & Marybone,
> Among the ruins of the Temple: and Vala who is her Shadow,
> Jerusalems Shadow bent northward over the Island white.
> At length he sat on London Stone, & heard Jerusalems voice . . .
>   (45.39–43, E. 195, K. 657)

Darkness and horrid solitude, the very conditions of the *il y a*, the neuter
state of no meaning, make this progress from west, to north of Oxford
Street, to the Temple, just east of the entrance to the City of London, and
then to London Stone within the City, like the 'Stone of Night' (*America*
5.1, E. 53, K. 197, see D. 130–1), posited as a place where Druids sacri-
ficed, a journey into the night, which is the shadow of Vala, the night
having the potential of the disarming feminine. London stone is 'where
Soldiers are shot', and it and Tyburn, with which it is equated, make up
the absent centre of London. Later, in *Jerusalem* 74, the loss of Reuben, a
figure for the male soldier, gives the added sense that 'London Stone' is
the place for the loss of masculinity as a result of the agencies of the
feminine in the city, a repeat of the alliance of Enitharmon with warfare
(*Jerusalem* 74.33–7, E. 230, K. 715).[37] A failure at the level of the masculine
(the appearance of the spectre) is complemented by a failure at the level
of the feminine: two sources of the city's distress and melancholia.

Autobiography in the city

We intend to call on Saturday afternoon in Hampstead, to take fare-
well, All things being now nearly completed for our setting forth on

Tuesday Morning; it is only Sixty Miles, & Lambeth was One Hundred, for the terrible desart of London was between.

(Catherine Blake to Mrs Flaxman,
14 September 1800, E. 708, K. 800)

Mrs Blake's letter shows London deranging a sense of place: Felpham is
sixty miles south of Lambeth, which is six miles south of Hampstead.
But between the latter two is a 'desart', an abstraction, a source of fear.
To name the places within it constructs the subject's autobiography,
and attempts to make something of the city, to build it, in writing, as
Jerusalem. In *Jerusalem* plate 38 (34), two new voices are heard, both
part of what London embodies. One is autobiographical, speaking from
South Molton Street (compare *Milton* 4.21, E. 98, K. 484; there is a pun
here: Milton/Molton) and naming other places, Lambeth, and Felpham
in Sussex. Autobiography, a word OED dates to 1797, appears in relation
to city spaces, houses, and streets. The voice feels responsibility, related
to precise locales.[38]

The voice responds to another voice, the city as masculine ('Cities are
Men' (34.46–7)), not Jerusalem ('a City yet a Woman', *FZ* 9.222, E. 391,
K. 362).[39]

I behold London; a Human awful wonder of God!
He says: Return, Albion, return! I give myself for thee:
My Streets are my, Ideas of Imagination...
My Houses are Thoughts: my Inhabitants; Affections,
The children of my thoughts, walking within my blood-vessels,
Shut from my nervous form which sleeps upon the verge of Beulah
In dreams of darkness, while my vegetating blood in veiny pipes,
Rolls dreadful thro' the Furnaces of Los, and the Mills of Satan.
For Albions sake, and for Jerusalem thy Emanation
I give myself, and these my brethren give themselves for Albion.

So spoke London, immortal Guardian! I heard in Lambeths shades:
In Felpham I heard and saw the Visions of Albion
I write in South Molton Street, what I both see and hear
In regions of Humanity, in Londons opening streets.

(*Jerusalem* 34.29–43, E. 180, K. 665)

London's network of communications feed it; as 'a Human awful
wonder of God' it is like the Tyger, unrepresentable. The passage shows
no negativity: rather, the city is always in transition, and as the work of

both Urizen and Los, it is the source of not only melancholia, as in 'London' but also, as here, wonder. On 2 July 1800, Blake in a letter to George Cumberland (1754–1848) comments on his plans for a National Gallery (Cumberland had, in 1793, written a 'Plan for Improving the Arts in England').[40] Blake says that he has begun to emerge 'from a Deep pit of Melancholy', and perhaps his change relates to London's readiness to accept the visual arts:

> It is very Extraordinary that London in so few years from a city of meer Necessaries . . . should have become a City of Elegance in some degree, and that its once stupid inhabitants should enter into an Emulation of Grecian manners.

For himself, he remembers when a printshop was 'a rare bird' and when he thought his 'pursuits of Art a kind of Criminal Dissipation & neglect of the main chance' (E. 706, K. 798). He also noted, in a letter to William Hayley (26 October 1803), signs of a new consumer-culture:

> The shops in London improve; everything is elegant, clean and neat; the streets are widened where they were narrow; even Snow Hill [near Smithfield] is become almost level, and is a very handsome street, and the narrow part of the Strand near St. Clement's is widened and become very elegant.
>
> (E. 738, K. 831)

Imagination, thoughts, and affections are placed at the heart of London: in Golgonooza, in metonymies which represent the people, 'the stones are pity, & the bricks, well wrought affections' (*Jerusalem* 12.20, E. 155, K. 632). It is the opposite of the witty literality of 'Prisons are built with stones of Law, Brothels with bricks of Religion' (*MHH* 8.1, E. 36, K. 151). (Stones were heavy to transport and came from outside London: everything about the prison and law, which is of Urizen, is heavy. Bricks were easy to make and to bring into London.) *Jerusalem* 34 concludes with London as Golgotha, destroying 'Victims to Justice', adding:

> There is in Albion a Gate of Precious stones and gold
> Seen only by Emanations, by vegetations viewless,
> Bending across the road of Oxford Street; it from Hyde Park
> To Tyburns deathful shades, admits the wandering souls
> Of multitudes who die from Earth: this Gate cannot be found
> By Satans Watch-fiends tho' they search numbering every grain

Of sand on Earth every night, they never find this Gate.
It is the Gate of Los.

(*Jerusalem* 34.55–9, 35.1–3, E. 181, K. 664, 666)

London in the early nineteenth century retains its ghosts of Tyburn, which is like London Stone: what official London stands for. Tyburn had been replaced by Newgate for executions after 1783, but in this writing nothing has changed.[41] As Hogarth showed in an engraving, 21 could be hanged at Tyburn at once.[42] On Rocque's map of London, South Molton Street gives onto Tiburn (Tyburn) Road, which to the east becomes Oxford Street. This had been laid out in 1739 on the site of a Roman road, with much development between 1763 and 1793.[43] At the intersection of South Molton Street and Stratford Place (*Milton* 4.21, and *Jerusalem* 74.55), created in the 1770s (contrasting with 'Old Stratford'), the Tyburn stream, which flowed through the village of Marylebone, disappeared underground. The place of execution was at the end of Tiburn Road, also by a stream called the Tyburn (present-day Park Lane was Tiburn Lane: the stream ran parallel to it). This perpetuation of names, showing that their significance is not predictable or stable, preserves memory of oppression, important when the builders and architects – who would reinterpret it – are of the class responsible for oppression. London is here Urizen's creation (the reference to Satan is significant) and holds its oppression within it.

The 'I' who heard London spoke from South Molton Street. The continuation of Regent's Street from Piccadilly – Blake was baptized at St James, Wren's Church of 1684 – to Oxford Street, and whose construction demolished streets and houses, has Glasshouse Street, first mentioned in the ratebooks in 1678, going off it to the right: Blake's father lived there from 1744 to 1753. North of this is Golden Square, laid out at the beginning of the eighteenth century.[44] Two blocks north of that is Broadwick Street on the right. It was then called Broad Street, at no. 28, demolished in 1963, and there Blake was born to James Blake (c. 1723–1784) and Catherine Harmitage (c. 1722–1792). After his father's death, he lived at 27 Broad Street for a year with James Parker, his partner. He moved to the next street to the left, 28 Poland Street (1785–1790), where *Songs of Innocence* were written. At no. 1 Broad Street, Fuseli lived from 1777 to 1781. After 1789, Thomas Butts lived on the north side of Great Marlborough Street, which runs between Regent Street and Poland Street, and which, laid out like Poland Street at the beginning of the eighteenth century, was named for Marlborough's victory at Blenheim in 1704.

Soho and Westminster constructed Blake, who attended Mr Par's drawing school in the Strand at the age of ten. At the further end of the Strand was Somerset House, then partly given to the Royal Academy, where he studied in 1779. His apprenticeship and lodging (1772–1779) were with James Basire at 31 Great Queen Street, on the way to Lincoln's Inn Fields. Going to Basire from Broad Street meant walking a mile south-east across Soho. His first married home was in rooms south of Leicester Square (23 Green Street, Leicester Fields, now Irving Street). Leicester Square was home to artists: Hogarth, Sir Joshua Reynolds, Sir Thomas Lawrence, and John Copley. North of Soho, running into Oxford Street, was South Molton Street, Blake's home from 1804 to 1821, but north of Oxford Street a road leads to Cavendish Square in Marylebone, where George Romney lived for twenty years from 1777 (in 1783, fifteen portraitists had an address there). Blake associated with Flaxman (1755–1826) who lived in Wardour Street, and with other artists including Thomas Stodhard (1755–1834), who lived in Newman Street, and perhaps George Cumberland, at 27 Rathbone Place, the house of Mrs Harriet Mathew, wife of the Rev Anthony Stephen Mathew of Percy Chapel, Charlotte Street, a Wilberforce Church. Charlotte Street, named after George III's wife, was an artists' colony. The milieu for *An Island in the Moon* (c. 1784) relates to this circle. North of this was Fitzroy Square and Warren Street, laid out in 1790–1791, home of more wealthy engravers, Cromek, and, later, Flaxman. Further east, Blake associated with the radical printer Joseph Johnson (1738–1809), at 72 St Paul's Churchyard, in the city (*SP* 110–17). Swedenborgianism in 1789 took him to the New Jerusalem Church, in Eastcheap, north of London Bridge. Blake's last move (see Chapter 7) was to Fountain Court, off the Strand. His widow kept house for John Linnell at his townhouse, 6 Cirencester Place, off Fitzroy Square (Linnell had moved his family to Hampstead), then for Frederick Tatham at 20 Lisson Grove in Marylebone; dying in 1831 in lodgings at 17 Charlton Street, off Fitzroy Square, and buried, like Blake's family, in Bunhill Fields.[45]

Thinking of this small space which stamped itself on Blake as he did on it amplifies Jean Hagstrum: 'The Dante of the parochial Blake is a work of a bold genius who continues to inspire; the Dante of . . . Flaxman (who illustrated Dante in Rome) now seems time-bound.'[46] The affirmatory point remains despite so much city-melancholia. In *Jerusalem* 83, Los bids the Daughters of Beulah: 'Found ye London! enormous City!' The 'River' weeps, and Los thinks, perhaps through Gray's 'Ode on a Distant Prospect of Eton College' (1747) of the Thames upstream at Windsor, of 'weaving bowers of delight on the current of infant Thames / Where the old Parent still retains his youth' (*Jerusalem* 83.23, 49–50, E. 241–2, K. 727–8). But a walk Los makes returns to 'trembling Thames', identified with the Euphrates (exile in Babylon). Albion's daughters call to 'wake' before continuing with a passage which names, in the first two lines, sites north of the river, before turning south to Lambeth:

Highgates heights & Hampsteads, to Poplar Hackney & Bow:
To Islington & Paddington & the Brook of Albions River
We builded Jerusalem as a City & a Temple; from Lambeth
We began our Foundations; lovely Lambeth! O lovely Hills
Of Camberwell, we shall behold you no more in glory & pride
For Jerusalem lies in ruins & the Furnaces of Los are builded there
You are now shrunk to a narrow Rock in the midst of the Sea
But here we build Babylon on Euphrates, compelld to build
And to inhabit, our Little-ones to clothe in armour of the gold
Of Jerusalems Cherubims & to forge them swords of her Altars
I see London blind & age-bent begging thro the Streets
Of Babylon, led by a child. his tears run down his beard
The voice of Wandering Reuben ecchoes from street to street
In all the cities of the Nations Paris Madrid Amsterdam
The Corner of Broad Street weeps; Poland Street languishes
To Great Queen Street & Lincolns Inn, all is distress & woe.

(*Jerusalem* 84.1–16, E. 243, K. 729)

'Lovely Lambeth' and the 'lovely hills of Camberwell' contrast with a passage in *Milton* on 'Lambeth vale' – dark, shadowed by death:

The Surrey hills glow like the clinkers of the furnace: Lambeths Vale
Where Jerusalems foundations began . . .

Return: return to Lambeths Vale O building of human souls
Thence stony Druid Temples overspread the Island white . . .

(*Milton* 6.14–19, E. 99–100, K. 485)

Lambeth Palace – a Druid Temple – sat by the horse ferry south of the Thames and Westminster. Lambeth Road runs away from the river with Hercules Road on its left, where a block of flats bears a plaque indicating that Blake lived from autumn 1790 to September 1800 at 13 Hercules Buildings, built in 1770. In *Milton* 25.48–50 (E. 122, K. 511), Lambeth is Jerusalem's 'inner court', 'ruin'd and given / To the detestable Gods of Priam [warfare preached from Lambeth Palace], to Apollo, and at the

Asylum / Given to Hercules' (type of the Zoas). The Asylum for Female Orphans stood at the junction Hercules Road makes at its other end with the road from Kennington, which becomes Westminster Bridge Road. In Edward Howard's autobiographical novel, *Rattlin the Reefer* (1836), the hero's early childhood in the 1790s is spent in Lambeth as an area abounding in saw-pits, and the novel gives testimony to the Archbishop's 'putting down all the jollity' by pulling down the 'Two Jolly Sawyers' inn and replacing it with a large wharf.[47] Lower Marsh road, where the Utilitarian Francis Place had lived in the 1780s, runs right from Kennington Lane. South of it, Place said, were only 'gardeners' grounds and open meadows' while Lower Marsh road was 'the only way from the Horse-ferry at Lambeth Palace to the Borough [i.e. Southwark], there was then no other horse or Carriage way excepting one close to the river. I have heard my father say that he has shot snipe in the marshes...A town has since been built on the Garden Grounds and meadows and the lane called the Marsh has been made into a street.'[48] The road meets Waterloo Road and Waterloo Bridge, which, Place noted in 1841, stood 'where there was a ferry and the Victoria theatre...where was a field. Lambeth Marsh, then a lane through the meadows, is now a street through the new town'.[49] Downstream from Lambeth is London Bridge and, further, Rotherhithe, where Blake's father was apprenticed as a hosier. The road south from London Bridge passes the site of the Tabard, the inn opening *The Canterbury Tales*. Blake's *The Canterbury Pilgrims*, which he exhibited in 1809, shows the landscape 'as it may be supposed to have appeared in Chaucer's time; interspersed with cottages and villages'. For Blake the antiquarian, Chaucer's Host, Henry Baillie, is 'the keeper of the greatest Inn, of the greatest City; for such was the Tabarde Inn in Southwark, near London' (*A Descriptive Catalogue* E. 532, 535, K. 567, 569).[50] And here was the medieval Southwark Fair, painted by Hogarth, suppressed in 1763; here, Dickens's Marshalsea prison.

The ground ascends from the river, towards Camberwell: Camberwell new road was opened in 1815. The south side of the hills, including 'Brockley Hills' (*Jerusalem* 90.24), includes Dulwich and, further east, another site: 'On Peckham Rye, (by Dulwich Hill)...while quite a child, of eight or ten perhaps, [Blake] has his "first vision". Sauntering along, the boy looks up and sees a tree filled with angels, bright angelic wings bespangling every bough like stars.... Another time, one summer morn, he sees the haymakers at work, and amid them angelic figures walking.' The associations of rye and harvesting are apocalyptic. The city in vision is equally divine: Gilchrist tells of the boy speaking of a city 'in which the houses were of gold, the pavement of silver, the gates ornamented

with precious stones'.[51] Palmer said that Blake was 'fond of the country
& particularly of that part surrounding Dulwich, he much preferred it
to Hampstead & would take long walks in that neighbourhood with
Palmer pointing *from* those passages of scenery he thought most beautiful'.[52] For Palmer, in a sketch-book note of 1824: 'When you go to
Dulwich it is not enough on coming home to make recollections in
which shall be united the scattered parts about those sweet fields into
a sentimental and Dulwich looking whole No but considering Dulwich
as the gate into the world of vision one must try behind the hills to
bring up a mystic glimmer.'[53]

In *Jerusalem* 84, London has not been built or transformed as
Jerusalem. Under the force of compulsion it is alienating and militaristic
and the power of the feminine (*The Four Zoas* 8.330, E. 379, K. 349),
controlling the masculine by 'Rational Morality', by which means it
traps Reuben (*Jerusalem* 74.32,34, E. 230, K. 715). London is reduced,
captive to Babylon, 'blind & age-bent, begging . . . led by a child'. Blind,
like Wordsworth's blind beggar in *The Prelude* 7, visionless, like Urizen
or Milton's Samson, London appears, in the illustration to plate 84, as
an old man who walks wearily on crutches and figures. The image recalls
the old man of 'Death's door'. To the left in the pictures rises a Gothic
Church with the dome of St Paul's behind it: perhaps a composite
image of Westminster Abbey and the city of London, 'a City & a Temple',
which also recalls the passage from *Jerusalem* 45.39–43. In the illustration
to plate 46, St Paul's appears on the left and a Gothic cathedral, perhaps
Westminster Abbey, is separate to the right; in the illustration to
plate 57, a dome is marked 'London' and, below, a Gothic Church is
marked 'Jerusalem'. The composite church in plate 84 puts Jerusalem
inside Babylon, confounding identity. Behind, a reddish half-seen sun
appears in the West (Westminster), or in the east (St Paul's, Babylon).

Another blind man and a boy pass a closed door in the picture for
'London', a picture with less relationship to the text but rendering weakness and woe. In *Jerusalem*, the old man weeps, but two lines further, so
do places associated with Blake's youth. The old man, passing a corner
('the Corner of Broad Street') – no corner in 'London' – embodies those
place names, representing their decay or their loss of meaning. Perhaps
the otherness of Paris, Madrid, and Amsterdam appear because of 'Poland'
Street, implying what lost otherness is folded into London. The old
man's fate is entwined with Reuben's whose voice echoes from street to
street. London appears as youth, maturity, and old age. The boy leads the
old man, in an act analogous to writing the poem. While in 'London'
his visibility represses the youthful harlot's, he may figure Blake's

childhood, having lived in these places, making him not separate from this London though he knows nothing of the sexual confusion caused by the presence of 'Babylon in the opening Street of London' (*Jerusalem* 74.16, E. 229, K. 714). The boy and the youthful harlot may be counter-posed images for Blake, their co-existence showing that both speak for the city, indicating that there is no single way to read it, nor a single time. Yet place names no longer relating, or conferring identity, or recording what has disappeared, or changed, engender the other night, space of madness and of the 'neuter', the loss of self in the act of writing the city. Two madnesses – one akin to mournfulness, or despair, the other created through midnight streets – make identities pale, deranged.

6

'Forests of the Night': Blake and Madness

> I begin to Emerge from a Deep pit of Melancholy, Melancholy
> without any real reason for it, a Disease which God keep you
> from & all good men'
>
> (E. 706, K. 798)

'Madmen see outlines & therefore they draw them'[1]

'Madness', as the possession or loss of identity, is a crisis fascinating
Blake's 'night thoughts'. What enables distinguishing and naming
discrete forms and identities? – as in *The Marriage of Heaven and Hell*
(1790)? This is cited by Bataille in *Literature and Evil*, associating it with
the French Revolution, in his argument of Blake's need to 'look Evil
[including madness] boldly in the face':[2]

> Without Contraries is no progression. Attraction and Repulsion, Reason
> and Energy, Love and Hate, are necessary to Human existence.
>   From these contraries spring what the religious call Good & Evil.
> Good is the passive that obeys Reason. Evil is the active springing
> from Energy.
>   Good is Heaven. Evil is Hell.

The language of the religious, paraphrased, betrays them. If 'Good' is
defined as passive, 'the active springing from Energy' must be preferable
to that (and gender-considerations might give priority to the active).
The religious equate evil with Hell, but the next passage, being called
'The voice of the Devil', asks, implicitly, who spoke earlier? The Devil's?
But he cannot have the right answers, since he is inside the system
he describes:

124

All Bibles or sacred codes have been the causes of the following Errors.

1. That Man has two real existing principles: Viz: A Body & a Soul.
2. That Energy. calld Evil, is alone from the Body. & that Reason. calld Good. is alone from the Soul.
3. That God will torment Man in Eternity for following his Energies.

But the following Contraries to these are True

1. Man has no Body distinct from his Soul for that calld Body is a portion of Soul discernd by the five Senses. the chief inlets of Soul in this age
2. Energy is the only life, and is from the Body and Reason is the bound or outward circumference of Energy
3. Energy is Eternal Delight.

(E. 34, K. 149)

For the Devil, all Bibles have perpetuated a body / soul dualism, responding to the Heaven / Hell dualism, but his talk of 'contraries' is equally dualistic. He sees both Energy and Reason as both of the body, so uniting them, but the previous section has made them contraries, so distinguishable. And if they could not be distinguished, there could be no *Marriage of Heaven and Hell*; nothing except what Hell represents. And apart from the voice of the Devil, the words 'Errors' and 'True' are problematic. Error, in the 'Proverbs of Hell', seems always productive, and if the Devil knows that his are 'contrary' truths, and that 'without Contraries is no progression', then he must grant error its truth.[3] Energy and reason are distinguishable; we cannot just speak from the standpoint of the devil's party.

'Reason is the bound or outward circumference of Energy' recalls 'The Tyger' and, like it, asks if the bound or outward circumference is on the inside or the outside. No poet is keener than Blake on the great and golden rule of art and life being 'the more distinct, sharp, and wiry the bounding line, the more perfect the work of art' (*A Descriptive Catalogue* E. 550, K. 585).[4] Though the line guarantees nothing since 'A fool sees not the same tree that a wise man sees' (*MHH* 7.8, E. 35, K. 151), it nonetheless puts certain things on the outside, and distinguishes between what is of the law and what is transgressive. The outline, opposed in Blake to abstraction (*Jerusalem* 74.25, 26, E. 229, K. 715), is outside the line, yet it is the line, the boundary, the limit which separates the inline from the outside line. That ambiguity informs 'The Tyger':

Tyger Tyger, burning bright,
In the forests of the night;
What immortal hand or eye,
Could frame thy fearful symmetry?

In what distant deeps or skies.
Burnt the fire of thine eyes?
On what wings dare he aspire?
What the hand, dare sieze the fire?

Drafts:
Burn in distant deeps or skies
The cruel fire of thine eye?
Could heart descend or wings aspire?
What the hand dare seize the fire?

[In what – *del.*] [Burnt in – *del.*] distant deeps or skies
[Burnt the – *del.*] [The cruel – *del.*] fire of thine eyes?
And what shoulder, & what art,
Could twist the sinews of thy heart?
And when thy heart began to beat,
What dread hand? & what dread feet?
[*or:* What dread hand Form'd thy dread feet?]
[or: forged][5]

What the hammer? what the chain?
In what furnace was thy brain?
What the anvil? What dread grasp,
Dare its deadly terrors clasp!

Drafts:
Could fetch it from the furnace deep
And in the horrid ribs dare steep
In the well of sanguine woe

In what clay & in what mold
Were thy eyes of fury rolld
When the stars threw down their spears
And water'd heaven with their tears:
Did he smile his work to see?
Did he who made the Lamb make thee?

Drafts:
And did he laugh his work to see

And dare he [smile – *del.*] [laugh – *del.*] his work to see;
[What the [shoulder – *del.*] ancle? What the knee? – *del.*]
[Did – *del.*] Dare he who made the lamb make thee?'

Tyger Tyger burning bright,
In the forests of the night:
What immortal hand or eye,
Dare frame thy fearful symmetry?

(E. 24–5, 794, K. 172, 214)

The tyger asserts a framed identity, designed by something organized
with hand, eye, wings, shoulder, art, and feet. Bataille (p. 93), focusing
on 'deadly terrors', makes the tyger the embodiment of heterogeneous
evil or cruelty. Its fearful symmetry – the tiger's markings, its outer
circumference – poses the issue; if this boundary is the marker of reason,
according to the Devil, is that produced from something inside the
body or from without? Bataille quotes 'The roaring of lions, the howling
of wolves, the raging of the stormy sea, and the destructive sword are
portions of eternity too great for the eye of man' (8.7, E. 36, K. 151). If
the tyger may be included here, what it embodies seems outside, part of
eternity, save that the word 'portion' – which may include 'proportion' –
may imply just such a separating and individuating as the poem shows.
Bataille's 'evil' is heterogeneous, outside and necessarily plural, while
reason is single, directed to one end, but here, what is within bounds
is the heterogeneous, and what is outside such bounds has identity. If
the outside of this inside constitutes and frames, reason is on the outside,
making it ambiguous because heterological. The reversal of a model
putting the transgressive and heterogeneous on the outside, and making
the framed the homogeneous, leaves it ambiguous whether energy is
transgressive or constitutive and the relation between energy and identity. Both energy and reason, in opposite ways, assert identity, which is
why nothing is said about the tyger in the poem.

It is ambiguous that the poem is framed by questions, altering from
first to last framing stanzas from 'Could frame' to 'Dare frame' as if,
after confronting the possibilities, it is decided that none dared frame;
that the model of a framer framing must go. While 'make' in line 20
may be a synonym for 'frame', 'frame' in OED vb.7c means 'to form, to
construct in the mind, to conceive, imagine', giving the idea of a framer
planning from the origin. Is it to be imagined that anyone could
plan the tyger's fearful symmetry? Could it be dared? One answer is
no, nothing has planned this symmetry: energy has neither origin

nor frame. A model framing passivity (the Lamb) could not work here.
But if the model disappears, so does the schema identifying energy with
the inside, which is puzzled about the border because though it is
constituted by reason, it must have something else outside the border,
which, if reason, makes that heterogeneous.

But perhaps the last line does not abolish what has been said; 'dare'
could affirm the lines preceding. Then it asks what *is* outside, a first
answer being 'the forests of the night', where the tyger burns, fire its
essence. These ancient trees are the nightwood of the lost, Dante's 'dark
wood' (*Inferno* 1, 1–3), the 'forests of night' (*Europe* 10.18, E. 63, K. 241).
And there is the space from where energy has come – 'distant deeps
or skies', requiring the 'he' who framed the tyger to 'aspire' – a word
associated with Icarus and Marlovian tragedy (the hand with the fire is
Promethean). Asking where the brain of the burning tyger burned,
draws on further realms of energy, evoked when the stars threw down
their spears, 'And water'd heaven with their tears' – the verb used in
'A Poison Tree' and *For the Sexes*, and quoting Adam, who wants to
'pardon beg; with tears/Watering the ground' (*Paradise Lost* 10, 1089–90).
While repentance and self-pity may be indistinguishable, it seems that
a prior 'repentance' to Adam's, in a different scene, has been exacted:
spears have become tears, stars pacified, feminized. When Urizen thinks
of the stars throwing down their spears (*The Four Zoas*, Night the Fifth),
there are no tears, nor fears, another significant, perhaps unconsciously
held rhyme-word which is supplied by the poem 'The Angel'. A Notebook
poem called 'Morning' hopes 'To find the Western path' to 'the break
of day':

> The war of swords & spears
> Melted by dewy tears
> Exhales on high
> The Sun is freed from tears
> And with soft grateful tears
> Ascends the sky

(E. 478, K. 421)

The tears put an end to the war; in 'The Tyger' the tears are part of that
war, which makes the poem of the night, not of a break of day. In the
line 'Did he smile his work to see?', there are no tears, like those of the
sun, and the question puzzles: is the 'work' the tyger? Then the smile is
directed at that artwork, as perhaps also at the lamb (which, as passive
may imply the female, while the tyger is male, so that the passive/

active order (Eve before Adam), replaces a typical gendering). Or is the 'work' the havoc wreaked in heaven, securing the tears of the spheres? If the first reading seems inadequate for the framer, the second makes him not only an overreacher and aspirer, but a rationalist, who has completed something and now stands as if saying 'Glad I see', like the man of tears in 'A Poison Tree'. Are the creator and the tyger implicitly opposed, as reason against energy? (That may be the point of the last line: 'Dare frame'. Perhaps the energy of the framer, now has become rationality, can stand up to a new energy. Framing the tyger may be the framer destroying itself, in which case, there is nothing but energy, destroying reason.) Or the smile may be implied superiority over a new energy.

Bataille senses in Blake's 'stare' 'both resolution and fear' yet if the poem's drafts are considered, the changes repress the tyger's fieriness, restricting these to 'deadly terrors'. But the monstrous is still emphasized: 'Did he who made the Lamb make thee?' stresses that the monstrous has been created, like the poem, which frames (its difficulties in framing becoming apparent through the revisions, never fully resolved). Tyger and poem are products of a *poeisis* presenting the unrepresentable. As an apostrophe, the poem gives the illusion of something to be addressed, conveying the speaker's mastery in being able to speak. But the tyger cannot reply, not being in the poem; the questions are addressed to what is outside, or at the circumference, while the tyger's essence is burning, which has no 'bound or outward circumference', no 'wirey bounding line'. The apostrophe to the tyger is not about the tyger but, metonymically, about its putative framer. Nothing can be said about the tyger because the tyger is not there. No wonder there is a gap between the tyger and its representation in the illustration. Steven Shaviro sees a repression at the heart of the text: 'the fixation which isolates and designates the tyger is also the repression which renders it inaccessible'.[6] The repression may be explained: that the tyger embodies one of the contraries without which is no progression, but the attitude speaking of these 'contraries' is situated, like the Devil's voice, on the side of energy. The other contrary is not spoken for by anything outside the system of contraries. 'The Tyger' tries to speak from an outside position about both contraries, energy and reason, but cannot, must identify with the tyger, and so with the first term of the contrary. Yet an identification with energy is over-simple. The poem, for instance, shows a virtual absence of the sexual, not just by individuating a single tyger, but also through non-sexual language, save perhaps the draft-word 'cruel' (compare 'A Divine Image' in *Songs of Experience* E. 32, K. 221). 'Cruel', like 'eyes', assumes another's presence, but 'cruel' was cut. Energy must be seen in plural terms: the tyger is a kind of energy, but not its essence, and if presented as that, there may be a repression.

Perhaps what *should* be the subject of the apostrophe is the framer, not the tyger. By making it the tyger, that is an absence within the poem, like the other subject, the framer, who may be reason. If nothing can be said about him then that is ambiguous because the framer stands in relation to the poem's speaker, also framing, forming, and making. Is the poet also then reason? The text cannot draw that conclusion. It seems rather, in the draft 'what dread hand formed thy dread feet', that hands and feet are drawn together into a single body, which is the poem (having stanzaic, symmetrical, feet), but which is incomplete, as this poem is not quite finished. The dread is of the single identity into which the framer and the framed are pulled into; the framer framed. 'Dread grasp' links with 'deadly terrors'. 'Dread' in *Songs of Experience* appears otherwise twice in 'Earth's Answer' ('the darkness dread & drear', and 'Stony dread!' (E. 18, K. 210) where dread petrifies energy. Fear of fiery energy and dread of stonification coalesce; fear of forming is of becoming what is formed and given identity (like Los binding Urizen), or of formation as abstraction. Fear of being formed is of being assigned a single identity.

In *Europe*, 'the nameless shadowy female' who obeys Enitharmon says:

> Unwilling I look up to heaven! unwilling count the stars!
> Sitting in fathomless abyss of my immortal shrine.
> I sieze their burning power
> And bring forth howling terrors, all devouring fiery kings.
>
> Devouring & devoured, roaming on dark and desolate mountains
> In forests of death, shrieking in hollow trees.
> Ah mother Enitharmon!
> Stamp not with solid form this vig'rous progeny of fires.
>
> *(Europe 2.1–9, E. 61, K. 238)*

Attention to the stars may recall the influential work of the astronomer Frederick William Hershel (1738–1822). The nameless shadowy female works like the framer, seizing the power of the stars and weakening them because, as agent of Enitharmon, she stamps on them a solid form, so limiting their spirit of liberty. *Europe* relates to 'The Tyger'. In 'When the stars threw down their spears', it seems that there must be more than the contraries. The framer (reason who is energy) produces the tyger (energy whose fearful symmetry is rational) and there is then another division apparent, when stars appear, simultaneously becoming impotent. The poem moves metonymically: tyger / framer / stars / spears rendered passive, with further ambiguities because of a fourth 'other', also passive, the Lamb. One unknowable succeeds and produces another. The tyger may also be a constellation. As 'deeps' are the further reaches of the cosmos, unfallen or fallen – 'the starry heighth, to the starry depth' (*Jerusalem* 11.12, E. 154, K. 630) – so Johannes Helvelius' seventeenth-century constellation of nineteen stars, the Lynx, was also called the Tyger'.[7] Does the poem apostrophize a constellation? Then constellating might suggest the work of the poem, in Wallace Stevens's sense, 'Fixing emblazoned zones and fiery poles / Arranging, deepening, enchanting night' ('The Idea of Order at Key West'). It would also recall Walter Benjamin's 'Ideas are to objects as constellations are to stars' – ideas, like constellations, being both fictitious and real.[8] The idea is being set against the night. But if the tyger is a constellation, the stars who throw down their spears show the stellar universe splitting, night becomes self-destructive in a torment of love and jealousy.

In *Europe*, 'the forests of the night' are not the cosmos but the place of oppression for those stars stamped with solid form. The action of creating identity is fearful, in reducing energy. 'To the Evening Star' (*Poetical Sketches*) concludes:

> Let thy west wind sleep on
> The lake; speak silence with thy glimmering eyes,
> And wash the dusk with silver. Soon, full soon,
> Dost thou withdraw; then the wolf rages wide,
> And the lion glares thro' the dun forest...
>
> (E. 410, K. 3)

'Silence' and 'silver' aligned give twilight, but the 'rage' of the wolf and the eyes of the lion evoke the madness of the night (the lion shares the same context as the tyger), while 'dun' also implies a loss of energy, the onset of melancholia.

One word dropped from 'The Tyger' drafts was 'fury' – 'were thy eyes of fury roll'd' – in the poem's second reference to eyes (often compared to stars). 'Fury' in the poem engenders 'furnace', and the Concordance has two pages of entries for it (another page for 'furies' and 'furious'), showing the potential of 'madness', 'anger', or 'rage' (the latter, with its cognates takes over two pages in the Concordance). It associates in the draft with the rarely used 'sanguine',[9] deriving from the hyacinth as 'that sanguine flower inscribed with woe' (*Lycidas* 106). Madness associated with blood is heterogeneous: the last version is less violent than the draft. Repression which creates identity and cuts 'horrid ribs' – visible, discernible form that causes horror – implies that the tyger's appearance in the forests of the night has traces of the traumatic, burning, tearing: wounding.

Madness: the lyric poetry

Madness may assert or refuse identity, be as much desired as feared. *Poetical Sketches* (1783) contains poems of madness, called 'Song'.[10] Their coda, self-reflective about lyricism, is called 'To the Muses'.[11] The first 'Song' seems an 'autobiography' – completed at fourteen – the gender unstable:

> How sweet I roam'd from field to field,
> And tasted all the summer's pride,
> 'Till I the prince of love beheld,
> Who in the sunny beams did glide!
>
> He shew'd me lilies for my hair,
> And blushing roses for my brow;
> He led me through his gardens fair,
> Where all his golden pleasures grow.
>
> With sweet May dews my wings were wet,
> And Phoebus fir'd my vocal rage;
> He caught me in his silken net,
> And shut me in his golden cage.
>
> He loves to sit and hear me sing,
> Then, laughing, sports and plays with me;
> Then stretches out my golden wing,
> And mocks my loss of liberty.
>
> (E. 412–13, K. 6)

Is the appeal of stanza 2 male- or female-directed, and does the prince of love (not Cupid, more Apollo, the sun, and poetry) appeal to the male or female? – For he does not behold the 'I', but the 'I' desires him, discerning him within something else. 'My vocal rage' links poetic inspiration and singing with the instability of passion, and through 'rage', with madness. The 'silken net' and 'golden cage' succeed the garden as enclosures for singing, houses for the mad. The prince of love, while heterogeneous, incarcerates, confining and maddening.[12] There is a sadism in the last stanza, as 'he' ensures the 'I' knows that it is trapped, and in a state of desire, however beautifully ('golden' appears three times, 'sweet' (very Blakean), twice). In *An Island in the Moon*, 'Matrimony' is the 'golden cage' (E. 460, K. 56). Is the last verse a woman commenting on her husband's 'male dominance and possessiveness' (so L.C. Knights, using *The Gates of Paradise* no. 7 for comparison)?[13] Or is the male complaining, when the last stanza makes the subject a victim? the 'wing' implying poetry, its wetness and dryness relating to the sexual, evidencing loss of liberty, evoking madness.

These 'Songs' alternate in passion and gender. 'My silks and fine array' shows the speaker feminine or feminized. With 'mournful lean Despair', there is no reference to song. The third, 'Love and harmony combine', where a change of 'her' to 'his' was made to describe love, celebrates 'innocence', a word also in the verb of the first line of the fourth, 'I love the jocund dance', where the speaker addresses 'Kitty'. The fifth, 'Memory, hither come / And tune your merry notes', quotes Amiens' 'song' in *As You Like It* (II. v. 1–8) which sounds positive, but makes memory a form of inspiration declining from energy, towards pensiveness, implying narcissism and a dreaming state, the opposite of song: 'And when night comes, I'll go / To places fit for woe, / Walking along the darken'd valley / With silent Melancholy'.[14] Memory, passive in its Lockean form, associates with melancholic night; and is addressed as something other ('*your* notes').[15] The sixth is 'Mad Song':

> The wild winds weep,
> And the night is a-cold;
> Come hither, Sleep,
> And my griefs infold [or unfold]:
> But lo! the morning peeps
> Over the eastern steeps,
> And the rustling birds of dawn
> The earth do scorn.
>
> Lo! to the vault
> Of paved heaven,
> With sorrow fraught
> My notes are driven:
> They strike the ear of night,

Make weep the eyes of day;
They make mad the roaring winds,
And with tempests play.

Like a fiend in a cloud
With howling woe,
After night I do croud,
And with night will go;
I turn my back to the east,
From whence comforts have increas'd;
For light doth seize my brain
With frantic pain.

(E. 415–16, K. 8–9)

Night appears in each stanza, in the second, breaking the rhyme to make
its entry. Night is cold, the time when sorrow is heard, the antithesis to
comfort. The poem is dramatic utterance, as if spoken by one of the
court exiles in *As You Like It*, or by Lear, the Fool, 'Poor Tom', 'old Tom
of Bedlam' (as in Percy's *Reliques*). The first four lines invoke sleep, which
will infold (repress) or unfold griefs (enlarge (upon) them, or release them).
The stanza's last four lines make light and consciousness the enemy, as
alienation appeared in the verb 'scorn' finishing the first verse (a word
noted in discussing jealousy in *The Four Zoas*). The line contrasts with
'the dawn in russet mantle clad / Walks o'er the dew of yon high east-
ward hill' (*Hamlet* I. i. 166–7). Perhaps the Ghost speaks here. Griefs in
the first verse become sorrow; neither active or passive, but 'driven' to
'the vault' of a heaven shut off (paved), like a modern city.

The lines beginning 'They strike', echoing 'make mad the guilty and
appal the free' (*Hamlet* II. ii. 564) by breaking the rhyme-scheme, assert
the power of his song to match the elements – the tempest – in echoes
of *King Lear*. The speaker does not admit to madness. In the last verse,
symmetrical with the first, the 'fiend in a cloud' – anticipating 'Infant
Sorrow', and associated with 'howling woe', like *The Sick Rose*'s 'howling
storm' – suits the night, identifying with it, desiring to lose identity
('croud' – he crouches with his back to the east which brings him pain).

The action seems to reject the lyric's simplicities. 'To Spring' invited
Spring to 'come o'er the eastern hills' (E. 408, K. 1). This would give (a)
the coming of the morning to end 'night thoughts' (b) the coming of
a season, and (c) the arrival of the apocalyptic, since it is Spring's 'holy
feet' (compare 'And did those feet') which must come, but which have
not yet come, in contrast to each of the other season-poems of Blake,

which address the seasons as present.[16] Spring, who with 'perfumed garments' is female, must deck forth a female 'love-sick land' with her 'fair fingers'. That female/female relationship echoes in *Jerusalem 77* (E. 233, K. 718), in a lyric whose first verse is written on the left-hand side of the page, and the second adjacent to it on the right, and the third in the centre, below, as though making for an Hegelian synthesis:

England! awake! awake! awake!
Jerusalem thy Sister calls!
Why wilt thou sleep the sleep of death
And close thee from her ancient walls?

Thy hills & valleys felt her feet
Gently upon their bosoms move:
Thy gates beheld sweet Zion's ways:
Then was a time of joy and love.

And now the time returns again:
Our souls exult, & London's towers
Receive the Lamb of God to dwell
In England's green & pleasant bowers.

Reading this late poem and comparing it with the early 'To Spring' asks: if in the first poem Spring has not yet come, *when* was the moment of the feminine tenderness uniting Jerusalem and England? The time returns, but never came round the first time. Is there any history here? An impossibility is pondered, happening in a time for which there is no time. So too, 'And did those feet' asks if those feminine feet walked, and if the holy Lamb of God was seen (was there ever the time of the *Songs of Innocence*?) and if the Countenance Divine shone (which might imply the presence of the 'prince of love'), and if Jerusalem was built among 'these dark Satanic Mills'. It is ambiguous whether the Mills exist where Jerusalem was, or whether Jerusalem has been built in Blake's London. Perhaps there never was such a time, nor, now, space for it in London's modernity, so that if anything comes, it will have no identity, being in antithesis to any predictable future.

For 'Mad Song', fulfilment of the lyrical, giving light, would give 'frantic pain'. Night thoughts are preferred, Spring is rejected before it comes, and the light of Enlightenment rationality is a source of madness. The other madness, like the tyger, stays with the night. So in the following 'Songs', In the first, 'my black ey'd maid' comes forth with 'holy feet', like Spring. The poem celebrates the impossible moment. In the second, 'the early morn walks forth in sober grey', darkening towards 'pensive woe', woe marked by thought, or thought necessitating woe – but also 'pleasing', a product of desire. In the first poem, the village and the woman's eyes in sleep prompt a violent poetry where 'innocence' seems akin to madness, since 'more than mortal fire / Burns in my soul, and does my song inspire'.[17] In the second, the woman drops a tear 'beneath the silent shade' (night's shade), which is a source of pleasure to him. The poem breaks down, as a song, in the contemplation of weeping, cursing, and death.

'To the Muses' follows, where the Muses live 'in the chambers of the East / the chambers of the sun' (lines 2, 3). Comparing that with the ending of 'Mad Song' and the rejection of the day implicit in the end of 'When early morn' it seems as if lyricism fails. Perhaps 'The languid strings do scarcely move! / The sound is forc'd, the notes are few' relates to a crisis which may be seen as madness.[18] Perhaps the lyric form belongs to Blanchot's first night which is the antithesis to day, but the essence of it is subverted or disturbed in the *Poetical Sketches* by a desire to turn the back to the east, desire for madness.

That appears in *Songs of Experience* too. 'The Fly' shows an impulse to argue towards being no other, or becoming no more or other than a fly, with no awareness of life or death. When it moved from its draft (E. 794, K. 182–3), the first verse quoted here, which had been at the end, was placed in its present position, so that the distinctive character of thought was added:

> If thought is life
> And strength & breath:
> And the want
> Of thought is death;
>
> Then am I
> A happy fly,
> If I live
> Or if I die.

(E. 24, K. 213)

Thought may be either a form of spontaneous knowing and being, its absence being death, including the death of others (thoughtlessness produces death).[19] It may be only a reflex, stimulus, and response, as with 'my thoughtless hand' and 'some blind hand'. But 'thoughtless' may also mean spontaneous knowing and being, as exists in the 'thoughtless' nests of the birds in 'Night' (E. 14, K. 119). Thought as reflex would make life no more than machinic, but its absence makes death indistinguishable from life. The speaker does not decide which meaning of thought is desired, but as with Gray who calls the 'moralist' 'a solitary fly', there seems a rejection of *all* thought as enlightenment, related to eighteenth-century rationality.[20] The desire is rather to be beyond life and death distinctions, a happy fly, thoughtless, in a commitment to madness, or a desire for it. It recurs in 'The Chimney Sweeper' saying 'I am happy, & dance & sing' (E. 23, K. 212), as though expressing an only possible mode of existence, in the knowledge of his exploitation, being like the fly (like it, black), rejecting the double bind of his parents' combination of piety and rationalism.

Blake and madness

The Prophetic works, such as *The Four Zoas*, are of the night though they are driven by a turn to the east, light, and 'sweet science'. Yet this is not unambiguous, if we follow through from the plate in *Milton* where the Blake of the poem, naked save for a sandal on the right foot, twists backwards towards the east in a kneeling position to see a naked Los stepping out of the sun, marking the line 'And I became One Man with him arising in my strength' (EV plate 21 (20) line 12, E. 116–17, K. 505). The illustration's content (see EV. 43 (21)), best commented on by 'The head Sublime, the heart Pathos, the genitals Beauty, the hands & feet Proportion' (E. 37, K. 152), is homoerotic, implying that a resolution of madness would have to be through changed perception in gender-terms.[21] The illustration flanks Milton's words:

> There is a Negation, & there is a Contrary
> The Negation must be destroyd to redeem the Contraries
> The Negation is the Spectre; the Reasoning Power in Man:
> This is a false Body: an Incrustation over my Immortal
> Spirit; a Selfhood . . .
>
> I come in Self-annihilation & the grandeur of Inspiration.
> To cast off Rational Demonstration by Faith in the Saviour
> To cast off the rotten rags of Memory by Inspiration
> To cast off Bacon, Locke and Newton from Albions covering
> To take off his filthy garments & clothe him with Imagination
> To cast aside from Poetry, all that is not Inspiration
> That it no longer shall dare to mock with the aspersion of Madness

Cast on the Inspired, by the tame high finisher of paltry Blots,
Indefinite, or paltry Rhymes; or paltry Harmonies.
Who creeps into State Government like a catterpiller to destroy
To cast off the idiot Questioner who is always questioning,
But never capable of answering; who sits with a sly grin
Silent plotting when to question, like a thief in a cave;
Who publishes doubt & calls it knowledge; whose Science is Despair
                    (EV. 42.32–6, 44 (43), 2–15, E. 142, K. 533)

The idiot questioner's science, like the 'idiot Reasoner' (32.6, E. 131, K. 521),
induces despair. In *Jerusalem* 54.21 (E. 203, K. 685) the Spectre seems the
same, and identifiable with the 'Dunce' at the end of *Night Thoughts* 8,
since he says 'Come hither into the Desert & turn these stones to bread',
not as a means of testing Jesus but, worse, because contending that it
cannot be done. The 'day' comes with a divine state called 'madness'
by mediocre contemporaries, Spectre-held. Blake's London, part of its
paranoia-inducing qualities, was peopled by 'reasoners' patronizing
him as mad.[22] Crabb Robinson, who seems to have thought him
a monomaniac (*BR* 536), searched for what he could of 'the insane
poet painter & engraver *Blake*' (*BR* 223). Yet Coleridge, preferring Blake's
poems of innocence over experience (the apparently morally uplifting
over the morally questionable), told H.F. Cary (who thought Blake
a 'wild enthusiast'):

> I have this morning been reading a strange publication – viz. Poems
> with very wild and interesting pictures .... [Blake] is a man of
> Genius – and I apprehend a Swedenborgian – certainly, a mystic
> *emphatically*. You may smile at *my* calling another Poet a *Mystic*; but
> verily I am in the very mire of commonplace common-sense compared
> with Mr Blake, apo – or rather anacalyptic Poet, and Painter.[23]

Robert Southey, recalling earlier events in 1847, called Blake then
'that painter of great but insane genius', quoting the 'Mad Song'
(*BR* 226). In 1811, Southey had visited Blake, and Crabb Robinson
reported of this that Blake 'spoke of his visions with the diffidence that
is usual with such people And did not seem to expect that he should be
believed. He showed S a perfectly mad poem called Jerusalem – Oxford
Street is in Jerusalem' (*BR* 229). Blake lived just off Oxford Street, of
course. Wordsworth, as reported by Crabb Robinson, commented on
Blake's poems in 1812: 'he was pleased with them and considered
Blake as having the elements of poetry – a thousand times more than

either Byron or Scott', but Alicia Ostriker notes that Wordsworth says nothing about the poetry; Blake was being treated as a case.[24] William Beckford (1759–1844), who collected Blake, reading Benjamin Malkin's on Blake in *A Father's Memoirs of his Child* (1806) called Blake as the 'mad draughtsman' and said of Malkin for quoting 'The Tyger' that 'the receiver and disseminator of such trash [is] as bad as the thief [i.e. Blake] who seems to have stolen them from the walls of Bedlam' (*BR* 431).

Charles Lamb (1775–1834), once confined himself, saw Blake's exhibition in 1810 with Crabb Robinson and Mary Lamb (who also endured periods of insanity). He sent 'The Chimney Sweeper' (*Innocence*) to a volume edited by James Montgomery, *The Chimney Sweeper's Friend, and Climbing Boy's Album* (1824), saying, in response to a request about the author, that he knew Blake's artwork and something of his criticism of Chaucer, but little of the poetry beyond 'The Chimney Sweeper' and 'The Tiger' [*sic.*] and added: 'alas! I have not the Book, for the man is flown, whither I know not, to Hades or a Mad House – but I must look on him as one of the most extraordinary persons of the age' (*BR* 284). Lamb's sense compares with Walter Savage Landor's, who in 1811 said that Blake was by no means a madman in common life but quite discreet and judicious, and in 1838 claimed Blake to be 'the greatest of poets'. Landor, who wanted to collect Blake's writings, 'protested that Blake had been Wordsworth's prototype, and wished they could have divided his madness between them; for that some accession of it in the one case, and something of a diminution of it in the other, would very greatly have improved both' (*BR* 229–30).

Imputation of madness aligns Blake with 'graveyard' melancholia and other casualties of Augustanism: William Collins (1721–1759), or Christopher Smart (1722–1771), whose confinement produced Johnson's commentary on the Age of Reason: 'My poor friend Smart showed the disturbance of his mind, by falling on his knees, and saying his prayers in the street, or in any other unusual place. Now although, rationally speaking, it is greater madness not to pray at all, than to pray as Smart did, I am afraid there are so many who do not pray, that their understanding is not called into question' and 'I did not think he ought to be shut up. He insisted on people praying with him, and I'd as lief pray with Kit Smart as any one else. Another charge was that he did not love clean linen; and I have no passion for it.'[25] Or John Clare (1793–1864), whose sufferings began four years after his first book: *Poems, Descriptive of Rural Life and Scenery* (1820). Clare, treated by Dr Matthew Allen in Epping from 1837 till he escaped in 1841 and then confined in an asylum in Northampton until he died, existed in a state of 'sad non-identity'.[26] But madness need not be confined to be mad, and need not be defined to separate it from nearly kindred states. George Romney (1734–1802) was marked by a 'melancholy malady' escape from which made him feel 'like one escaped from an enchantment'.[27] James Barry (1741–1806), expelled from the Royal Academy in 1799 for attacking his fellow-members and the memory of Reynolds, spent the last seven years of his life in profound melancholia.[28]

William Hayley explained in 1805 his wish to help Blake being for motives that the 'angelic Cowper would approve, because this poor dear man [Blake] with an admirable quickness of apprehension & with uncommon powers of mind, has often appeared to me on the verge of insanity' (*BR* 164). William Cowper (1731–1800), melancholic all his life, became Evangelical in 1764, his friendship with John Newton (1725–1807) engendering the *Olney Hymns* (1779). Cowper met Hayley in 1792: Hayley's biography containing the posthumous appearance of 'The Castaway' appeared eleven years later.[29] In 1776, Hayley had befriended Romney, who had painted Cowper in 1792: Romney's biography followed in 1809, with Hayley's *Cowper's Latin and Italian Poems of Milton* (1808) and *Cowper's Milton* (1810).

Blake's Cowper

Blake, observing Hayley with Romney, wrote: he 'thinks to turn me into a Portrait Painter as he did Poor Romney, but this he nor all the devils in hell will never do' (E. 725, K. 819). For Blake, becoming a portrait painter would take him out of history, making him a melancholy-mad tool of the wealthy classes. His poem 'William Cowper Esqre' appears in the Notebook of 1808–1811:

> For this is being a Friend just in the nick
> Not when hes well but waiting till hes sick
> He calls you to his help be not you movd
> Untill by being Sick his wants are provd.

> You see him spend his Soul in Prophecy
> Do you believe it a Confounded lie
> Till some Bookseller & the Public Fame
> Proves there is truth in his extravagant claim

> For tis [most wicked – *del.*] atrocious in a Friend you love
> To tell you any thing that he cant prove

> And tis most wicked in a Christian Nation
> For any Man to pretend to Inspiration
>
> (E. 507, K. 551)[30]

Cowper's madness is aligned to prophecy and inspiration, readiness to speak without proof. Blake shows a growing elective affinity with Cowper, who appears in Blake's notes (1819) on Johann Caspar Spurzheim's *Observations on the Deranged Manifestations of the Mind, or Insanity* (1817). Spurzheim had moved to London in 1814 as a phrenologist, believing 'that the mental powers of the individual consist of separate faculties, each of which has its organ and location in a definite region of the surface of the brain, the size or development of which is commensurate with the development of the particular faculty' (OED). For Spurzheim, bodily organs are responsible for states of the soul or states of mind. However, 'whatever occupies the mind too intensely... is hurtful to the brain' and religion – including Methodism – is therefore 'a fertile cause of insanity'.[31] Blake comments by a story which compares with Cowper telling Hayley in 1793 of a dream he had had of Milton, who said that he knew Hayley's writings. 'He then grasp'd my hand affectionately and with a smile that charm'd me, said – Well – you, for your part will do well also.'[32] Blake's narrative gives, implicitly, Blake's critique of Cowper's poetry when most introverted (OED credits the word to Cowper):

> Cowper came to me & said. O that I were insane always I will never rest. Can you not make me truly insane. I will never rest till I am so. O that in the bosom of God I was hid. You retain health & yet are as mad as any of us all – over us all – mad as a refuge from unbelief – from Bacon, Newton & Locke[33]
>
> (E. 663, K. 772)

Does the desire for insanity – the quotation shows Blake reading himself – mean Cowper had failed to be truly insane? Cowper posthumous sounds like his 'night' poem, 'The Castaway':

> Obscurest night involved the sky
>   Th'Atlantic billows roar'd,
> When such a destin'd wretch as I,
>   Wash'd headlong from on board,
> Of friends, of hope, of all bereft,
> His floating home for ever left.

The poem's 'I' is the victim of Calvinist predestination, while the sailor washed overboard and drowned understudies him:

> No voice divine the storm allay'd,
> No light propitious shone,
> When, snatch'd from all effectual aid
>   We perish'd, each alone;
> But I, beneath a rougher sea,
> And whelm'd in deeper gulphs than he.[34]

The 'I' says he has already perished, in more than the Atlantic. But he remains spectral, for the rest of his natural life, through the poem's posthumous publication, and when dead, visiting Blake, still 'outcast' – a castaway (I Corinthians 9.27) – like the oxymoronic 'outcast mate' of 'They left their outcast mate behind' (line 23), where the sailor is not only the victim of accident, but cast out. Since Cowper had no 'mate' his condition is worse. The outcast state, recalling 'Help! Help!' in *For the Sexes* (no. 10), is like being dead, spectral, 'castaway' from God's presence, in the sea, at night. It is part of a retreat from normative values that made Hazlitt find 'an effeminacy about [Cowper] which shrinks from and repels common and hearty sympathy'.[35] Cowper comes to Blake from 'the outside, the night', in Blanchot's phrase. But a similar sense of being of the tomb – below Judas, placed by Dante at the centre of Inferno – and yet alive, above ground, alienated from his 'rightful' place, even after four suicide attempts, appears in this poem of 1774:

> Hatred and vengeance, my eternal portion,
> Scarce can endure delay of execution:-
> Wait, with impatient readiness, to seize my
>   Soul in a moment.
>
> Damn'd below Judas; more abhorr'd than he was,
> Who, for a few pence, sold his holy master.
> Twice betray'd, Jesus, me, the last delinquent,
>   Deems the profanest.
>
> Man disavows, and Deity disowns me.
> Hell might afford my miseries a shelter;
> Therefore hell keeps her everhungry mouths all
>   Bolted against me.

> Hard lot! Encompass'd with a thousand dangers,
> Weary, faint, trembling with a thousand terrors,
> Fall'n, and if vanquish'd, to receive a sentence
> Worse than Abiram's:

> Him, the vindictive rod of angry justice
> Sent, quick and howling, to the centre headlong;
> I, fed with judgments, in a fleshly tomb, am
> Buried above ground.[36]

The first two stanzas anticipate being in hell, as 'The Castaway' makes the Atlantic a prelude to hell, where the sailor 'drank / The stifling wave, and then he sank' (lines 47, 48). The ending contrasts those sent to hell 'headlong' (the word of 'The Castaway', echoing *Paradise Lost* 1.45) with the soul 'in a fleshly tomb...buried above ground': As with 'The Castaway', Cowper is not yet in Hell. The poem contains its own madness, making Jesus only twice betrayed, by Judas and by Cowper, 'the *last* delinquent'. The poem's close, condemning him to his own body, alienates him from it.

Cowper may say 'we perished' but he appears to Blake as what Foucault writing on Blanchot calls 'the thought from outside', from the 'void' outside the language which communicates, outside the rational discourse, for which Bacon, Newton, and Locke, named in the passage quoted from *Milton* (above, pp. 137–8), are metonymies.[37] Cowper's ghost longs for a disappearance that neither Calvinism – not mad enough – nor internment in a madhouse could give. He wills to be the castaway, to be on the outside, to be the ice-island in 'Cimmerian darkness' that cannot be warmed by the sun.[38] *Milton* opposed rationalism by Methodism, a movement inside and outside the Church of England, Calvinist and Evangelical, for Rintrah tells Los: 'I rais'd up Whitefield, [George Whitefield (1714–1770)] Palamabron raised up Westley' [John Wesley (1703–1791)]:

> He sent his two servants Whitefield & Westley; were they Prophets
> Or were they Idiots or Madmen? shew us Miracles!

> Can you have greater Miracles than these? Men who devote
> Their lifes whole comfort to intire scorn & injury & death
> (*Milton* EV. 21 (20) 55–62 (22) 1–2, E. 118, K. 506)

Blake defends Whitefield in 'To the Deists' in *Jerusalem* 52, against the play by Samuel Foote (1729–1777), *The Minor* (1760), which satirized

Methodism: 'Foote in calling Whitefield, Hypocrite, was himself one; for Whitefield pretended not to be holier than others, but confessed his Sins before all the World' (E. 201, K. 682).[39] The passage, including the words 'Man is born a Spectre or Satan & is altogether an Evil', which are at the heart of *Jerusalem*, attacks Rousseau as hypocritical, thinking 'Men Good by Nature; he found them Evil & found no friend. Friendship cannot exist without forgiveness of Sins continually. The Book written by Rousseau calld his Confessions is an apology & cloke for his sin & not a confession' (*Jerusalem* 52, E. 201, K. 682). In this defence, Whitefield loses energy, while Blake seems to adhere to Calvinist Methodism, in spite of Spurzheim on its insanity, but instead of being more mad than Cowper (heterogeneous, wholly outside), he wants more confession, being held by an argument imposing a belief in sin, in refuge from eighteenth-century rationalism. The madness which is enthusiasm is replaced by something more abject, confessional.

Something of 'Hatred and Vengeance' appears with the Spectre of Los:

> the Reasoning Power
> An Abstract objecting power, that Negatives every thing
> This is the Spectre of Man: the Holy Reasoning Power
> (*Jerusalem* 10.13–14, E. 153, K. 629)

Negation, Contrary, and Selfhood were new terms in *Milton*, which identified Selfhood, Spectre, and Satan (*Milton* 14.30–1, E. 108, K. 496). 'Holy reasoning power' makes the Spectre Evangelical and Deist, with the Calvinist's and the rationalist's melancholias. As Cowper has 'a wish that I had never been. A wonder that I am. And an ardent but hopeless desire not to be',[40] the Spectre says that God 'feeds on Sacrifice & Offering, / Delighting in cries & tears & clothed in holiness & solitude...' continuing:

> O that I could cease to be! Despair! I am Despair
> Created to be the great example of horror & agony: also my
> Prayer is vain I called for compassion: compassion mockd
> Mercy & pity threw the grave stone over me & with lead
> And iron, bound it over me for ever: Life lives on my
> Consuming: & the Almighty hath made me his Contrary
> To be all evil, all reversed & for ever dead
> (*Jerusalem* 10.47–8, 51–7, E. 153–4, K. 630)

The complaint echoes Adam before he waters the ground with tears:

> Did I request thee, Maker, from my clay
> To mould me man, did I solicit thee
> From darkness to promote me?
>
> (*Paradise Lost* 10.743–5)

The sentiment is quoted by Frankenstein's monster, who is contemporary with the Spectre. Milton's God has produced a creature definable by complaint.[41] The sense of sin gives him an identity which is the Selfhood, which has its own 'pride' (*Jerusalem* 38.53, E. 185, K. 673). Life lives on his consuming others, a sadistic form of negating, like the Devourer. But the Spectre wants not to be because he is Despair, which as an allegorical identity is an abstraction, like the 'dumb despair' Albion is named in his melancholy (*Jerusalem* 36.60, E. 183, K. 668). The Spectre's obsession is sin, so he defines himself by his worthlessness. He is abstract, 'knowing / And seeing life yet living not' – so that his qualities are abstract, allegorical, shadows of something else, but threatening with the thought that there is nothing else. He dominates, as in this fragment:

> [This world – *del*.] Each Man is in [the – *del*.] his Spectre's power
> Untill the arrival of that hour,
> [Untill – *del*.] When [the – *del*.] his humanity awake
> And cast [the – *del*.] his own Spectre into the Lake.
> And there to Eternity aspire
> The selfhood in a flame of fire
> Till then the Lamb of God....
>
> (E. 810, K. 421)

The words reappear at the end of *Jerusalem* plate 41. A male fairy has written the first verse backwards on a scroll, of paper or stone, part of a page or tablet on which sits a Ugolino-like giant Despair. Plate 42 opens:

> Thus Albion sat, studious of others in his pale disease:
> Brooding on evil: but when Los opend the Furnaces before him:
> He saw that the accursed things were his own affections...
>
> (*Jerusalem* 42.1–3, E. 189, K. 669)

Brooding and despair are commented on by the parergal writing telling Albion that he is in his Spectre's power, become like the Spectre in *Jerusalem* 10. Yet to say 'I am Despair' is impossible: it elides the person who speaks with the 'I' of his speech; to say that 'I am Despair' is a rhetorical move: the person speaking is much more than 'just' Despair. He can only say he is Despair (i.e. that is the identity he wishes) because he is not wholly Despair. Cowper's 'I' pronouncing his own damnation in 'Hatred and Vengeance' is something other than his own statement. The effort to reach that impossible absolute would indeed impose madness.

For Levinas and Blanchot, the 'I' has no power to die because dying requires the cessation of my 'I', my willpower. For Cowper to be the 'outcast' 'castaway' shows the power of the will; it asserts the self, accepting the position of the ice-island that does not float south, is never melted. Desiring a release from will's power and the Spectre's insanity, Cowper, posthumous, has achieved neither, but in saying Blake is more mad, he offers him an identity which is not that of the Spectre, one which is of the outside, the night, and since it has no absolute identity, that of the death Cowper wanted, he gives him in his madness an identity which is not final.

Blake's spectre

'My abstract folly hurries me often away while I am at work, carrying me over Mountains & Valleys, which are not Real, in a Land of Abstraction where Spectres of the Dead wander' (E. 716, K. 809).

Blake's letter describes 'night thoughts', a state removed from daytime prudentialism (as indicated by two further uses of 'abstract' further on). If creativity is sexual, the Spectre, like Satan, operates in that sphere, as a letter of 23 October 1804 indicates:

> I have entirely reduced that spectrous Fiend to his station, whose annoyance has been the ruin of my labours for the last passed twenty years of my life. He is the enemy of conjugal love and is the Jupiter of the Greeks, an iron-hearted tyrant, the ruiner of ancient Greece. I speak with confidence and certainty of the fact which has passed upon me. Nebuchadnezzar had seven times passed over him; I have had twenty; thank God I was not altogether a beast as he was; but I was a slave bound in a mill among beasts and devils; these beasts and these devils are now, together with myself, become children of light and liberty, and my feet and my wife's feet are free from fetters'.
>
> (E. 756, K. 851–2)[42]

He adds: 'I thank God that I courageously pursued my course through darkness', characterizing his work, from 1784 to 1804, as of the night.

Blake's Spectre opposes conjugal love, and perhaps heterosexuality. He is implicitly aligned with Urizen, explicitly with Nebuchadnezzar, a familiar figure for Blake (the colour-printed drawing of 1795; depicted in 'There is No Natural Religion'; seen in *The Marriage of Heaven and Hell* above 'One Law for the Lion & Ox is Oppression' (E. 44, K. 158)).[43] The mad king illustrates 'abstract folly'. Like George III, the madman is crowned, just as in the picture of Bedlam in *The Rake's Progress* which shows a naked man with a crown holding a mock sceptre.[44] It is mad to be a king: it is mad to think you are a king: the king who thinks he is a king is mad. Nebuchadnezzar relates to Ugolino in *The Marriage of Heaven and Hell* (plate 16). The 'devourer' asserts his subjectivity by destroying the other, as if 'One King, one God, one Law' (2.40, E. 72, K. 224) will establish his being. But law-making and binding of energies makes the wise man mad. Thinking together, Ugolino, Urizen, Nebuchadnezzar, and the Spectre evokes images of giants embodying energy but enchained, devourers who consume energy in its excess, patriarchs responsible for the death of sons, madness a dream of kingship, kingship a mad dream.

Nebuchadnezzar appears in no. 299 of Blake's illustrations to *Night Thoughts*, in a passage framed by two which were quoted in Chapter 4 (above, pp. 92–3), where Young discusses the sexuality of the male and of 'wanton Eve'. Young is defending male passion:

> Like the proud *Eastern*, struck by Providence,
> What tho' our *Passions* are run mad, and stoop
> With low, terrestrial Appetite, to graze
> On Trash, on Toys, dethron'd from high Desire;
> Yet still, thro' their Disgrace, no feeble Ray
> Of Greatness shines...
>
> (*NT* 7.533–8)

Blake makes Nebuchadnezzar a fallen faun, Dionysiac; in the print, going on all fours, his limbs like tree-trunks, he is more bare as if flayed.[45] He implies the passions, but, heroically, he may be associated with the artist John Hamilton Mortimer (1741–1779), 'call'd a Madman' (E. 635, K. 445), as Blake wrote, annotating the second of Reynolds's *Discourses* (1769). For Reynolds:

> The artist who has his mind thus filled with ideas, and his hand made expert by practice, works with ease and readiness, whilst he who would have you believe that he is waiting for the inspirations of Genius, is in reality at a loss how to begin; and is last delivered of his monsters, with difficulty and pain.[46]

Blake called this allying of individuality and imagination with the monstrous: 'A Stroke at Mortimer!', adding, 'Painters are noted for being Dissipated and Wild' (E. 646, 644, K. 457, K. 454). Mortimer painted Nebuchadnezzar as an outcast, like Timon, with a wild animal's fingernails and toenails, but human, insofar as he walks upright.[47] The outcast artist paints the mad figure of passion. Blake's Nebuchadnezzar compares with his Newton, the bowed status of both recalling Adam's abject head, judged by God. Nebuchadnezzar complements Newton, who recalls the 'Ancient of Days', the Frontispiece to *Europe* (see D. pp. 161–8). So Nebuchadnezzar's madness complements the madness of the rationalists; Urizen's rationalism being a fallen state.[48] Urizen at the end of *The Four Zoas* is called to 'come forth from slumbers of thy cold abstraction' (9.129, E. 389, K. 360). The line fuses Nebuchadnezzar's outcast state with the night, with Ugolino's coldness, which is that of Cowper's ice-islands, and masculinity enslaved to rational jealousy.

Rationalism seems inseparable from the passion that fascinates it. A rational figure condemning or preventing heterosexual passion, the Spectre images the degradation of passion it brings about. The letter makes the Spectre opposed to marriage, but marriage introduces his power. Madness seems plural, one state coming from the spectrous force, as a melancholia inducing sexual impotence or aggression. Another state shows when Blake continues: 'Dear Sir, excuse my enthusiasm or rather madness, for I am really drunk with intellectual vision . . . .' as indeed he has been so 'drunk' throughout his 'course through darkness', like a star or a tyger, so affirmative in energy. Yet this madness is not Spectre-free: 'Tuesday, Janry. 20, 1807, between Two & Seven in the Evening – Despair' (K. 440). Night thoughts, indeed.

The Spectre abstracts, inducing despair and loss of the emanation, but that is not valueless. The Prolific creates, but that must be given a form by being chained. The place given to the Devourer, who receives 'the excess of his delights' and who is compared to an inherently prolific 'sea', implies the priority of forming something even if with chains. The Devourer's priority enables the Prolific, even if the image of Ugolino and his sons, prolific and devouring together, implies the cost at which this spectrous power which enables creation is bought. Abstracting, like the night which is 'the very experience of the *il y a*',[49] abstract folly may be the void allowing thinking.

7
Dante's 'Deep and Woody Way'

Fountain Court

In autumn 1824, when beginning his Dante illustrations, Blake was living up a wainscotted staircase, in a two-roomed apartment in 3 Fountain Court on the south side of the Strand, surrounded by warehouses. From the back window he peered 'down a deep gap between the houses of Fountain Court and the parallel street, in this way commanding a view of the Thames with its muddy banks, and of distant Surrey or Kent hills beyond'. While the river was 'like a bar of gold', Crabb Robinson referred to 'the squalid air, both of the apartment and [Blake's] dress', and to the 'dirt, I might say filth' that Blake and his wife existed in (*BR* 564–7, *SP* 393). Here he worked – 'too much attach'd to Dante to think of much else' (letter to Linnell, 25 April 1827, E. 784, K. 879) – until his body, 'the Machine' (E. 778, K. 873), as though it, like the tyger, was part of an industrial manufacturing process, proved 'incapable' in August 1827.

The Dante Illustrations are cultural productions of the 1820s. The first 69 are of *Inferno* and are night-scenes, for Dante and Virgil enter on the road to Hell in the evening. Nos 70–89 depict *Purgatorio*, beginning with the sun rising (no. 70): nos 76 and 77 give the first night in Purgatory, and no. 86 the third: these are pastoral moments. In Paradise, there are no considerations of night and day. In no. 2, Dante and Virgil penetrate the forest, 'lo cammino alto e silvestro' (*Inferno* 2, 142), which H.F. Cary, Dante's main translator for the Romantics, renders 'the deep and woody way'. The phrase recalls Dante coming to himself in a dark wood (*Inferno* 1.1–3), and the journey to hell being called the 'deep (or high) way' (2, 12) and the journey through hell being called 'silvestro' (woody: *Inferno* 21, 84). Blake recalls the forests in nos 24, 25, as does Dante, and

149

also in no. 4, no. 8, no. 28, no. 76, and no. 77, and even in nos 85, 86, and 87 (as Dante also connects the forest of the Earthly Paradise with the original dark wood). Forests precede entry into the Inferno, making *all* the *Commedia* 'night thoughts'.

Also in 1824, Byron died, and this finds a response, whether conscious or not, in shifts between aristocratic and middle-class sentiment, and approaches to punishment. Byron's death acts as a metaphor for the ascendancy of middle-class approaches to morality, and for the rule of the bourgeois conscience. This chapter uses not only Byron, but also Dickens as a bourgeois writer with a special relation to 1824, so that the Illustrations are strung between the differences evoked by what Byron represents and what Dickens. This is not bracketing off the Illustrations' relationship to Dante, but avoiding a view of both 'Dante' and 'Blake' as having texts outside history, immediately interpretable as systems of thought, as if a determinate reading of Dante's text could be compared with Blake's reading, or as if a separate, non-historically confined reading of Dante was available outside historical constructions, of which Blake's is one. How Blake read Dante is better discussed as the question of what was the 'Blake' that was constructed by the 1820s, and what was the 'Dante'. These Illustrations relocate Dante's text and hint at buried narratives within themselves, leading their reader to associate Dante and Blake as if in montage.

Policing London

That the Illustrations form a document of the 1820s finds support from the incident of Dante and Virgil, in *Inferno* canto 7, 1–15 encountering Plutus. As Blake renders this (no. 14),[1] Dante and Virgil look down on Plutus, who, unlike his counterpart in *Inferno*, has his right hand resting on a money-bag, with 'Money' written upon it. His left hand stretches up the side of the page with his fingers in a position of blessing, though his vicious look contradicts that. Though Blake's working life was lived under the shadow of poverty and financial crisis, national and personal, perhaps money became refocused as an issue for Blake after the Napoleonic Wars. At the time of engraving the Laocoon (c. 1820),[2] he calls money 'the life's blood of Poor Families' which is identified with 'Caesar or Empire' – a reminder that in 1815 'the boundaries of the British empire were so extensive that they included one in every five inhabitants of the globe'.[3] Money is 'The Great Satan or Reason, the Root of Good and Evil in The Accusation of Sin' (E. 275, K. 776). According to Asa Briggs, economic historians see the years 1824–1825 as 'the first truly modern cyclical boom in British economic history',[4] ending with a collapse in the autumn of 1825, much of it to do with failures in investment in South America, and attended by bank failures, the collapse of the stock exchange, suicides and bankruptcies.[5] The Goddess Fortune, as the emblem of the new spirit of speculation (no. 16), Blake does not even begin to describe in Dantean terms as in a state of bliss, unconscious of what men say about her (*Inferno* 7, 94–6), an agent of a creative mutability. He agrees that she 'has the goods of the world in her paws' (*Inferno* 7, 69), from which view Dante is immediately corrected by Virgil. Blake's portrayal goes much further: her position is cloacal, in a pit full of excrement, like the mud of *Bleak House* accumulating 'at compound interest'.[6] The stress on the excremental is of course not new – for example, the comment on the moral law, 'The Hebrew Nation did not write it / Avarice and Chastity did shite it' (E. 516, K. 187), comes from the 1790s, but seeing Fortune this way comments on urban money and the new capitalist economics of the post-Waterloo years, just as the Laocoon engraving and the comments around it link money-power to rationalism, and so to Utilitarianism.

The *Westminster Review* began promulgating the 'dismal science' of political economy in January 1824, and the Dante Illustrations span the years from then till 'Utilitarianism' became a newly coined term in 1827 (OED). The emergent values of utility and the felicific calculus connected with the oppressiveness of a government and national ideology whose control was by both secular and religious 'Accusation of Sin' – and the suggestion that both these arms of the national ideology were involved in accusation, another word for which would be surveillance – are a reminder that links between the Utilitarians and the Evangelicals became a feature of everything that was joyless for the Victorians.[7] Hazlitt stresses Bentham's moralism in his secular accusation of the subject:

> Mr Bentham takes a culprit and puts him into what he calls a *Panopticon*, that is, a sort of circular prison, with open cells, like a glass beehive. He sits in the middle and sees all the other does. He gives him work to do and lectures him if he does not do it. He takes liquor from him, and society, and liberty; ... and when he has convinced him, by force and reason together, that this life is for his good, he turns him out upon the world, a reformed man ....[8]

Blake saw Dante as an accuser of sin – telling Crabb Robinson that 'Dante saw devils where I see none' (*BR* 541) – yet Blake's Fortune is diabolic, not Dante's, and Blake outdoes Dante with devils – in over 12 illustrations out of the 69 which portray *Inferno* (nos 32–4, 37–44 particularly). The occasions in Dante where an implicit critique of divine punishment emerges disappear. No. 21 shows Dante confronted by Farinata, rising out of the tomb and looking like Hamlet's father's ghost (no. 21), but does not evoke his secular atheism and the challenge that provides, unlike *Inferno* 10. Brunetto Latini does not appear in the space devoted to the sodomites in Dante, so that Blake omits the dialogue between master and pupil, and of the tensions existent in Dante's text (*Inferno* 15) where it is possible to read it as self-reflexive, questioning its own judicial procedures. Though Ulysses (*Inferno* 26) is pictured, his narrative of desire and transgressiveness, so important for raising questions about the rightness of his damnation, is not. Elements of dramatic monologue are not important for Blake, Ugolino's narrative being the exception.

Roe's version is that Blake sees Dante as the uninspired poet subservient to Empire, influenced by classical poets representing only Memory. This inclines Dante towards a stasis whereby he believes in people being held in fixed states and in vengeance for sins. (Blake's portrayals of Limbo (nos 7, 8) critique Homer and a poetry based on memory, but have nothing to say about the problem of divine justice and the ethic of Christianity that Limbo raises.) The 20 illustrations of *Purgatorio* end with the domination of Beatrice; Dante's surrender to the powers of Nature, Priestcraft, and the woman, the embodiment of the Female Will, of materialism and of the loss of imagination. On this reading, there is no equivalent of the diabolic / deconstructive 'Bible of Hell' in these illustrations, for the dispute between Reason and Desire governing *The Marriage of Heaven and Hell* corresponds to nothing in Dante. And Dante's God is virtually absent in Dante and in Blake, save for no. 3 where he is made Urizenic; Satan who is also there, kneeling before him, is most clearly seen in no. 69, as a frozen form in the bottom of the ice. Since for Blake, as for most of his contemporaries, the *Commedia* was mainly *Inferno*, a hostile view of Dante seems implicit in 'Whatever Book is for Vengeance for Sin, & whatever Book is Against the Forgiveness of Sins is not of the Father, but of Satan the Accuser & Father of Hell' and in 'Dante's supreme Good...could never have built Dante's Hell, not the Hell of the Bible neither...it must have been originally Formed by the devil Himself', in a text added to the diagram of hell circles, no. 101 (E. 690, K. 785). This, implying that language inverts reality under the power of ideology, is the basis for the third Illustration, 'The Mission of Virgil', where state-power unfolds between Urizen, and a crowned figure kneeling with his back to the viewer, whose censer ('Caesar' written near it in pencil) evokes Empire, and state religion, while his left hand points down to a giant tormented in flames. Another, younger, giant sits manacled and in flames on the right. Between these two giants, framing the lower part of the picture, Virgil escorts Dante into hell. The beasts – as accusing as the left-hand forefinger of the kneeling crowned figure – menace Dante as he enters.[9] Dante is framed twice, first by the giants, who have been successfully accused so that their power is gone, second by what is above him which also encloses these giants: that is the sphere of 'The Angry God of this World, and his Porch [or Throne] in Purgatory' (the superscription). Purgatory becomes a negative image: of life as a matter of paying for sins. The Illustration not only shows what Dante sees (he has visions of four women who appear above him, and who in his text [*Inferno* 2] answer to the Virgin, Lucia, Rachel and, Beatrice, but they are transposed here) but also shows what he does not see. The illustration unveils the power of the state to accuse.

The figures of rule in no. 3 replay arguments in *The Marriage of Heaven and Hell*, applied there to *Paradise Lost* and to the *Book of Job*, which for Blake could be *Paradise Lost* Book 13. Satan who began in Milton as a Titan, desiring and energetic, prolific, is reduced by the Book of Job to a figure of Nietzschean *ressentiment*, marked by the envy that other people are doing better materially which for Nietzsche motivates the nineteenth-century bourgeoisie. Satan's demand of God 'Does Job fear God for naught?' evokes the principle of Utility, as that which motivates both the accuser and the accused: Job fears God because he fears physical pain. By appealing to the felicific calculus, the figure who tortures Job is a rationalist. In no. 11 of those engravings, Job dreams of the figure who torments him, and pushes him away with his hands. The tormentor's rationalism shows as his right hand points back to arched stones inscribed with Hebrew lettering, suggestive of a Law he wishes to embody.[10] His face answering to that of Job, he points up the Utilitarianism of Job's worship by being the Utilitarian of restricted vision himself. Though *Paradise Lost* included Satan's energy, Job's Satan is a rationalist as is Job's God. In the second engraving of the *Book of Job*, he is old, enfeebled, Job's double, reading. The only energy he can point to is that of creation, but this involves the Urizenic techniques of binding 'the sweet influences of Pleiades' (illustration no. 14), dividing or devouring. According to *The Marriage of Heaven and Hell*, 'In the Book of Job Miltons Messiah is call'd Satan' (E. 34, K. 150) meaning that the figure of reason, who restrains desire, is the lower, activating force of a more repressive deity on whose behalf he acts. He is Blake's Selfhood, the Spectre, the Accuser who is the God of this world.

At the beginning of the Illustrations to the *Book of Job*, Satan and God conflict, but by no. 11, they have become one, Utilitarian meeting Utilitarian, and by the end, there is no more Satan. The margin contains at the base of no. 17 (the vision of God) the words 'And the Father shall give you another Comforter that he may abide with you for ever, even the Spirit of Truth whom the world Cannot receive.' This is also evoked in *The Marriage of Heaven and Hell* – as though this God acknowledged his deficiency in desire, his lack, as rational, of something else, while the Messiah knows he is parasitic on the Satanic energy he has appropriated, and it is he, the principle of government, the restrainer, who has fallen, not the devil. Fallen reason – constricted, dominating, aware of its lack – must steal from the abyss, the sphere of night thoughts, to possess desire and energy. Hell provides some of the 'portions of existence' that the Devourer grabs. The devil stands outside the text, an alternative to the official archive whose ideological form is that God necessarily had to exclude the subversive. His own archive, the 'Bible of Hell' (E. 43, K. 158), is what Bataille sees Blake as beginning to write. What this figure of energy is, escapes representation, the point made in reference to 'The Tyger'. The Bible of Hell could not be written: there is a textual repression that will not look at the energy because to represent it would be to form it. Blake supplements the 'Voice of the Devil' in *The Marriage of Heaven and Hell*: 'The reason Milton wrote in fetters when he wrote of Angels & God, and at liberty when of Devils & Hell, is because he was a true Poet and of the Devils party without knowing it' (E. 35, K. 150). And sex in Milton? Was Milton in fetters when he wrote about that? Presumably, because sex in *Paradise Lost* is not related to 'Devils and Hell', though it is worth noting that Blake's opposition, between angels and devils, which is not quite Milton's, leaves out men as a species, and women as a gender and species altogether, as if Blake was also in fetters. Nonetheless, granting Blake's point about Milton, the only way to see the power of energy is through reading the text symptomatically to see the presence of its absence. But whereas *Paradise Lost*, because Milton the prolific was in fetters, slowly eliminates the doubleness Satan evoked, the *Book of Job* shows a desire for desire, and for that otherness which has been excluded and which cannot be represented.

As in Job, so in the *Commedia*, Dante is held by Urizen. But in contrast to the representation in no. 3, he appears in a different visualization in the engraved version of no. 58, 'The Pit of Disease: The Falsifiers'. Dante and Virgil stand on a ledge above the figures in hell, with their garments lifted to their noses to keep out the smell. The gesture responds to the 'puzzo' (stench) that comes from rotting flesh that Dante refers to (*Inferno* 29, 50, 51), yet its prominence also in Blake makes Virgil and Dante two figures of the bourgeoisie keeping up their difference from what is beneath them, from what is 'low'. On the floor, figures lie or crawl. Immediately below Dante and Virgil two sinners sit back to back, scratching their own backs furiously. These figures are quite outside the heroic or the mythological or the ghostly. They are like the petit-bourgeois property-owners, the Smallweeds in *Bleak House*, or the forger Uriah Heep in *David Copperfield*, belonging to an urban realism Dickens defined.

The bourgeois background encourages a look at the punishments and the crimes non-eschatologically, by reflecting that forgery was, controversially, in the 1820s, a capital offence. A Parliamentary committee in 1819, including such Benthamite reformers as Sir James Macintosh and Thomas Buxton, had recommended retention of the death penalty only for forgery of Bank of England notes. Norman Gash, writing on Robert Peel, Home Secretary during most of the 1820s, emphasizes that forgery was regarded as middle class, and that Peel was reactionary in insisting on the death penalty for it in 1828, and in passing new Forgery laws in 1830. No one was executed for forgery after 1830,[11] showing the triumph of middle-class opinion in the decade of the Reform Bill.

A social history behind punishment for forgery places the Illustrations within the debate on capital punishment and law and order running through Britain post-Waterloo, and Peel's belief in 'preventive policing'. This, involving new rationalizations and more calculated approaches to crime and the criminal, was not a new idea, for the notion of a police force had been present since the time of the magistrate Patrick Colquhoun's *Treatise on the Police of the Metropolis* (1795). In the engraved illustration (58E), Urizen sits writing, hidden by a rock, near the back-scratchers. His placement indicates how many levels of awareness the Dante Illustrations assume. Since writing and forgery fit together as fraudulent practices, it is easy to justify his position anyway, but as the spirit of accusation, perhaps he could be seen as the agent of the police. In 1829, after a series of experiments which had lasted for most of that decade with whatever policing was already available for the city, Peel introduced a new police force for London. That year saw the replacement of the night watchman, satirized from the time of *The Rake's Progress* no. 6, by the power of the police: night was coming under a surveillance different from the 'watchman of the night' of 'A Dream', with the other 'watch' in 'my Angel-guarded bed'. Night in the city changes its meaning, as the city becomes more rationalized, and lessens its difference from day.

Passing from Blake's 'midnight streets' to Dickens's, in 'The Streets – Night' (*Sketches By Boz* 1836), there are gas-lamps – gas lighting began in 1812 – shops are lit, and the policeman is there. The setting is Lambeth, the Marsh Gate, near the newly re-named Royal Victoria theatre (1833, the Royal Coburg, 1816). The evening continues until late and if the activities taking place at three in the morning are declared 'by no means pleasing' they are not recorded (80). The 'streets of London' are 'at the height of their glory' on a winter night.[12] In *David Copperfield*, set in the 1820s, the hero watches the 'youthful harlot' Martha go down to the water's edge at Millbank to drown herself. 'As if she were a part of the refuse it had cast out, and left to corruption and decay, the girl we had followed strayed down to the river's brink, and stood in the midst of this night-picture, lonely and still, looking at the water.'[13] The woman's night thoughts come under the surveillance and control of the hero, who makes them a 'picture'.

Urizen in the engraving implies keeping records and files on those who were to be named and labelled as criminals. As if stressing the new importance of record-keeping, Blake's no. 92 shows the recording angel of *Paradiso* 19, 112–41, a figure Dante only implies (books are mentioned, not the writer). The angel, his legs covered with a scaly pattern, and with his left foot forward – the familiar markers of Urizen, or of debased state-power – implies the power of state surveillance to see and to keep incriminating documents, and Blake, noting the note-taker, shows his perception of the power of accusation. The two Urizens of nos 3 and 58E imply two faces of English power – imperial power, and newer forms of control. These, in the very years of 'the making of the working-class', were furnishing the emergent middle class with the means of establishing itself. The stress on noting and archiving produces the clerk, prototype of the new city petit-bourgeoisie. Dickens's *Sketches by Boz* notes how the metropolis produces people who belong 'exclusively' to it, making character the effect of the urban: 'shabby-genteel' (303) males, misanthropes, bachelor-types, friendless office-clerks, and the drunkard. The melancholy adds to the sense that the city remains yet to be created. Opening up public spaces, it produces people more and more secretive, and unsexed, whose anomie can only be staved off by mad little rituals which enable them to survive, but which ask how much of a toll is exacted on lives by city existence which continues in a way people within it cannot read.

Byron

Though there is realism and factuality in no. 58, the pictures are also full of ghosts, since they represent confrontations with the dead. Even Dante looks shadowy, lacking in energy. Byron's is one ghost lingering in the Illustrations: he died in April 1824 at Missolonghi. After his exile, his body was brought back to London, up the Thames to Westminster, arriving on July 5 to rest there, virtually lying in state till July 12. Clare, his mind already suffering, witnessed the event.[14] Then, with 47 coaches in attendance, the funeral procession left London for the north. That was the return of one ghost and its disappearance, but another ghost – a Blakean Spectre – appears in Blake's almost last poetic text, *The Ghost of Abel* (1822), written as part of an open letter to 'Lord Byron in the Wilderness'. Foster Damon's *Blake Dictionary* (p. 63) says that Byron was the only contemporary poet named by Blake in work for publication. *The Ghost of Abel* comments on Byron's atheistic *Cain: A Mystery* (1821), as does Blake's tempera work, 'The Body of Abel Found by Adam and Eve' (c. 1826), which foregrounds the black open grave, dug for Abel, marker of the night thoughts which Cain has now entered into. In the space within the painting, it divides Cain from Adam and Eve. Everything now, of the future, is to come from the grave, the gap in rational continuity, and is inseparable from it. Cain's right foot emerges from the grave (he has been inside, digging it). As with Dante: everything depends upon entrance into the tomb. Cain recalls *Night Thoughts* no. 316 (7.874–93) where a black cloud overshadows a figure in similar anguish, who may be standing over a grave. 'What is that dreadful wish? [the wish for death] – The dying Groan / Of Nature murder'd by the blackest Guilt' (lines 884–5). (An earlier pen and water-colour on the subject is referred to in the *Descriptive Catalogue* no. 11 [E. 548, K. 584].)

Saying, in *The Ghost of Abel*, 'What doest thou here Elijah? Can a Poet doubt the Visions of Jehovah?' (E. 270, K. 779) dignifies Byron as prophet and poet in his exile since 1816, and endorses the absolute virtue of his position, while deploring his absence. As shown in the play that Blake wrote, which succeeds the letter, he is to be compared with the *ressentiment*-laden virtue of Abel, demanding vengeance. Perhaps Blake knew of Byron's reputation, his homosexuality included, and identified him with aristocratic rebellion threatened by middle-class morality. It would fit with the arguments of Louis Crompton's *Byron and Greek Love* which stresses the class-based nature of prejudice against homosexuality in the early nineteenth century: that radicals, for instance, tried to increase resentment of class by claiming that aristocrats behaved effeminately.[15]

Cain's rebellion is directed at the God who demands sacrifice, and his last speech, ending 'Now for the wilderness' (Act 3, line 544), keeps him as an exile. As Blake read this, in Northrop Frye's terms, 'imaginative vision has something diabolic attached to it, and . . . the visionary is not only doomed to be an outcast and an exile, but . . . even crime may well be an inseparable part of a genius above the law, as illustrated in a murder which was the product of an intellectual awakening'.[16] Blake's text, though asking why the poet should be in the wilderness, accepts that marginality since it begins from Cain's words addressed to the dead Abel, saying that Abel will forgive him (*Cain* Act 3, lines 528–33). The irony is that Abel does *not* forgive. Demanding vengeance, he becomes Satan, the Accuser (it is not Cain who has been contaminated by Lucifer). In *Cain*, the murderer's violence is a Promethean dream of freedom, connected to his desire to escape the implications of Abel's altar, which demands the violence of blood-sacrifice. He strikes out against the reifications of the law replacing a personal God by the God who demands that he is approached only through sacrifice. It is the ground of the Prologue to *For the Sexes: The Gates of Paradise* (1818). Cain's violence tries to displace this stress on the necessity of a scapegoat (the gallows and the altar are the same), but in the Dante Illustrations, possibilities of resistance are set aside by damned figures in chains, or prison.

Abel in *The Ghost of Abel* and *For the Sexes* suggests that the 'Christian' must believe in capital punishment. Rearing the crucified Christ on altars – and in public places – sanctifies the notion of a life for a life, or life to be given to the state when property has been taken. The point is underscored when it is remembered that seven bishops voted against the bill that the Whig reformer and anti-Evangelical Samuel Romilly (1757–1818) introduced in 1810 to abolish the death penalty for stealing from shops if the theft was less than five shillings in worth. Romilly commented on his defeat at their hands:

> I would rather be convinced of their servility to government than that, recollecting the mild doctrines of their religion, they could have come down to the House spontaneously to vote that trans-portation for life is not a sufficiently severe punishment for the offence of pilfering what is of five shillings value, and nothing but the blood of the offender can afford an adequate atonement for such transgression.[17]

David Cooper points out that in the ten years following Romilly's initiative, six bills introduced to abolish the death penalty for such a level of shoplifting were thrown out. Nonetheless, though there was powerful state reaction against diminishing the use of Albion's 'fatal tree' (*Jerusalem* plate 27, E. 172, K. 650), and though Peel was a pro-hanging Home Secretary, with the numbers of people who were executed averaging 1,336 per annum over the years 1825–1830,[18] the dominant trend in criminal law-making was in another direction: towards mechanistic Utilitarian methods of surveillance and regulation of criminality, and the use of records. Peel professed himself aware of Panopticism and he knew Bentham: John Stuart Mill says he was then 'entering cautiously into the untrodden and peculiarly Benthamite path of Law Reform'.[19] Peel's police challenged an older discourse, whose character could be summarized when an 1822 Select Committee, oppositional to the very notion of the police, referred to 'that perfect freedom of action and exemption from interference which are the great privileges and blessings of society in this country' (Gash, p. 313). Through the police, accusation of sin was to become more calculated, more aimed at producing a rational confession. Satan, the accuser in *The Ghost of Abel*, is Urizen in no. 58.

In this engraving, Dante and Virgil's delicacy makes them faintly comic, non-heroic, bourgeois figures. Byron's own self-identifications with Dante as exile, 'malinconico e pensoso' – melancholic and thoughtful, as Boccaccio described him – do not carry over into the portrayal of Dante. Though the poet was a titanic, Promethean figure for Byron, and his head, as depicted in Renaissance portraiture, offered for the Romantics a powerful image of heroism,[20] Blake rejects this for his Illustrations. Instead of Byronic withdrawal and exile, Blake de-heroizes Dante, as it may be noted that the Illustrations de-politicize his text too, just as much as they also make him not a poet. In contrast to Flaxman's illustrations of the *Commedia*, neither Dante nor Virgil in Blake wear laurel-crowns. While they may be informed by a sense of Dante as – in Blake's words to Crabb Robinson – 'a mere politician busied about this world' (*BR* 543), the Illustrations also give no sense of Dante as a political exile, excluded from the city and evoking in his poetry not bourgeois wealth but 'that humble Italy' (*Inferno* 1, 106).

Blake's giants

The Byronic world of what *David Copperfield* calls 'thunder and the gods' appears in the Illustrations, not in Dante but in non-feminine figures of loss, the giants in flames crouching at the base of the page (no. 3), or in pictures showing the energy of the angel who opens up the City of Dis (nos 19, 20). Some of the punished display heroism, such as Farinata (no. 21), or as in the case of the dignity and innocence given to the naked upside-down simoniac Pope (no. 35). Here, the well confining him has been made transparent, allowing a focus on the body, seen especially when the page is inverted, seen as muscular (note the legs, and the length of the fingers), which gives an appeal at least in part homoerotic. Flames from his feet evoke passion which cannot be escaped, while, in contrast, Dante is held by Virgil so that he has the least power and autonomy in the scene. Titanic grandeur appears with Ciampolo (no. 41) and with the obscene Fucci 'making the figs' against God (no. 49), where Dante and Virgil, looking on at the right, their hands held up in horror, make a strong contrast with Fucci's nakedness and energy and, as in no. 58, look almost Victorian in their modesty, that dangerous word for Blake, as in *Visions of the Daughters of Albion* 6, 3–20 (E. 49–50, K. 193–4).

Heroism is visible in the schismatics (no. 56), even though their bodies are fragmented, as much as though they had stepped out of the early pages of *Discipline and Punish*. The torture – the violence performed on them – is also an ennobling. For the soul of Mohammed, a devil, unseen in Dante, cuts him and other 'schismatics' with his sword (*Inferno* 28, 37–40), but Blake brings this figure of the devil centre-stage, elevates him above the others and raises his right arm with the sword so that he cuts the line of vision as he cuts the sinners, and dominates the scene completely. This figure of accusation, this critic with the sword, is ambiguous: devilish in the shape of his wings only, angelic otherwise, a figure seen doubly too, for he is seen with his back to the viewer in no. 57, showing a later moment in the same canto. This implies the modernity of Blake's art which seems as if cinematic, catching figures in different positions as a narrative proceeds, with different perspectives assumed for the viewer. First time seen, this devil seems heroic and magnificent, but, twice seen and in the same posture, he seems more machine-like, the mechanical force of state-power. In seeing him twice, so that the reader of the Illustrations is asked to think about him twice, this devil, foregrounded and then put in the background but negligible in neither position, represents the ambiguity of punishment that characterizes these Illustrations – titanic, ennobling, belonging to an aristocracy based on heroism, or mechanical, middle class, and homogenizing.

Grandeur is seen with the giants (nos 61, 62, 63) and with Lucifer (no. 69). The most outstanding of these gigantic forms is Antaeus (no. 63), a Michelangelesque nude, a rendering of pure phallic power. This is the more accentuated because he is also, in the sense of strain and in the right arm and hand movement, which it takes the reader to turn the page round by ninety degrees to see, both the God of Michelangelo's 'God Creating Adam' *and* the Adam who reaches forward to touch God's finger. He is both patriarch and Oedipal son, the latter demonstrated in the body's twisted state (he must just have brought the right arm round and towards and away from the viewer through an angle of 180 degrees) and in the emphasis on effort in the grasp on the rock with the left hand, just as every muscle is extended in the splayed-out right foot and in the right arm. The torsion of the silent giant shows that he is already under torture: the previous illustration shows Ephialtes as one of the giants who lives in the world in chains. The point about grandeur holds too with Capaneus (no. 27), classic figure of Byronic rebellion. The Illustrations stress the male nude and titanic power: and to notice the homoeroticism recalls the point that women throughout are less individualised. In no. 33, the flatterers emerge out of the excrement, their habitat (Dante and Virgil cover their noses). Thais, the prostitute who flattered her client by saying he pleased her marvellously (*Inferno* 18, 135), is on the right; above, a pander or a seducer flees pursued by a female devil. The comedy of the woman's presence – and the grotesque nature of her body – is missed by Blake in a depiction which is more 'moral' and anti-woman; just as Myrrha (no. 59), another woman who is running, is made demonic with a dog's face.

Violence in the *Inferno* illustrations looks not titanic but trivial and demeaning. Many punishments belong to a world antithetical to that of Cain – and oftentimes imply the excremental – with the wrathful sinners fighting in the Stygian lake (no. 15), Filippo Argenti being ducked in the water (no. 18), the usurers (no. 30) and some of the portrayals of sinners and devils together: the Devil carrying the Lucchese magistrate (no. 37), or tormenting Ciampolo (no. 41), or fighting in a state of bafflement (no. 42). The acts of violence in the lower hell – Dante pulling Bocca's hair or kicking (nos 65, 66) – also suggest levels of violence that are degrading, that belong more to a frustration of power and to the overtaking of spontaneous action by *ressentiment*. Admiration in the Illustrations is for figures of energy not reduced to such debased violence. There is a conflict between those figures who seem aristocratic, even in torment, and those who seem bourgeois, where that may evoke femininity or asexualism. Here the episode of the thieves (*Inferno* 24 and 25) is relevant. It produced Blake's most extensive work in the series (nos 45–54) and interest in following an intricate narrative development as he moved through the incidents in picture after picture: ten illustrations (two engravings), eight focusing on the metamorphoses with the snakes. These illustrations show a politics divided in their ambiguity as to whether the thieves' rebellion can be seen as bourgeois or aristocratic; that is, whether they are confined by the surveillance of the state, or can make something out of their transgression, which would give to them a kind of innocence. Class, status, identities, gender are in flux. In no. 51, when the six-footed serpent attacks Angolo Brunelleschi, the soul immediately to the right becomes feminine-looking, and both souls look scared: this gender ambiguity is not there, however, in the engraving (51E). Brunelleschi half transformed by the serpent (no. 52) becomes giant-like, and Guercio Cavalcanti retransformed from a serpent into a man (no. 53) attains a heroic nobility by doing so, but elsewhere the status of these sinners looks more unstable, the noble sinner becoming a creeping snake. It becomes impossible here to assess behaviour or personality because both are in the process of change.

Another example of change at work in a characterization comes in the three illustrations for Ugolino, also following the movement of a narrative closely, gradually focusing on him, as though partaking of the pre-history of cinema. In no. 66, Ugolino is just coming into view on the left, glimpsed at behind Virgil, while Dante tugs Bocca's hair. At this point, Ugolino is biting into the back of Archbishop Ruggieri's neck in a posture suggestive of anal rape. The viciousness of the homoeroticism is followed up in no. 67, where the Archbishop now looks even more abject and Ugolino in the centre looks back at Dante and Virgil with his hands spread open in a gesture of self-justification. This compromises him, making him a cringer, a whiner, disavowing his own actions, as though he has been caught out by surveillance and accusation. In the following illustration, however, which responds to his account of his death by starvation, and which lifts the repression upon him when he gives an account of his death, he is a dignified dying patriarch, with his children in prison and angels overhead. Here, uniquely, Blake responds to a character's monologue and the illustration goes outside Hell, showing a prison on earth, Ugolino framed by two forms of confinement: in prison and in a cave in Hell. The secular prison conveys an oppression which ennobles the passive Ugolino. The three pictures are marked by a split in characterization, as though neither identity nor position were fixed. R.D. Laing writes that in many schizophrenics, the self-body split remains basic, but that when the 'centre' fails to hold, neither self-experience nor body-experience can retain identity, integrity, cohesiveness, or vitality. He calls the result 'chaotic nonentity', finding its description in Blake. 'In the Greek descriptions of Hell, and in Dante, the shades or ghosts, although estranged from life, still retain their inner cohesiveness. In Blake, this is not so. The figures of his Books undergo divisions within themselves.'[21] Whether true of Dante or not, Laing's point illuminates Blake's work with Ugolino, his prime example of 'night thoughts'.

Dickens

In February 1824, John Dickens, the father unable to maintain patriarchal status, went to the Marshalsea prison, while the 12-year-old Charles Dickens was put to work in a blacking-factory in the Strand, 'at old Hungerford-stairs. It was a crazy, tumble-down old house, abutting, of course on the river, and literally overrun with rats. Its wainscotted rooms and its rotten floors and staircase, and the old grey rats swarming down in the cellars, and the sound of their squeaking and scuffling coming up the stairs rise up before me as if I were there again. The counting-house was on the first floor, looking over the coal-barges and the river...'[22] In this autobiographical fragment, written in the late 1840s, and absorbed into *David Copperfield* (1849–1850) and into Forster's *Life of Dickens* (1872), Dickens describes the working conditions of the manufactory in terms suggestive of the underworld, where it is not possible to distinguish between the rats rising up and the memory surfacing.

Associating the boy Dickens and the 67-year-old Blake in 1824 invites speculation: was Blake's one of the faces in the crowd for Dickens? Blake fetching porter for his evening meal from the public house (cut by the Royal Academician William Collins (1788–1847), father of Wilkie Collins, who saw him doing this) might have coincided with the original of the deprived boy in *David Copperfield* who roamed about the Strand and the Adelphi and Covent Garden as documented in *David Copperfield*. Did Dickens ever read Blake? Three accounts help on the history of Blake's reception in the nineteenth century.[23] Crabb Robinson, Samuel Rogers, Walter Savage Landor, Charles Lamb, all suggest that Blake's reputation between his death in 1827 and Gilchrist beginning his researches on Blake in 1855 was not as forgotten as it was thought. But the issue of a possible relation between Dickens and Blake might be better expressed in terms of both their relationships to Utilitarianism. In 1965, Steven Marcus, who said that the early chapters of *Oliver Twist* were like the *Songs of Experience*, pointed out how the conjunction of the chimney sweep and the coffin that Dickens makes in moving Oliver Twist from Gamfield to Sowerberry had already been made by Blake in

Songs of Innocence.[24] In 1967, F.R. Leavis linked Dickens with Blake, continuing the secularization of Blake that Erdman began. Raymond Williams continued when he saw in Blake's 'London' and its sense of the ubiquity of trade a 'forcing into consciousness of' 'suppressed connections' which he said was 'a new way of seeing the human and social order ... a precise prevision of the essential literary methods and purposes of Dickens'. Blake's London, its streets, chimney sweeps, chapels, charity school-children, prisons and orphans, becomes Dickens's.[25]

Dickens enables a reading of Blake's Dante because the events of 1824 produced a narrative afterwards exploited in his novels. *David Copperfield*, Chapter 11, fusing the factory and the prison as the bases of a vision of the nineteenth century, returns to this moment by thinking of 'the slow agony of my youth' so that when in memory, 'I tread the old ground, I do not wonder that I seem to see and pity, going on before me, an innocent romantic boy, making his imaginative world out of such strange experiences and sordid things' (*DC* 11, 165). Even without the suggestions of Dante, the passage is full of ghosts of 1824. The mid-century writer, Copperfield, looks back, saying the stones of the streets may even now be worn down by the ghost of himself as a boy, and constructs a figure who says he pities the child's innocence, romanticism, and imagination. The desire is for a particular kind of childhood, defined as bourgeois, non-sexual, which appears, ambivalently, in the Dante Illustrations. In no. 1, Dante flees the three beasts, running into the arms of a feminine-looking Virgil, who stretches out his arms as though the two were joining in a dance. Virgil does not touch the ground; he is pure spirit: Dante is man, but also made young like a boy.[26] The beasts occupy the right half of the picture, and they could be allegorized as accusing passions, perhaps as elements of sexuality that are being fled from by the bourgeoisie. Yet the second, third, and fourth illustrations – 'Dante and Virgil Penetrating the Forest', 'The Mission of Virgil', 'The Inscription Over Hell Gate' – do not imply escape, but rather initiation, under the guidance of Virgil. In each, Dante and Virgil move back, away from the viewer, into the picture itself, as though merging with areas they have not confronted before, and drawing attention to the textual nature of experience, as they walk as if into the page. Initiation into the forest means going into the area of night thoughts; initiation into Urizen's world is into the sphere of state-violence, produced by night-fear. The gates of hell because of their invitation to melancholia with the words written 'Lasciate ogni Speranza, voi ch'entrate' translated by Blake as 'Leave every Hope you who in

Enter' – reveal sunken worlds beyond them (perhaps Atlantis), the sphere of the past, the territory of the repressed. Each of these three initiatory pictures frames the two poets Virgil and Dante. Not till they are inside hell (no. 5) is the frame taken back and two slender forms of the poets, willowy and feminine-looking, are positioned against the immediate world of the souls in hell, and from then on the pictures largely show the poets looking, from the side or from above, panoptically. There is one exception: no. 9, which shows Minos, sitting as at a Last Judgment, with his right hand upraised and holding a phallic-looking spear. Blake's Minos, even more than Dante's in *Inferno* 5, judges the carnal sinners, and it is a scene of tempest and fire. Virgil draws Dante towards Minos as though leading him towards sexual initiation, which he had fled from at the first. This further initiation, which takes place in no. 9, overwhelms Dante in the tempest depicted in the illustration and engraving that form no. 10 and 10E, 'The Circle of the Lustful: Francesca da Rimini'.

A parallel initiation takes place in *David Copperfield* when the orphaned boy is told, 'What is before you, is a fight with the world, and the sooner you begin it, the better' (*DC* 10, 149). David Copperfield comments: 'I think it occurred to me that I had already begun it, in my poor way: but it occurs to me now, whether or no.' This statement invites pity, but the reader who suspects the investment in this particular form of childhood knows that by this stage, Copperfield has not only bitten the father-figure Mr Murdstone, but has fallen in love with Little Em'ly and been exposed to the patronage of the Byronic Steerforth, whose insulting behaviour to the pauper Mr Mell Copperfield is complicit in, as his innocence is already overcoded with elements of the sexual tragedy – Emily's seduction by Steerforth – which he forwards through his attraction to Steerforth. Andrew Elfenbein discussing Byronism makes Byron's homosexuality an 'open secret' in the 1820s for those who were 'in the know', amongst whom he includes Bulwer and Disraeli.[27] Something of that carries into the portrayal of Steerforth; Byron living on in the sexual ambiguity structuring *David Copperfield*.[28]

Sexuality

Blake's Illustrations are as aware as Dickens of bourgeois unease with the sexual. No. 10 gives the whirlwind of the lovers, with Paolo and Francesca. Here, in a first culminating narrative of the Illustrations, Dante is overcome, though not through his own sexual delight. Indeed, in the phallic wind and fire that rises as in a dream from his inert body (as if he is dissociated from that energy, as though consciously he cannot let himself be aware of his phallic urges), his dream-influence – which is overall ultimately accusatory – seems to pull Francesca back from rising higher with Paolo. She is a figure caught in the middle; Paolo – a figure of positive energy, reversing his position in Dante, weeping and trembling – would draw her higher, but she looks back, away from him, almost looking towards Dante, as though turning away from passion, under the dominance of the poet's thoughts whose sexual inertia is apparent in his position on the ground. The two lovers cannot become their other image, seen to the right, embracing within the sphere of the sun. In the wind and fire rising from Dante's body, Francesca seems caught in a tug-of-war between Paolo and Dante, two types of males. The difference of this from *Inferno* 5 needs no underlining.

Within the impossible adventure of reading Blake's Illustrations to Dante as though they provided the narrative of *David Copperfield*, this tension fits. When the emotional storm breaks in a chapter called 'Tempest', and Steerforth and Ham, the rivals for Emily, are drowned, the scene is preceded by David Copperfield's night thoughts:

> There was a dark gloom in my solitary chamber...but I was tired now, and getting into bed again, fell, – off a tower and down a precipice – into the depths of sleep. I have an impression that for a long time, though I dreamed of being elsewhere and in a variety of scenes, it was always blowing in my dream. At length, I lost that feeble hold upon reality, and was engaged with two dear friends, but who they were I don't know, at the siege of some town in a roar of cannonading.
>
> (55, 727)

In these falling images, appears a dream-memory of the English Civil War, which suggests a condition divided, psychically and nationally, where the friends, perhaps both Steerforth and Ham, despite their class-differences, are pictured with David Copperfield, participants in the assault on Emily as though she was the town and all three were responsible for her seduction.[29] The dream connects to an earlier one: in Chapter 19, David Copperfield arrives in London, watches *Julius Caesar*, re-meets Steerforth (an aristocratic Roman), and falls asleep at the inn 'and dreamed of ancient Rome, Steerforth, and friendship, until the early morning coaches, rumbling out of the archway underneath, made me dream of thunder and the gods' (19, 273). Waking from these night thoughts, he 'peer[s] out of window at King Charles on horseback'

(20, 273). The dead King Charles has obsessed the madman, Mr Dick. David Copperfield lives in an accumulation of images of power and rule from which he is excluded. Steerforth / David Copperfield differences are like a memory of the 1820s, giving a politics split between the sexually powerful, masculine Byronic aristocrat and the weaker bourgeois, whose political power-basis is different. Middle-class ideology looks nostalgically towards child-like innocence, evoking a de-sexualized woman, opposite of Francesca. But Blake's Dante cannot escape the consequences of his sexual repression. The protagonist seems sexually innocent, timid in nos 9 and 10, yet in nos 87 and 88 he sees Beatrice, whose chariot wheels, in no. 88, are circling flames, in form recalling a vortex or whirlpool, and recalling the whirlwind of lovers in no. 10. The feminine-looking, shockable figure who goes through hell has, it appears, a pre-history of passion and the sexual, which seems to be evaded in no. 85 ('Dante at the Moment of Entering the Fire' – yet not actually standing inside the fire) but finally reasserted in the meeting with Beatrice. It is as though everything in no. 88 was designed to show Dante as phallicly weak because repressed and Beatrice as empowered and overpowering by her entourage. She is sexual, knowing, accusatory: no wonder the wheels are full of eyes, with eyes looking at Dante from the chariot. Roe's sense of Blake's Beatrice as the negative Female Will can be modified: she is rather that which enables the Illustrations to confront what is inadequate in the romantic/bourgeois imagination Dante possesses. The illustration following the appearance of Beatrice is therefore apt, showing the harlot and the giant (no. 89) – no restraint in sexuality or phallic power there – and as Roe (p. 172) suggests, 'the coils of the serpent's body recall the vortex of the preceding design' and connect back to souls caught up within a sexuality which seizes and whirls them.

Blake follows Dante in giving these two narratives: of facing up to the sexual, as that which the bourgeois, in its establishment of power, has repressed, another, which is the preferred narrative from the protagonist's standpoint, a journey to meet Beatrice. When the encounter with Beatrice takes place in *Purgatorio*, it demands a re-reading, a reassessment, of 'Dante'. The then significant narrative – rendering his past, making him face it – is not quite the one so far witnessed, of initiation and growth in the company of Virgil. Beatrice in the *Commedia* releases what has been silenced thus far in Dante's narrative. The sexual anticipation (*Purgatorio* 30, 46–8), the disappearance of Virgil, the tears, the references to ice melting (*Purgatorio* 30, 96–9), the requirement to confess to an all-knowing accusing woman – these elements require a re-reading of the earlier part of the text, and ask about the status of the narrator who must take on a new position, produced as a new subject by the requirement to confess to the name given to him, 'Dante' (*Purgatorio* 30, 55–63). That moment of naming recalls Derrida's point: 'the name is a wound, and there is no other origin of the work of art'.[30] Since he is named, even this re-unification includes loss, a sense of incompletion, of being caught between two narratives, one of which, including Virgil, must vanish. The two narratives barely fuse: in Dante, Virgil's disappearance, as the poet marked by loss and limited to Limbo, virtually acknowledges their incompatibility. But while Dante's text marks the crisis moment of the narratives by emphasizing the tragedy implicit in Virgil going at the point of meeting (*Purgatorio* 30, 49–53), Blake puts no stress on it at all. There is much less engagement with the narrative of the *Commedia* after the meeting with Beatrice: the illustrations to the *Paradiso* are much less worked over. Blake's primary interest is in *Inferno*, and in the figure whose approach to experience suggests a desire to be separate, implying fears which are caught in a partly unconscious politics split between admiration for male power and a turning away from the body and from experience in conscious accusation.

Melancholia

In no. 4 of the Dante Illustrations, 'The Inscription over Hell-Gate', Virgil stands on the threshold of hell and beckons Dante to what is beyond. This recalls 'Death's Door'. Dante looks at the inscription and points to it. Standing outside, he can see what is written on the outside upper lintel. There seem to be two messages in this illustration: the lost world beyond the gates of hell, which suggests new experience and hope, and the melancholic writing of loss of hope. These messages are not identical and the split makes melancholy a leitmotif within the Illustrations. If Virgil has not read or not paid heed to the writing, there is a reason within the Blakean text itself for his departure: though a figure of Limbo, he cannot see the despair and the sadness Dante knows.

The Illustrations are full of melancholy, the mental state coming from awareness of repressed psychic material. The Illustrations give hints of an otherness to be found in them. The differing architectural styles and different historical periods of Blake's hell imply an absorption with experiences which are unattributable in the subject's own historical time or place. Art-historians have found Persian suggestions in the portrayal of Nimrod (no. 61) and other antiquarian interests; the City of Dis has Eastern-style domes and a building with Doric columns (no. 21), Capaneus looks like an antique torso,[31] while Roe quotes Blunt on the Old Man of Crete (no. 28) as a version of an antique statue of Helios; while Butlin (p. 578) finds in Lucifer the possible influence of the Indian goddess Durga from Moor's *Hindu Pantheon*. Hell is the repository of different experiences, some oppositional to the limited conscious vision of the subject: again, giving point to the divided vision of Dante and Virgil, one just seeing the world beyond, the other aware of the rubric of melancholia with which it is necessary to go beyond.

Byron's Dante and the Byron formed by the image of the Dante he constructed are melancholy, but this melancholia is different, being not self-dramatizing, like, possibly, Byron, but because the subject is self-divided. In no. 58, immediately beneath Dante and Virgil looking down upon the sinners is the sleeping Albion. Roe compares this to *Jerusalem* 41 where Albion sits hunched 'studious of others in his pale disease' (42.1, E. 189, K. 669), discussed in Chapter 6. Albion's state links accusation of others (and later of himself) with melancholy. In *Jerusalem* 27, Albion seems associated with a connivance at capital punishment; in no. 58E, his 'Spectre', in whose power he is (and he is his own Spectre), is round the corner: it is Urizen. To be a melancholic, in the grip of the Spectre in the 1820s, is to be held by Utilitarian rationalism. Albion appears in an Italian *Inferno* to make the subject of the Illustrations Britain, held in the grip of an accusatory power. Since Albion is beneath Dante and Virgil, his placing suggests that his melancholia – a caving inwards, a collapse – is what, if anything, supports them. Dante is not separated from Albion's pale disease, a form of madness.

But as night thoughts bring discrete identities, times, and places into question, Albion and Urizen are not separable. Albion in no. 58E returns in nearly the same posture as Ugolino in no. 68, for in these Illustrations characters change so much that the Illustrations suggest that any state described could also be depicted in terms of its opposite. Urizen as the name for a repressive Utilitarian rationalism gains a new dignity as Ugolino. The last sight of Urizen in the *Inferno* illustrations is as a shadowy figure beneath Lucifer's right foot (no. 69): just above him, lying the opposite way, is a sleeping man. These are figures virtually sunk beyond trace, held in night thoughts, anonymous, as they are in Dante's text (*Inferno* 34, 10–15). In no. 3, assuming that the crowns are enough to identify the two figures in both illustrations, Urizen was above and Satan below. In that case, what narrative – Oedipal revolt? – is implied from the reversal of roles that Urizen now appears below Lucifer? Urizen, sunk, like the despairing Albion, in sleep and kept in ice in no. 69, but again with a certain dignity, suggests an unconscious – perhaps an unconscious guilt – subtending what can be brought to formal representation. Forms of the past, fitting that unconscious, are suggested in the landscape of dead humanity, in nos 34 and 58, and in 58E. They are visible in the petrified figures in the ice in the side walls and hills of no. 65, and in the suicides turned into trees (no. 24).[32] In no. 82, Dante and Virgil see engraved in the rock Lucifer, fallen, and a fallen Urizen above him (continuing the subject-matter of no. 69) with Nimrod, supine, bound to a brick pillar, on the ground to their right. Virgil points upwards, Dante downwards, ignoring the angel above, as though the melancholy bourgeois sees a collapse of proud, titanic energy into melancholic thought. These figures lie beneath, yet because of the perspective of the illustration, seem to rise above, as though agents of his own accusatory powers. These examples, no. 82 in particular, fit the new meanings developing round consciousness in the decade of the Illustrations: OED cites De Quincey in 1823 for the first use of 'subconsciously' and then ten years later for 'subconscious'.[33]

After Blake

The working-class London of the Strand – different from Bentham's Westminster[34] – is a context for many of the Blake Illustrations, but apart from the City of Dis, only urban fragments appear, crowds in no. 5, the wharf and a factory-like building in no. 5, a wharf in no. 6, buildings in no. 32 with a chain hanging and large cogged wheels, wall and masonry, and a prisonous sense in no. 61, and the prison for Ugolino in no. 68. These metonymies, seen from odd perspectives, anticipate cinema. Blake's *Inferno* has fires, seen in the distance in different places, testifying to ruin. The expansion of the urban that Blake knew is complemented by a sense of the world burning, ghostly, filled with ruins from the past. These fragments suggest melancholy, but with the fires, imagination, and sexual energy which the melancholic drive to punishment – punishing the imagination – cannot allow itself to be fully aware of.

If Blake's London educed melancholia and madness, what of London now, a 'world city' (Patrick Geddes) since 1915, when it stood the world's largest? By 1938, its suburbs had pushed out fifteen miles. Its seven million is 12 per cent of the UK population, 42 per cent of the ethnic minority population.[35] For Saskia Sassen, London is a 'global city' – one of those 'which are strategic sites in the global economy because of their concentration of command functions and high-level producer-service firms oriented to world markets...cities with high levels of internationalization in their economy, and in their broader social structure.'[36] The city is directed from elsewhere, being at the centre of global finance, or global, because its population, partly migratory, another effect of globalization, makes it a city which must come to terms with its colonial past, the imperial city becoming postcolonial. That London was to be part of a global economy was epitomized in creating 'Docklands', an homogenizing pastoralizing neologism of Peter Walker, in Edward Heath's government (1970–1974), after flying – a contrast to Los's walking – over ten square miles, 5000 acres, of discrete neighbourhoods, Wapping, the Isle of Dogs, Surrey Docks, Shadwell, Beckton – areas north and south of the river. The London Docklands Development Corporation followed in 1981 to supplement the finance companies of the City of London. 'Docklands' has been criticized for appealing to only outside interests. For geographer Roger Lee, its redevelopment 'has little to do with an attempt to redistribute wealth to the inhabitants of a deprived inner-city district and everything to do with the sustenance and expansion of Britain's and London's role in the global economy.'[37] This, which goes with the claim that London, with Tokyo and New York, remains a world city because of its financial opportunities, its language, and its favourable position in the differing time-zones, makes Anthony D. King argue that the abolition of the GLC in 1986, successor since 1965 to the LCC, and brought in with a Blakean appropriation, 'Awake Albion' (*Jerusalem* 38), was necessary to permit de-regulation within the City and Docklands.[38] The 'Big Bang', which freed the City's institutions from regulation, indeed followed. King sees an irony whereby the city that was at the heart of empire is now owned and sold to other multi-national interests, which makes him compare it to a colonial city.[39] This part of London stands separate from its boroughs which it dominates architecturally, as with Canary Wharf, its name a reminder of fruit from the Canary islands, its position on the 'Isle of Leutha's Dogs', the site of the West India Docks, and its Cesar Pelli-designed tower dominating the skyline. Docklands and the City have engendered non-modernist architecture, as with Norman Foster (Lord Foster of Thames Reach) – whose name allegorizes how architecture and capitalist private industry reach for keeping the Thames 'chartered', building 'luxury' apartments crowded close to the water's edge, cutting the river off.[40]

An information economy based on telematics, the apparent reverse of night thoughts in making information visible, threatens to dispose of an economy rooted in place. Some forms of politics would disperse the city altogether, since the global economy attracts 'edge cities', 'exopoles', outside the suburbs ringing the inner city. The inner city is no longer the centre. Perhaps, as Habermas has intimated, the notion of the city has been superseded. Manuel Castells talks of 'the space of flows' rather than the 'space of places', thinking of the city as part of the 'network society'. Bernard Tschumi discusses the 'exploded', Paul Virilio the 'overexposed' city. For Guy Debord, in *The Society of the Spectacle* #168, banality has made it disappear: world cities, identical tourist-cities, mean visitors arrive nowhere.[41]

A reading of Blake needs to be placed against this. While it is true that Blake produced his works 'to answer the needs of his times' (W. p. 7), criticism cannot remain historicist, in an imagined sense that it knows what those times were, as opposed to having constructed them, nor can it remain isolated from the present which its subject enables it to read. Criticism cannot ignore the untimeliness of poetic utterance, which imposes on it the need to read allegorically. Peter Ackroyd, in *Hawksmoor* (1985) or *Chatterton* (1987), or his biographies of Dickens (1990) and Blake (1995), and *London: The Biography* (2000), attempts to find a permanence in an unknown or secret, earlier London.[42] So too, Ian Sinclair, attempting to stabilize a sense of the city with leylines and the permanence of the 'London Stone'. Ackroyd, in *London: The Biography*, and Sinclair, in *Lights Out for the Territory*, speak of 'psychogeography', and Blake as 'the godfather of all psychogeographers'.[43] Psychogeography in Guy Debord studies 'the precise laws and specific effects of the geographical environment, consciously organized or not, on the emotions and behaviours of individuals'[44]: Debord detects psychogeography through the *dérive*, 'the practice of a passional journey out of the ordinary through rapid changing of ambiances' (24). The theory of the *dérive* draws up 'maps of influence' in the city, and it does so by drifting, walking through city-streets without a 'proper' focus.[45] But situationism begins with the proposition that life presents a series of different situations which affect consciousness, and it wants to become aware of these. Looking at streets contrasts with Le Corbusier's planning, where the city suppresses the street in favour of the abstract and rational, which has no place for the idea of another form of abstract (non-definable) form of influence. The planner begins by erasing the city, creating a *tabula rasa*, and this creates the spectacle – Debord's theme – in contrast to which Debord interrogates the city by psychogeography.

Ackroyd's *London: The Biography* in contrast personifies the city, attributes to it as human a single identity, and – since biography assumes the subject's stability – makes the life dead, finished, knowable. This means rejecting those other aspects of London it cannot discuss, its ethnic diversity and difference. Like Sinclair, Ackroyd's support is Blake, 'London Blake' – 'he left the city only once and most of his life was spent in the same small area bounded by the Strand. He did not need to travel any further because he saw, literally *saw*, Eternity there' (92). Blake is 'one of the great artists of London'. To say that Blake saw Eternity in London is merely journalistic, however, and though *London: The Biography* assumes the constancy of places, that some place names still exist, some with a relation to Blake's moment, others where the contrast offers a fascinating montage does not erase the point that the present can only be alienated from Blake's city. And the historicism in Blake studies cannot – as historicism never can – ever make that knowable. While Salman Rushdie's *The Satanic Verses* quotes the 'Proverbs of Hell' (305–6, 318), the 'modern city' is the place of 'incompatible realities' (314). Evoking 'London', Gibreel Farishta wanders the streets of that 'tortured metropolis whose fabric was now utterly transformed, the houses in the rich quarter being built of solidified fear, the government buildings partly of glory and partly of scorn, and the residences of the poor of confusion and material dreams' (320). He attempts to walk the city following the A to Z, as if imposing order on it, but 'the city in its corruption refused to submit to the dominion of the cartographers, changing shape at will and without warning, making it impossible for Gibreel to approach his quest in [a] systematic manner'. Further, 'in this pandemonium of mirages he often heard laughter: the city was mocking his impotence, awaiting his surrender, his recognition that what existed here was beyond his powers to comprehend, let alone to change.... It was in this sorry condition that he arrived at the Angel Underground.' A Blakean pun,[46] 'Babylondon' (459) produces the 'paranoid schizophrenic' (338).

London's multi-cultural population is different from Ackroyd's 'Londoners', who were like his version of Blake, and Blake's Londoners, who 'were in fact like Londoners of all times and all periods' (*Blake* p. 33). It contains histories which introduce difference, while questioning who are meant by 'Londoners'. Urizen's London contained Urizen's religion. Present London shows the inadequacy of Christianity as a centre in the face of global capitalism with which it remains, as then, complicit, and multiculturalism. Night thoughts, markers of heterogeneity, outside what can be thought, are threatened by the modern city, whose global modernity, in making everything visible, would exclude the outside, the night. As Blake's city, known and unknown, fades out, can his London work allegorically for thinking multi-cultural, postcolonial, heritage London?

Notes

1 Introduction: 'The sun is gone down'

1. Pencil-drawing of 1780, colour-printed line engraving in 1794. See B 73. For images associated with 'Glad Day' and 'And did those feet' see Blake's pen and watercolour for Milton's 'L'Allegro' lines 57–68, 'The Sun at his Eastern Gate' (B 543.3). The 'bow of burning gold' and the 'arrows of desire' recall the watercolour for Gray's 'The Progress of Poesy' where poetry is the Sun as Apollo. The 'Countenance Divine' is the sun-god, recalling Blake's illustration to *Paradise Lost*, 'The Rout of the Rebel Angels'. See B 335.46, 536.7.

2. See Jeremy Dibble, *C. Hubert H. Parry: His Life and Music* (Oxford: Clarendon Press 1992), pp. 483–5, and Patrick French, *Younghusband: The Last Great Imperial Adventurer* (London: Harper Collins 1994), pp. 294–303. Five years after 'Rule Britannia', there appeared 'God Save the King', becoming in the early 1800s the 'national anthem', Linda Colley, *Britons: Forging the Nation 1707–1837* (London: Vintage 1996), p. 47, so linking patriotism and religion. See Shirley Dent and Jason Whittaker, *Radical Blake: Influence and Afterlife from 1827* (London: Palgrave 2002), pp. 88–95.

3. David V. Erdman (ed.), *A Concordance to the Writings of William Blake* (Ithaca: Cornell University Press 1967), 2 vols.

4. David Wagenknecht, *Blake's Night: William Blake and the Idea of Pastoral* (Cambridge, Mass.: Harvard University Press 1973). See Philip Brockbank, ' "Within the Visible Diurnal Sphere": The Moving World of *Paradise Lost*', in *The Creativity of Preception: Essays in the Genesis of Literature and Art* (Oxford: Basil Blackwell 1991), pp. 59–64, for day and night in Milton. (His account of *Paradise Lost* in C.A. Patrides (ed.), *Paradise Lost 1–2*, London: Macmillan 1972, pp. 13–74, excellently intersects Milton with Blake.)

5. Valentine Cunningham, *Everywhere Spoken Against: Dissent in the Victorian Novel* (Oxford: Clarendon Press 1975) discusses the Irvingites, reprinting Dickens's satirical poem on them, p. 197. See also Columba Graham Flegg, *'Gathered Under Apostles': A Study of the Catholic Apostolic Church* (Oxford: Clarendon Press 1992).

6. See BR pp. 256–347. On Linnell, see Alfred T. Story, *The Life of John Linnell*, 2 vols (London, Richard Bentley 1892); on Samuel Palmer, see Raymond Lister, *The Paintings of Samuel Palmer* (Cambridge: Cambridge University Press 1985) and Raymond Lister, *Samuel Palmer and 'The Ancients'* (Cambridge: Cambridge University Press 1984). See also Gerald E. Bentley Jr, Robert N. Essick, Shelley M. Bennett, and Morton D. Paley, *Essays on the Blake Followers* (San Marino: Huntington Library and Art Gallery 1983).

7. No. 10 in Colin Harrison, *Samuel Palmer* (Oxford: Ashmolean Museum 1997), pp. 24–5.

8. See the waning moon in 'A Rustic Scene', Harrison no. 5, pp. 1–15, Lister no. 7, and Lister's commentary in *Samuel Palmer and 'The Ancients'*, pp. 5–6. A full moon is in 'The Valley Thick with Corn', Harrison no. 9, pp. 22–3, Lister no. 9, and a waning moon in the watercolour 'A Hilly Scene' (1826, Lister no. 10) with a bright star shining through tree branches. A full moon against cloud appears in 'Moonlit Scene with a Winding River' (Lister no. 11), and a crescent moon in the watercolour 'Cornfield by Moonlight, with the Evening Star' (1830, Lister no. 21). There is 'Harvest Moon, Shoreham', c. 1830, watercolour (Lister no. 22); another harvest moon, with a constellation of huge bright stars accompanies the peasants harvesting in the oil work 'The Harvest Moon' (1833). In 'The Gleaning Field' (oil, 1833, Lister no. 26) a full moon emerges above a ridge at the back, to illuminate the women working together in the field.

9. Poem by Palmer of 1824; Lister no. 20 includes it in the commentary.

10. Ulro is Death, dehumanized thought, marked by belief in the 'natural cause' (*Milton* 26.45, E. 124, K. 513). Generation establishes the masculine and the feminine, as opposed to the hermaphroditic (*Jerusalem* 58.18–20, E. 207, K. 690). Beulah, from Isaiah 62.4, and, important for Palmer, also from *The Pilgrim's Progress*, is the married state and comparatively feminine; Eternity is the 'world of Imagination' (*A Vision of the Last Judgment* E. 554, K. 605).

11. See John Barrell, *The Dark Side of the Landscape: The Rural Poor in English Painting 1730–1840* (Cambridge: Cambridge University Press 1980), pp. 32–3, discussing Linnell's 'Woodcutting in Windsor Forest' (1834–1835). See Linnell's London illustrations, *John Linnell: A Centennial Exhibition*, catalogued Katharine Crouan (Cambridge: Cambridge University Press and Fitzwilliam Museum 1983).

12. On Blake's influence, see Robert J. Bertholf and Annette S. Levitt, *William Blake and the Moderns* (Albany: State University of New York 1982).

13. See *Reynolds*, ed. Nicolas Penny (London: Weidenfeld & Nicolson 1986), pp. 251–4.

14. See *Henry Fuseli, 1741–1825* (London: Tate Gallery 1975), pp. 99–104, for the impact of Reynolds and Fuseli on Gericault's *The Raft of the Medusa*, see Patrick Noon (ed.), *Constable to Delacroix: British Art and the French Romantics* (London: Tate Publishing 2003), p. 84.

15. For Dante in English, and the material for this paragraph, see Paget Tonybee, *Dante in English Literature*, 2 vols, London, 1909; Werner P. Frederich, *Dante's Fame Abroad*, Rome: Edizioni di Storia e Letteratura, 1950 – which includes work on German translations and plays derived from Ugolino material; Frances Yates, 'Transformations of Dante's Ugolino', *Journal of the Warburg and Courtauld Institutes* 14 (1951), 92–117, William de Sua, *Dante into English* (Chapel Hill, NC: University of North Carolina Press 1964), esp. pp. 8–14, 18–20 on the Gothic horror stressed in the eighteenth-century translations, Steve Ellis, *Dante and English Poetry: Shelley to T.S. Eliot* (Cambridge: Cambridge University Press 1983), V. Tinkler-Villani, *Visions of Dante in English Poetry* (Amsterdam: Rodopi, 1989), Ralph Pite, *The Circle of our Vision: Dante's Presence in English Romantic Poetry* (Oxford: Clarendon Press 1994), John Roe, 'Dante, Ugolino and Thomas Gray' in Nicholas Havely (ed.) *Dante's Modern Afterlife* (London: Macmillan), 1998.

16. Compare Byron, *Don Juan*, Canto 2.82, on the cannibalism of Pedrillo at sea:

> And if Pedrillo's fate should shocking be,
> Remember Ugolino condescends
> To eat the head of his arch-enemy
> The moment after he politely ends
> His tale: if foes be food in hell, at sea
> 'Tis surely fair to dine upon our friends
> When shipwreck's short allowance grows too scanty,
> Without being much more horrible than Dante.

17. See Ricardo Quinones, *Foundation Sacrifice in Dante's Commedia* (Philadelphia, PA: Pennsylvania University Press 1994), p. 29.
18. Freud connects narcissism with melancholia: see Freud, Sigmund, *On Metapsychology: The Penguin Freud vol. 11* (Harmondsworth: Penguin 1977), pp. 258–9.
19. Lacan discusses this fantasy of fragmentation: the mirror-stage seems to convey wholeness to 'inchoate desires', gendered identity divides these again: Jacques Lacan, *Ecrits: A Selection* trans. Alan Sheridan (London: Tavistock 1977), pp. 4, 11; *The Psychoses: The Seminar of Jacques Lacan Book III: 1955–1956* ed. Jacques Alain-Miller, trans. Russell Grigg (London: Routledge 1993), p. 39.
20. See Theodor Spencer, 'The Story of Ugolino in Chaucer', *Speculum* 9 (1934), pp. 295–301; Piero Boitani, 'The Monk's Tale: Chaucer and Boccaccio', *Medium Aevum* 45 (1976), 50–9, and see his reading of Canto 26 in Kenelm Foster and Patrick Boyde (eds) *Cambridge Readings in Dante* (Cambridge: Cambridge University Press 1981), pp. 70–89, and Boitani (ed.), *Chaucer and the Trecento* (Cambridge: Cambridge University Press 1983), pp. 115–40.
21. John Beer finds the 1818 revisions more 'personally oriented' than the earlier version: see his 'Influence and Independence in Blake' in Michael Phillips, *Interpreting Blake* (Cambridge: Cambridge University Press 1978), p. 210. In *Blake's Humanism* (Manchester: Manchester University Press 1969), p. 237, he takes Ugolino and his four sons as the five senses. If Ugolino represents despair, yet in Blake's last illustrations of Dante (1824–1827), in the pencil drawing of Ugolino and his sons, two angels hover. Albert Roe, *Blake's Illustrations to the Divine Comedy* (Princeton: Princeton University Press 1953), p. 153, links these angels with 'Man's Perceptions are not bounded by organs of perception, he perceives more than sense (tho' ever so acute) can discover' from 'There is No Natural Religion' (E. 2, K. 97).
22. David Erdman, *The Illuminated Blake* (Oxford: Oxford University Press 1975), p. 113.
23. Blake's reading of Fuseli overturns his own reading of the text. The reaction to Ugolino is split, and involves Blake in gender-blindness. He adds: 'The child in [Ugolino's] arms, whether boy or girl signifies not (but the critic must be a fool who has not read Dante and does not know a boy from a girl). Whether boy or girl *signifies* not' (my italics); but it does signify, especially as the figure lying in the lap of Ugolino, like Cordelia dead in Lear's arms, with hair hanging down and falling back from the head like the woman in the Fuseli 'Nightmare' seems to be female, a daughter-figure. Blake's reading of the picture and his defence of it implies a certain repression. The father in

Fuseli's painting cannot be considered outside the contexts of Romantic interest in incest, which, reworking the motif of technophagia, sexualizes the patriarch. Compare Fuseli's picture with James Barry, 'King Lear Weeping over the Body of Cordelia' (1786–1787); see Scott Paul Gordon, 'Reading Patriot Art: James Barry's *King Lear*', *Eighteenth-Century Studies* 36 (2003), 491–510.

24. Jeremy Tambling, *Dante and Difference: Writing in the Commedia* (Cambridge: Cambridge University Press 1988), pp. 82–3.

25. See my 'Dante and Benjamin: Melancholy and Allegory', *Exemplaria* 4.2. (1992) 341–63, and my *Allegory and the Work of Melancholy: The Late Medieval and Shakespeare* (Amsterdam: Rodopi 2004).

26. Note the militarism when Enitharmon rouses Sotha and Thiralatha (*Europe* 14.26–31, E. 66, K. 244). See Northrop Frye, *Fearful Symmetry: A Study of William Blake* (Princeton: Princeton University Press 1947), p. 262.

27. The illustration following Enitharmon's message, however, showing a London interior with two women with a dead child and with the possibility that they are going to eat it, hardly suggests the triumph of the woman – see D. pp. 185–90, on plate 7 (8).

28. The draft (E. 26, K. 162) begins line 7 with 'And' before this became 'so', thus making seven lines out of the twelve that begin this way (Compare 'A Poison Tree'). It spells 'gowns' 'gounds': OED gives 'foul matter, especially that dwelling in the eye' for 'gound', associating it with 'redgum' – rashes spotting the body. Compare 'blackning' ('London').

29. Even the green is created: 'Unorganizd Innocence: An Impossibility / Innocence dwells with Wisdom but never with Ignorance' (E. 697, K. 380).

30. The subject desiring its own death in the death drive is from *Beyond the Pleasure Principle*. Derrida draws out the implications of the subject centring itself through its approach to a death which is considered its own, belonging to it, in *The Postcard: From Socrates to Freud* trans. Alan Bass (Chicago: University of Chicago Press 1987), p. 355.

31. Andrew Lincoln compares the binding of the graves with *Night Thoughts* illustrations nos 34, 35, and 96, L., p. 191.

32. Freud, 'Beyond the Pleasure Principle', *On Metapsychology: The Penguin Freud 11* (Harmondsworth: Penguin 1977), p. 306.

33. Nicholas Abraham and Maria Torok, *The Shell and the Kernel* trans. Nicholas T. Rand (Chicago: University of Chicago Press 1987), pp. 125–38.

34. See my *Lost in the American City: Dickens, James, Kafka* (New York: Palgrave 2001).

35. See Peggy Meyer Sherry, 'The Predicament of the Autograph: William Blake', *Glyph 4* (Baltimore: Johns Hopkins 1979), pp. 130–55.

36. Gilles Deleuze and Felix Guattari, *Anti-Oedipus: Capitalism and Schizophrenia* trans. Robert Hurley, Mark Seem, and Helen R. Lane (London: Athlone Press 1984), p. 362. Cited, Paul Youngquist, *Madness and Blake's Myth* (University Park, Penn.: Pennsylvania State University Press 1989), p. 180.

37. Nietzsche, *The Birth of Tragedy* section 10, trans. Francis Golffing (New York: Doubleday Anchor 1956), p. 66.

38. Emmanuel Levinas, *Totality and Infinity: An Essay on Exteriority* trans. Alfonso Lingis (Pittsburgh: Duquesne University Press 1969), p. 25.

39. Maurice Blanchot, *The Step Not Beyond* trans. Lycette Nelson (Albany: SUNY Press 1992), pp. 21–2.

40. Martin Heidegger, *On the Way to Language* trans. Peter D. Hertz (New York: Harper & Row 1982), p. 160.
41. Emmanuel Levinas, *Existence and Existents* trans. Alphonse Lingis (The Hague: Martinus Nijhoff 1978), p. 65. A vigil is a watch kept through the night before a religious festival. See my 'Strange Images of Death: *Macbeth* and Levinas', *Essays in Criticism* 54. 4 (2004).

2 'In the silent of the night'

1. Thomas Mann, *Doctor Faustus* trans. John E. Woods (New York: Vintage 1997), p. 176. Further references in text.
2. W.H. Auden, 'Psychology and Art Today' (1935) reprinted in *The English Auden* ed. Edward Mendelson (New York: Random House 1977), p. 339. See also 'The Prolific and the Devourer' (1939), pp. 394–406. Benjamin Britten has set Blake's poems, for instance, *Songs and Proverbs of William Blake* op. 74 (1965), while 'The Sick Rose' appears in his nocturne, *Serenade for tenor, horn and strings* (1943), as the loss of an unquestioned innocence.
3. Compare the draft for 'The Lilly': 'The [rose puts envious – *del.*] [lustful – *del.*] modest rose puts forth a thorn' (K. 171). There is no rose in *Songs of Innocence*.
4. See Georges Bataille, *Literature and Evil* trans. Alastair Hamilton (London: Marion Boyars 1973). Further references in text.
5. See ME, p. 44 (Night 3), discussion p. 50, for the interrelationship of sexual and religious idolatry that appears in the portrayal of a naked woman with a sanctuary, altar, and cathedral in the genital area.
6. For Blake and psychoanalytic thought see Morris Dickstein, 'The Price of Experience: Blake's Reading of Freud', in Joseph H. Smith (ed.) *The Literary Freud: Mechanisms of Defence and the Poetic Will* vol. 4 (New Haven: Yale University Press 1980).
7. See Martin Bidney, *Blake and Goethe: Psychology, Ontology, Imagination* (Columbia: University of Missouri Press 1988), p. 67.
8. W.J.T. Mitchell, 'Dangerous Blake', *Studies in Romanticism* 21 (1982), 410–16, sees the last two lines forecasting Blake's tendency towards obscenity. E.P. Thompson, *Witness Against The Beast: William Blake and the Moral Law* (Cambridge: Cambridge University Press 1993), pp. 171–2, interprets the chapel as the Swedenborgian Church after it had moved politically to the right in 1791 and sees Blake as disenchanted, disgusted, turning away to secular advanced radicalism associated with Thomas Paine, Joel Barlow and Joseph Johnson the dissenting publisher. The group were identified, and they identified themselves, as the 'swinish multitude'.
9. See John Brenkman, *Culture and Domination* (Ithaca: Cornell University Press 1987), pp. 111–21 (see also his analysis of 'London', 121–38).
10. Freud, 'Instincts and their Vicissitudes', *The Penguin Freud: On Metapsychology* (Harmodsworth: Penguin 1977), pp. 136–7.
11. See Henry Yule and A.C. Burnell, *Hobson-Jobson: A Glossay of Colloquial Anglo-Indian Words and Phrases and of Kindred terms, Etymological, Historical, Geographic and Discursive* (1886, London: Routledge 1988), entry under 'upas'. See the reference to Java in E. 499, 861, K. 185 (and note the pun, in the following line, 'And a great many suckers grow all around', which makes the

tree-image so comprehensive). For Blake's tree, see Jon Mee, *Dangerous Enthusiasm: William Blake and the Culture of Radicalism in the 1790s* (Oxford: Clarendon Press 1992), pp. 7–8, 97–103.

12. Virgil vol. 1, trans. H. Rushton Fairclough (Cambridge, Mass.: Harvard University Press 1957), p. 563. See also *Eclogues* 7.62 – the myrtle is 'most dear to lovely Venus' *ibid.*, p. 53. The myrtle's appearances in *Paradise Lost* 4.262 and 9.431 associate it with Venus; Alastair Fowler notes for the latter that when 'satyrs surprised Venus bathing, she hid behind a myrtle' – see Ovid, *Fasti*, 4.138ff. In Shakespeare, *Venus and Adonis* 865: John Roe, editing *Shakespeare: The Poems* (Cambridge: Cambridge University Press 1992), p. 123, says as a tree it was 'similar in status to the rose among flowers'.

13. Compare Laertes in the graveyard:

> Lay her i' th' earth.
> And from her fair and unpolluted flesh
> May violets spring. I tell thee, churlish priest,
> A ministering angel shall my sister be
> When thou liest howling. (*Hamlet* V. i. 235–8)

and 'howl, howl, howl' (*King Lear* V. iii. 257).

14. See my *Becoming Posthumous: Life and Death in Literary and Cultural Studies* (Edinburgh: Edinburgh University Press 2001), pp. 37ff.

15. Samuel Richardson, *Sir Charles Grandison* vol. 3 letter 22. The novel's heroine, Harriet Byron, for whom this woman is a double, quotes *Night Thoughts*, calling Young 'my favourite author' (vol. 2 letter 7). *Sir Charles Grandison* ed. Jocelyn Harris (Oxford: Oxford University Press 1986), pp. 298, and pp. 153 and 157. Richardson's interest in women's history also appears in Clarissa's distracted readings of what has happened to her after her rape by Lovelace:

> Thou pernicious caterpillar, that preyest on the fair leaf of virgin fame, and poisonest those leaves which thou canst not devour!
> Thou fell blight, thou eastern blast, thou overspreading mildew, that destroyest the early promises of the shining year! that mockest the laborious toil, and blastest the joyful hopes of the painflul husbandman!
> Thou fretting moth that corruptest the fairest garment!
> Thou eating canker-worm that preyest upon the opening bud, and turnest the damask rose into livid yellowness! . . .
> (*Clarissa* letter 261, ed. Angus Ross (Harmondsworth: Penguin 1985), p. 892).

Clarissa works through images of Ophelia and of the passage in *Twelfth Night*. Compare Laertes to Ophelia, *Hamlet* 1. iii. 39–42. For other Shakespeare echoes in 'The Sick Rose' see *Macbeth* on 'nature's mischief' (1. v. 50) for 'the invisible worm' and 'come thick night'.

16. The plural nature of secrecy may be expanded on by seeing it politically. Thomas Holcroft (1745–1816), the radical author who knew Blake, makes his hero, Hugh Trevor, become involved in political and religious intrigue: 'It might well be expected that at this age I should fall into a mistake common to mankind, and consider secrecy as a virtue; yet I think it strange that I did

not soon detect the duplicity of my conduct, nor imagine there was any guilt in being the agent of deceit' – *Hugh Trevor* ed. Seamus Deane (1794: Oxford: Oxford University Press 1973), p. 137.

17. Compare George Herbert's 'Vertue':

> Sweet rose, whose hue angrie and brave
> Bids the rash gazer wipe his eye;
> Thy root is ever in its grave,
> And thou must die.

18. See Stephen C. Behrendt, *The Moment of Explosion: Blake and the Illustration of Milton* (Lincoln: University of Nebraska Press 1983) plates 16, 17, discussion pp. 160–1.

19. See Bette Charlene Werner, *Blake's Vision of the Poetry of Milton* (Lewisburg: Bucknell University Press 1986), pp. 86–90. In Blake's Crucifixion in the *Paradise Lost* series, the serpent winds round the cross, its bruised head just under the foot (the heel) of Christ: see pp. 94–8.

20. Freud discusses the 'sadism of the superego', which secures single identity, in *The Penguin Freud: vol. 11: On Metapyschology* (Harmondsworth: Penguin 1977), p. 425.

21. Freud, 'The Ego and the Id', *The Penguin Freud: vol. 11: On Metapsychology* (Harmondsworth: Penguin 1977), p. 387.

22. See Philip J. Gallagher, 'The Word Made Flesh: Blake's "A Poison Tree" and the Book of Genesis', *Studies in Romanticism* 16 (1977), 237–49.

23. See S.H. Clark, *Sordid Images: The Poetry of Masculine Desire* (London: Routledge 1994), pp. 160–1.

24. The last six lines, reminiscent of 'London', putting London in the human brain, appear only in the Notebook. Phillips, pp. 69–70, says that the Notebook poem came from a cancelled five lines which it followed:

> How came pride in Man?
> From Mary it began
> How Contempt & Scorn
> What a world is Man
> His Earth . . .

(E. 472, K. 173)

The lines trace the origins of emotions. S 157 thinks Blake was continuing this poem, making the issue of gender pertinent to 'the human image'.

25. Phillips, pp. 39–41, derives the poem in the Notebook 'I heard an Angel singing' (E. 470, K. 164) as a response to 'The Divine Image' in *Songs of Innocence* (E. 12, K. 117), though he concedes that 'A Divine Image' (E. 32, K. 221), etched but not included by Blake in *Experience* may be an earlier response to 'The Divine Image'. (I reviewed Phillips, *MLR* 98 (2003), pp. 438–40.)

26. For this poem and *King Lear*, see John Danby, *Shakespeare and the Doctrine of Nature: A Study of King Lear* (London: Faber 1948), pp. 117–20.

27. See C.B. MacPherson, *The Political Theory of Possessive Individualism: Hobbes to Locke* (Oxford: Clarendon Press 1962).

28. Geoffrey H. Hartman, 'Envoi: "So Many Things"', in Nelson Hilton and Thomas A. Vogler (eds) *Unnam'd Forms: Blake and Textuality* (Berkeley: University of California Press 1986), pp. 242–8.

29. Compare Cowper's 'Hope' 746: 'When night has quenched the pole', or 'On the Death of Mrs Throckmorton's Bullfinch': 'Night veil'd the pole – all seem'd secure' (31).

3 Young and 'weary night'

1. *Poems* (1870), from Comte de Lautréamont, *Maldoror and Poems* trans. Paul Knight (Harmondsworth: Penguin 1978), p. 255.

2. André Breton, 'Manifesto of Surrealism' (1924) in *Manifestoes of Surrealism* trans. Richard Seaver and Helen R. Lane (Michigan: Ann Arbor Paperbacks 1972), p. 26.

3. Maurice Blanchot, 'The Outside, the Night', *The Space of Literature* trans. Ann Smock (Lincoln: University of Nebraska Press 1982), p. 163.

4. 'Thel's Motto', E. 3, K. 127.

5. 'Worldliness and Other-Worldliness: The Poet Young' (1857) in Thomas Pinney (ed.) *Essays of George Eliot* (London: Routledge & Kegan Paul 1963), pp. 335–85.

6. Karl Philipp Moritz, *Anton Reiser: A Psychological Novel* trans. Ritchie Robertson (Harmondsworth: Penguin 1997), pp. 180–1, 186, 189, 201–2 for Young.

7. Quotations from Dick Higgins (trans.), *Novalis: Hymns to the Night* (New York: McPherson 1988). Novalis was Friedrich von Hardenberg (1772–1801).

8. Simon Critchley, *Very Little... Almost Nothing: Death, Philosophy, Literature* (London: Routledge 1997), p. 63.

9. Maurice Blanchot, *The Writing of the Disaster* trans. Ann Smock (Lincoln: University of Nebraska Press 1986), p. 49.

10. See Nicholas Powell, *Fuseli: The Nightmare* (Harmondsworth: Penguin 1973), and Kristen Strom, *Making History: Surrealism and the Invention of a Political Culture* (Lanham: University Press of America 2002), p. 144.

11. In 1795, Blake received a commission to illustrate a new *Night Thoughts*, comprising 537 watercolours, the basis for a selection of engravings. The first of the four volumes appeared in 1797, using 43 designs, which Blake engraved himself out of 156, but no others. For commentary, B. vol. 2, pp. 178–294. See H.M. Margoliouth, 'Blake's Drawings for Young's *Night Thoughts*', in Vivien de Sola Pinto (ed.) *The Divine Vision: Studies in the Poetry and Art of William Blake* (London: Victor Gollancz 1957), pp. 191–204, Morton D. Paley, 'Blake's *Night Thoughts*: An Exploration of the Fallen World', in Alvin H. Rosenfeld (ed.) *William Blake: Essays for S. Foster Damon* (Providence: Brown University Press 1969), pp. 131–57, Thomas H. Helmstadter, 'Blake and Religion: Iconographical Themes in the *Night Thoughts*', *Studies in Romanticism* 10 (1971), 119–212 and his 'Blake's Night Thoughts: Interpretations of Edward Young', in Robert N. Essick (ed.) *The Visionary Hand* (Los Angeles: Hennessey and Ingalls 1973), pp. 381–418, reading Blake as criticizing Young's rationalism. See W.J.T. Mitchell, review of 'William Blake's Designs for Edward Young's *Night Thoughts*' in *Modern Philology* 80 (1982–1983), 198–205, John E. Grant, 'Jesus and the Powers that Be in Blake's Design for Young's *Night Thoughts*', in

David Erdman (ed.) *Blake and his Bibles* (West Cornwall, CT: Locust Hill Press 1990), pp. 71–116, Christopher Heppner, *Reading Blake's Designs* (Cambridge: Cambridge University Press 1995), pp. 147–70, J.M.Q. Davies, 'Variations on the Fall in Blake's Designs for Young's *Night Thoughts*' and Jon Mee, ' "As Portentous as the Written Wall": Blake's Illustrations to *Night Thoughts*' and Peter Otto, 'From the Religious to the Psychological Sublime: The Fate of Young's *Night Thoughts* in Blake's *The Four Zoas*', all in Alexander Gourlay (ed.) *Prophetic Character: Essays on William Blake in Honor of John E. Grant* (West Cornwall, Conn.: Locust Hill Press 2002), pp. 27–50, 171–203, 205–62. Young is quoted in the edition by Stephen Cornford, *Night Thoughts* (Cambridge: Cambridge University Press 1989).

12. See *Collected Poems of Thomas Parnell* ed. Claude Rawson and F.P. Lock (Newark: University of Delaware Press 1989), and C.H. Peake, *Poetry of Landscape and the Night* (London: Edward Arnold 1967). See also David W. Lindsay, *English Poetry 1700–1780* (London: Dent 1974). For night in relation to the sublime, see section III. 3, 'Obscurity', in Edmund Burke, *A Philosophical Inquiry into the Origin of our Ideas of the Sublime and Beautiful* ed. Adam Phillips (1757, Oxford: Oxford University Press 1990), pp. 54–5.

13. David Bindman, *Blake as an Artist* (Oxford: Phaidon 1977), Bindman, pp. 454–5.

14. See Horace W. O'Connor, 'The Narcissa Episode in Young's *Night Thoughts*', *PMLA* 34 (1919), 130–49.

15. Richardson, *Sir Charles Grandison* vol. 6 letter 31 (ed. Jocelyn Harris, Oxford: Oxford University Press 1986), p. 143. Richardson's use of dreams in *Clarissa* and *Sir Charles Grandison* (vol. 6 letter 32, pp. 148–9) extends Young.

16. See Roger Lonsdale (ed.), *Thomas Gray and William Collins: Poetical Works* (Oxford: Oxford University Press 1977), pp. xiii, 33–4.

17. Compare Lacan on the *aphanasis* of the subject: 'Hence the division of the subject – when the subject appears somewhere as meaning, he is manifested elsewhere as "fading", as disappearance' – Jacques Lacan, *The Four Fundamental Concepts of Psychanalysis* (Seminar XI) trans. Alan Sheridan (Harmondsworth: Penguin 1977), p. 218.

18. Blake began watercolours of Gray's poetry, in late 1797, for Flaxman's wife. See Frank A. Vaughan, *Again to the Life of Eternity: William Blake's Illustrations to the Poems of Thomas Gray* (Selinsgrove: Susquehanna University Press 1996), pp. 109–10.

19. Blake quotes the passage in describing the watercolours for 'L'Allegro' and 'Il Penseroso' made c. 1816 for Thomas Butts (K. 618). See Melancholy in B. cat. 543.7.

20. Robert F. Gleckner, *Gray Agonistes: Thomas Gray and Masculine Friendship* (Baltimore: Johns Hopkins University Press 1997), George E. Haggerty, 'Gray's Tears', *Men in Love: Masculinity and Sexuality in the Eighteenth Century* (New York: Columbia University Press 1999), pp. 113–35, Robert L. Mack, *Thomas Gray: A Life* (New Haven: Yale University Press 2000), pp. 31–40 for Gray's attachments, for example, to Charles Victor de Bonstetten.

21. T.S. Eliot, 'Poetry in the Eighteenth Century', in Boris Ford (ed.) *From Dryden to Johnson* (Harmondsworth: Penguin 1965), pp. 273–4. F.R. Leavis, *Revaluation* (1936, Harmondsworth: Penguin 1964), pp. 118–20, takes Eliot's discussion of eighteenth-century poetry to be complicit with what it attacks, since Eliot

holds that poetry must have the 'virtues of good prose', which would align it with eighteenth-century poetry. Leavis reads the 'Introduction' to the *Songs of Experience* to show that Blake 'essentially disdains the virtues of prose'; see Leavis's further comments in *The Common Pursuit* (1952, Harmondsworth: Penguin 1962), pp. 217–19; see also 'Justifying One's Valuation of Blake', in *The Critic as Antiphilosopher* ed. G. Singh (Chicago: Elephant 1998), pp. 1–23. See also *The Living Principle: English as a Discipline of Thought* (London: Chatto & Windus 1975), pp. 89–93. For Eliot on Blake, see *Selected Essays* (London: Faber 1951), pp. 321, 322, criticizing him for not taking hold of the 'advantages of culture'.

22. John Leonard, 'Milton, Lucretius and "the Void Profound of Unessential Night"', in Kristin A. Pruitt and Charles W. Durham (eds) *Living Texts: Intepreting Milton* (London: Associated University Presses 2000), pp. 198–217.

23. H.S. Harris, *Hegel's Development: Night Thoughts (Jena 1801–1806)* (Oxford: Clarendon Press 1983), quoting first from *Difference Between the Systems of Fichte and Schelling*, pp. 194–5. See also p. 348, and Preface to the *Phenomenology of Spirit* trans. A.V. Miller (Oxford: Oxford University Press 1977), p. 9.

24. Jacques Derrida, *The Ear of the Other: Otobiography, Transference, Translation* trans. Avital Ronell and Peggy Kamuf (Lincoln: University of Nwebraska Press 1985), p. 38.

25. Frank M. Parisi, 'Emblems of Melancholy: For Children: *The Gates of Paradises*', in Michael Phillips, *Interpreting Blake* (Cambridge: Cambridge University Press 1978), pp. 70–110 (p. 71). See also, on the *Gates*, George Wingfield Digby, *Symbol and Image in William Blake* (Oxford: Oxford University Press 1957), pp. 5–53; and Gail Kmetz, 'A Reading of Blake's 'The Gates of Paradise', *Blake Studies* 3 (1971), pp. 171–85, and Brenda Webster, *Blake's Prophetic Psychology* (Athens, GA: University of Georgia Press 1983), pp. 181–202. See also David Erdman, with Donald K. Moore, *The Notebooks of William Blake: A Photographic and Typographic Facsimile* (Oxford: Clarendon Press 1973), pp. 14–44, and *The Illuminated Blake* (Oxford: Oxford University Press 1975), pp. 268–79.

26. His limitation is keeping himself within the influence of Milton, and Pope. (Blake's no. 35 appears in *The Four Zoas*, p. 123). See Daniel W. Odell, 'Young's *Night Thoughts* as an Answer to Pope's *Essay on Man*', *Studies in English Literature, 1500–1900*, 12 (1972), 481–501, which brings out Young's confidence; see also Steve Clark, '"Radical Insincerity" in Edward Young's *Night Thoughts*', *British Journal for Eighteenth-Century Studies* vol. 20 (1997), 173–86.

27. John E. Grant, 'Envisioning the First *Night Thoughts* in David V. Erdman and John E. Grant (eds) *Blake's Visionary Forms Dramatic* (Princeton: Princeton University Press 1970), p. 322.

28. See G, pp. 42, 43. The editors compare Dürer's *Melencolia* holding compasses. A soul holding compasses in the right hand (contrast 'The Ancient of Days') appears in no. 227, illustrating: 'To rise, in Science, as in Bliss, / Initiate in the Secrets of the Skies' – 6.94, 95. See also no. 62.

29. Marshall Brown, *Preromanticism* (Stanford: Stanford University Press 1991), p. 36. See also Shaun Irlam, *Elations: The Poetics of Enthusiasm in Eighteenth Century Britain* (Stanford: Stanford University Press 1999). See also John Dolan, *Poetic Occasion from Milton to Wordsworth* (London: Palgrave 2000) for Blair, Young, Gray, and Cowper, and Amy Reed, *The Background to Gray's Elegy, 1700–1751* (New York: Russell & Russell 1962).

30. Quoted, Cornford, p. 338. See also Georges Minois, *History of Suicide: Voluntary Death in Western Culture* trans. Lydia G. Cochrane (Baltimore: Johns Hopkins University Press 1999), pp. 179–209.

31. Freud, 'Civilization and its Discontents', *The Penguin Freud 12* (Harmondsworth: Penguin 1985), p. 313 (see pp. 256–60 for the 'oceanic feeling' of 'oneness with the universe').

32. This recalls where the senses 'Take in, at once, the Landscape of the world, / At a small inlet, which a Grain might close, / And half create the wonderous World, they see' (6.425–8). This provides both Wordsworth with a phrase in 'Tintern Abbey' – 'Both what they half create / And what perceive' (lines 106–7) – and Blake with the beginning of 'Auguries of Innocence': 'To see a World in a Grain of Sand' (E. 490, K. 431). Note the echo of Young's section 5. 172–6, quoted above, in 'Tintern Abbey' 28 and 94–5.

33. Nelson Hilton, *Literal Imagination: Blake's Vision of Words* (Berkeley: University of California Press 1983), p. 265.

34. Emmanuel Levinas, *Existence and Existents* trans. Alphonso Lingis (The Hague: Martinus Nijhoff 1978), p. 66.

35. Gerda S. Norvig, *Dark Figures in the Desired Country: Blake's Illustrations to The Pilgrim's Progress* (Berkeley: University of California Press 1993), p. 114 (see pp. 109–17 for discussion). See Erdman and Moore (p. 9) for Bunyan and no. 14.

36. From Quid's song in *An Island in the Moon* (E. 463, K. 60), which has no answering 'The Little Boy Found'. Cp. 'The Little Girl Lost' and 'The Little Girl Found' (E. 20, 21, K. 112–14) in *Innocence* (later moved to *Experience*) and 'A Little Girl Lost' in *Experience* (E. 29, K. 219) and 'A Little Boy Lost' in *Songs of Experience* (E. 28, K. 218).

37. For Death's Door see Irene H. Chayes, 'Picture and Page, Reader and Viewer in Blake's *Night Thoughts* Illustrations', *Studies in Romanticism* 30 (1991), 437–71, discussing nos 40, 61, 118, 119, 535. Michael Wheeler, *Death and the Future Life in Victorian Literature and Theology* (Cambridge: Cambridge University Press 1990), pp. 298–9 connects Blake and Blair and Dickens' *Our Mutual Friend* Book 2 Chapter 5.

4 Night dreams: *The Four Zoas*

1. E. 818, quoting the uncollected inscription in the edition by E.J. Ellis and W.B. Yeats (1893).

2. The manuscript of *The Four Zoas* is of 70 pages, written on both sides, including seven pictures without text. Its first 42 pages were written in copperplate on blank sheets, comprising part of the proofs for *Night Thoughts*, while pages 43–84 and 111–12 were written in more ordinary handwriting on the recto of proof sheets for *Night Thoughts*, so that the illustrations for *Night Thoughts* accompanied Blake's poem which was placed inside the boxes left blank for the inclusion of Young's poem. On the verso, Blake produced new designs. The third section, pages 85–140, was like the second, but not stitched together as the second was stitched together by Blake. Pages 87–90, exceptionally, were made by cutting in half a print of 'Edward and Elinor'. Altogether, there are 85 new drawings to accompany the poem. It is assumed that while Blake

began work in 1797, the third section, introducing Christian imagery, may be of 1803–1805.

3. For scholarship on *The Four Zoas*: Brian Wilkie and Mary Lynn Johnson, *Blake's Four Zoas: The Design of a Dream* (Cambridge, Mass.: Harvard University Press 1978), Donald Ault, *Narrative Unbound: Revisioning William Blake's The Four Zoas* (Barrytown: Station Hill 1987), Vincent De Luca, *Words of Eternity: Blake and the Poetics of the Sublime* (Princeton: Princeton University Press 1991), George Anthony Rosso Jr, *Blake's Prophetic Workshop: A Study of the Four Zoas* (London: Associated University Press 1993), Andrew Lincoln, *Spiritual History: A Reading of William Blake's Vala or The Four Zoas* (Oxford: Clarendon Press 1995), John B. Pierce, *Flexible Design: Revisionary Poetics in Blake's Vala or The Four Zoas* (Montreal: McGill-Queen's University Press 1998), Peter Otto, *Blake's Critique of Transcendence: Love, Jealousy and the Sublime in The Four Zoas* (Oxford: Oxford University Press 2000). For other work on the manuscript: H.M. Margoliouth, *William Blake's 'Vala': Blake's Numbered Text* (Oxford: Clarendon Press 1956); G.E. Bentley Jr, *'Vala' or 'The Four Zoas': A Facsimile of the Manuscript, a Transcript of the Poem and a Study of its Growth and Significance* (Oxford: Clarendon Press 1963). The dominating difficulties are over the revisions: whether the poem begins with the First or Second Night (the second is never so named by Blake), and over the two versions of Night 7. Keynes prints these separately, whereas Erdman (regarding 7b as earlier, a point which has not achieved consensus) puts 7b inside 7a, at 7a.331, plate 85, line 22 (E. 360, K. 328). Blake had written 'End of the Seventh Night' at this point. S follows E, but prints 7b in reverse order, lines 124–301 before 1–122. These are only two of several possibilities. Another question rises over the designs, some of which were partially erased, at some stage in the nineteenth century (on account of their obscenity?). For an early attempt to relate the illustrations to Young, see John Beer, *Blake's Visionary Universe* (Manchester: Manchester University Press 1969), pp. 343–452, about which John E. Grant is intemperate in his 'Visions in *Vala*: A Consideration of Some Pictures in the Manuscript', in Stuart Curran and Joseph Anthony Wittreich Jr, *Blake's Sublime Allegory: Essays on The Four Zoas, Milton, Jerusalem* (Madison: University of Wisconsin Press 1973), pp. 141–202. The revisions mean that *The Four Zoas* contains material from the Lambeth books (much of it in pages 43–84) overlaid with material from *Milton* and *Jerusalem* imported at a later stage. Much criticism of the poem takes the form of distinguishing the revisions. I have worked with the poem as far as possible as if it was complete, continuous, even self-consistent, while recognizing it is none of these things. I have disregarded questions of chronology, which assume a narrative force to the events in the text; Ault could be cited as an ally for his reading of the text as 'anti-Newtonian narrative' – but I do not assume an agreement with Ault for leaving aside chronology, for I do not want to argue particularly that the breaks are modes of foiling linear narrative.

4. Pierce, p. 93, points out how this image, combining the temporal and corporeal, is a revision created from its use in *Milton* and *Jerusalem*.

5. On stonework in London and the bricks and the brickfields that marked out suburban London, see James Ayres, *Building the Georgian City* (New Haven: Yale University Press 1998).

6. For discussion, see Christopher Z. Hobson, *Blake and Homosexuality* (London: Palgrave 2000), pp. 56–8.

7. Georges Bataille, *Eroticism* trans. Mary Dalwood (London: Marion Boyars 1987), p. 11; 'The Notion of Expenditure' in *Visions of Excess: Selected Writings 1927–1939* ed. Allan Stoekl (Minneapolis: University of Minnesota Press 1985), pp. 116–29. For experience, cp. E. 622, K. 89.

8. 'Masculine virtue': a complex pun, 'virtue having at the same time its ordinary modern sense of morality.... and its etymological sense of virility' – Wilkie and Johnson, p. 74.

9. 'Tharmas as a "raging ocean" [47, 4.16, E. 331, K. 298] devours life because he, like it, cannot die. The random, directionless motion of stormy waters reinforces the idea of confused emotionalism, and the destructive energy of water that seems bent on destroying itself and whatever it crashes into develops the notion of a figure who would destroy himself and others. Further, water is an element that, in itself, is basically formless. It always takes the form of that which contains it' – Pierce, p. 115.

10. G.A. Rosso (1993), p. 68, shows the prevalence of 'indolence' and 'repose' in the accounts given of the Fall.

11. The passage is heard again in *Jerusalem*, where the account of the industrial revolution is followed by accounts of pressganging 'from London... Westminster & Marybone' (65.32–6, E. 216–17, K. 700).

12. Chronologically, this may be the first appearance of the Spectre in Blake, though compare *French Revolution* 171 (E. 293, K. 142) and *America* 5.6 (E. 53, K. 198). The spectre of Tharmas is seen in *FZ* (5, 1.78, E. 302, K. 266) brought about by Enion's weaving. The daughters of Beulah call it 'in every man insane and most / Deform'd' (5, 1.103–4, E. 303, K. 267, repeated 84, 7a. 304–5, E. 360, K. 327). This Spectre rapes Enitharmon, bringing about the birth of Los and Enitharmon. It seems, however, as if this passage was revised later than the Spectre of Urthona. Pierce, p. 185, notes the first datable use of 'Spectre' to be in a letter to Thomas Butts of 11 September 1801, and (p. 186) Blake's first use of the idea of the fourfold to be in Blake's letter to Thomas Butts, 22 November 1802: 'Now I a fourfold vision see, / And a fourfold vision is given to me; / 'Tis fourfold in my supreme delight / And threefold in soft Beulah's night / And twofold Always. May God us keep / From Single vision & Newton's sleep' (E. 722, K. 818).

13. Cp. E. 601, K. 938. For Blake's illustrations to *A Midsummer Night's Dream* see B. cat. 245, 246.

14. Gregory Bateson, 'Towards a Theory of Schizophrenia' in *Steps to an Ecology of Mind* (New York: Ballantine Books 1972), pp. 201–27.

15. Jacques Derrida, *The Postcard: From Socrates to Freud and Beyond* trans. Alan Bass (Chicago: University of Chicago Press 1987), pp. 355, 389 for the reference to Bateson.

16. PE 367–9. Dickens connections are made by Northrop Frye, *Fearful Symmetry: A Study of William Blake* (Princeton: Princeton University Press 1947).

17. Compare page 41, where the hermaphrodite has male sex organs. See Brenda Webster, *Blake's Prophetic Psychology* (Athens: University of Georgia Press 1983), p. 204, John Beer, p. 101.

18. 'Satan's hermaphroditic quality refers simultaneously to the arms' alternating beast and human forms, to the perversion of male sexuality in war signified

by the warriors' dragon shapes, and to the hiding of "male" sexualized aggression within the "female" "veil" of Vala's war and religious mystery' – Christopher Z. Hobson, *The Chained Boy: Orc and Blake's Idea of Revolution* (Lewisburg: Bucknell University Press 1999), p. 191.

19. On Tirzah see S. 415–16, who sees her first appearance in *Milton* 30. 19 (E. 130, K. 520). Her song is heard in *Jerusalem* 67.44–68.9, and the *FZ* passage may revise that. She does not appear in Night the Ninth, an instance of the text's indeterminateness. The date of 'To Tirzah' in *Songs of Experience* is disputed, but is later than the other Songs: see L., p. 18.

20. Pierce, p. 17, discusses the draft of 8.268 (105, 8.268, E. 378, K. 348), changed to 'The Lamb of God stood before Satan opposite' by replacing Satan for Urizen: see E., p. 842.

21. Andrew Efelbein, *Romantic Genius: The Prehistory of a Homosexual Role* (New York: Columbia University Press 1999), p. 152. For a critique of Efelbein see Christopher Z. Hobson, *Blake and Homosexuality* (London: Palgrave 2000), p. 219.

22. Compare: 'Correggio is a soft and effeminate, and consequently a most cruel demon' – *Descriptive Catalogue* no. IX (E. 548, K. 583). Absence of line proclaims femininity.

23. Julia Kristeva, *Powers of Horror: An Essay on Abjection* trans. Leon Roudiez (New York: Columbia University Press 1982) discusses fear of the loss of boundaries defining the subject: 'the places of joy and love' are, of course, borders.

5 'I see London, blind...'

1. Djuna Barnes, *Nightwood* (London: Faber 1936). Page-numbers in text.
2. Maurice Blanchot, 'The Outside, the Night', *The Space of Literature* trans. Ann Smock (Lincoln: University of Nebraska Press 1982), p. 169.
3. Lewis Mumford, *The City in History: Its Origins, Its Transformations and Its Prospects* (New York: Harcourt, Brace and World, 1961), p. 46.
4. Golgonooza appears first in *Four Zoas* 5.75 (E. 340, K. 307), 'named Art & Manufacture by mortal men' (*Milton* 24.50, E. 120, K. 509).
5. Dostoyevsky, *Notes from Underground* trans. Jessie Coulson (Harmondsworth: Penguin 1972), pp. 17–18.
6. George Rudé, *Hanoverian London 1714–1808* (Berkeley: University of California Press 1971), p. 4.
7. Ralph Hyde (ed.), *The A to Z of Georgian London* (Guildhall Library: London Topographical Society 1982), reproduces Roque. Phillips, p. 58, reprints a 1793 map of Lambeth; see also Stanley Gardner, *Blake's Innocence and Experience Retraced* (London: Athlone 1986), pp. 137–41. For Blake's houses, see *BR* 550–69. For maps of London c. 1810, S. 624–6.
8. Celina Fox (ed.), *London – World City 1800–1840* (New Haven: Yale University Press 1992); Dana Arnold, *Representing the Metropolis: Architecture, Urban Experience and Social Life in London 1800–1840* (Aldershot: Ashgate 2000). See Julian Wolfreys, *Writing London: The Trace of the Urban Text from Blake to Dickens* (London: Macmillan 1998), Dana Arnold (ed.), *The Metropolis and its Image: Constructing Identities for London, 1750–1950* (Oxford: Blackwell 1999).

9. Illustrations to Egan were by George Cruikshank (see *Sketches By Boz* and *Oliver Twist*). See Guilland Sutherland, 'Cruikshank and London', in Ira Bruce Nagel and F.S. Schwarzbach (eds) *Victorian Artists and the City: A Collection of Critical Essays* (New York: Pergamon Press 1980), pp. 106–25.

10. Linda Clarke, *Building Capitalism: Historical Change and the Labour Process in the Production of the Built Environment* (London: Routledge 1992), pp. 114–18.

11. Revised (Phillips, pp. 10–12) from when Obtuse Angle sings it in *An Island in the Moon* (E. 462, K. 59). On *An Island in the Moon* see Nick Rawlinson, *William Blake's Comic Vision* (London: Palgrave 2003), pp. 98–162. See David Fairer, 'Experience Reading Innocence: Contextualizing Blake's *Holy Thursday*', *Eighteenth-Century Studies* 35 (2002), 535–62.

12. See Heather Glen, *Vision and Disenchantment: Blake's Songs and Wordsworth's Lyrical Ballads* (Cambridge: Cambridge University Press 1983), p. 128, on 'cherish' as 'entertain kindly'.

13. D.G. Gillham, *Blake's Contrary States: The Songs of Innocence and Experience as Dramatic Poems* (Cambridge: Cambridge University Press 1966), p. 196, sees the speaker as abstractly moralizing.

14. Sir John Summerson, 'The Mind of Wren' in *Heavenly Mansions and Other Essays on Architecture* (New York: W.W. Norton 1998), pp. 51–86, compares Wren and Locke.

15. For this and the separation of 'An ancient proverb' (E. 475, K. 176), see Phillips, 54–8, 60, 64–7, and see also pp. 32–3 for the design. See also Erdman p. 796.

16. Thomson, *Works* (Oxford, 1951), pp. 422–3.

17. Tom Paine, *Rights of Man* ed. Henry Collins (Harmondsworth: Penguin 1969), p. 242. See E.P. Thompson, 'London', in Michael Phillips (ed.) *Interpreting Blake* (Cambridge: Cambridge University Press 1978), pp. 5–31. Cp. 'Why should I care for the men of Thames / Or the cheating waves of charterd streams' (E. 473, K. 166).

18. See Vivian de Sola Pinto, 'William Blake, Isaac Watts and Mrs Barbauld', in Vivian de Sola Pinto (ed.) *The Divine Vision: Studies in the Poetry and Art of William Blake* (London: Victor Gollancz 1957), pp. 65–88. See J.H. Pafford (ed.), *Isaac Watts: Divine Songs: Attempted in Easy Language for the Use of Children*, facsimile reproductions of the first edition of 1715 with an illustrated edition of c.1840 (London: Oxford University Press 1971), pp. 154–5.

19. S. 214 reads 'ban' as 'an angry swear-word', cp. 'curse'; E. 796 compares 'Bow-street's ban' in *Don Juan* XI. 19.

20. For details, see *PE* 216–17. For Thurlow by James Gillray (1756–1815), see *James Gillray: The Art of Caricature* ed. Richard Godfrey (London: Tate Publishing 2001), fig. 2 and no. 105.

21. See Sean Shesgreen, *Hogarth and the Times-of-the-Day Tradition* (Ithaca: Cornell University Press 1983).

22. Quoted from the criminologist Gotthold Lehnerdt in Joachim Schlör, *Nights in the Big City: Paris, Berlin, London 1840–1930* trans. Pierre Gottfired Imhof and Dafydd Rees Roberts (London: Reaktion Books 1998), p. 23.

23. On history painting, see Morris Eaves, *The Counter-Arts Conspiracy: Art and Industry in the Age of Blake* (Ithaca: Cornell University Press 1992).

24. For the acrostic, see Nelson Hilton, *Literal Imagination: Blake's Vision of Words* (Berkeley: University of California Press 1983), p. 64.

25. In Wilkie Collins, *Basil*, the dying Margaret in her delirium refers to her unconsummated marriage as 'the funeral of our wedding', ed. Dorothy Goldman (Oxford: Oxford University Press 1990), p. 291. See also John Harvey, *Victorian Novelists and their Illustrators* (London: Sidgwick & Jackson 1970), pp. 139–41, on the funeral in Phiz's illustration to the wedding-scene, 'Coming Home from Church' in *Dombey and Son*.

26. Blake produced five copies of *Jerusalem*, A, C, F, and D, E; the latter the one copy he coloured. The groups vary in the order of Chapter 2. Erdman follows the first, Keynes D and E (putting plates 43–6 after plate 28). See Morton D. Paley, *The Continuing City: William Blake's Jerusalem* (Oxford: Clarendon Press 1983), pp. 1–12.

27. See the picture by David Wilkie (1785–1841), 'The Chelsea Pensioners Reading the Waterloo Dispatch', painted for Wellington, 1816–1822: this, contrasting with Blake's portrayal of the 'hapless soldier's sigh', shows four or five pensioners but emphasizes the young serving soldiers: see Nicholas Tromans, *David Wilkie: Painter of Everyday Life* (London: Dulwich Picture Gallery 2002), pp. 88–91.

28. See Francis Place, on tea gardens as 'places of amusement and dissipation', *The Autobiography of Francis Place (1771–1854)* ed. Mary Thale (Cambridge: Cambridge University Press 1972), pp. 28–9; see also M. Dorothy George, *London Life in the Eighteenth Century* (Harmondsworth: Penguin 1966), pp. 18, 162, 279, 296.

29. Roy Porter, *London: A Social History* (Harmondsworth: Penguin 1994), p. 122. Porter says that Highgate in 1793 had only 200 houses; see pp. 116–23 for sites discussed.

30. For Primrose Hill, see *Milton* 39.37, E. 140, K. 531, and *Jerusalem* 73.54, E. 229, K. 714. Here Blake saw the spiritual sun, as told to Crabb Robinson, *BR* 541.

31. See *PE* 472–5, and Morton D. Paley, *The Continuing City: William Blake's Jerusalem* (Oxford: Clarendon Press 1983), pp. 73–8.

32. The Jew's Harp House was where the radical London Corresponding Society held its last general meeting, 7 December 1795: John Barrell, *Imagining the King's Death: Figurative Treason, Fantasies of Regicide 1793–1796* (Oxford: Oxford University Press 2000), p. 597. The political presence robs the passage of nostalgia, creating, instead, organized innocence. Barrell's book suggests the extent of political paranoia infecting London from Pitt's government.

33. Maldon was supposed '(since Camden), to be the site of the Roman Camulodounum. Aylett Sammes, in *Britannia Antiqua Illustra* (1676) identifies a god Camulus with Mars; "Camalodunum" is "*Mars-Hill*", now *Maldon* in *Essex*; the goddess Venus Adraste also had a temple there' (S. 684). Paired with Colchester, Maldon appears in *Jerusalem* 21.37 (E. 166, K. 644) as in a state of unrest; paired with Canterbury in *Jerusalem* 37.6 (E. 183, K. 668) associated with cruelty, with primitivism in 57.6 (E. 207, K. 689), associated with the east it looks towards the dawn in 65.38 (E. 217, K. 700, in the context of press-gangs, where sailors would have gone through Maldon), it appears with Camberwell, Wimbledon, Walton and Esther (Surrey hills) and Stonehenge in *Jerusalem* 68.44 (E. 222, K. 706), and associated with primitive worship in 90.62 and 94.24 (E. 250, 254, K. 737, 742).

34. See Dana Arnold, pp. 1, 6–7. Hilton, *Literal Imagination: Blake's Vision of Words* (Berkeley: University of California Press 1983), pp. 141–2, sees a pun on Baby*lon* and Lon*don*.

35. David Punter, 'Blake and the Shapes of London', *Criticism* 21 (1981), 1–23, p. 17. See Kenneth R. Johnston, 'Blake's Cities: Romantic Forms of Urban Renewal', in David Erdman and John E. Grant (eds) *Blake's Visionary Forms Dramatic* (Princeton: Princeton University Press 1970), pp. 413–42.

36. S. 719 says that Blake refers to the Moorfields hospital, 'site of scandals about maltreatment in 1807 and 1814'. The associations of Lam*beth* and Beth*lehem* are also there, however, and it is unwise to date this section of the poem from Los's itinerary.

37. See Erdman, pp. 464–5. For London Stone's sexual oppressiveness: the Daughters of Albion 'sit naked upon the Stone of trial' (*Jerusalem* 66.19, E. 218, K. 702). 'Reuben and Hand mean the ordinary man and his Selfhood respectively, and Reuben purified of his Selfhood would become a prophetic imagination' – Frye, p. 376. Paley, p. 270, makes Reuben mother-fixated, quoting *Jerusalem* 93.8 (E. 253, K. 740), relating to Reuben finding mandrakes (Genesis 30.14), and plate 1 of *For the Sexes*, where the mandrakes are souls subject to the mother.

38. Paley, p. 312, indicates the passages – apart from the Prefaces to each chapter – where the 'I' speaks in Jerusalem: 4.3–5 (E. 146, K. 622), 5.16 (E. 147, K. 623), 38 (K) or 34 (E) line 40 (E. 180, K. 665), 47.18 (E. 196, K. 677), 74.14 to end (E. 229, K. 714–15), 97.5 (E. 256, K. 744), 98.40 (E. 258, K. 746), 99.5 (E. 259, K. 747).

39. See Max Byrd, *London Transformed: Images of the City in the Eighteenth Century* (New Haven: Yale University Press 1978), pp. 157–72, for this.

40. For the pre-history of the National Gallery (architect: William Wilkins, opened 1838), on a square cleared in 1830, see Nick Prior, *Museums and Modernity: Art Galleries and the Making of Modern Culture* (Oxford: Berg 2002), pp. 63–96. The nucleus of the collection had belonged to John Julius Angerstein, a founder of the British Institution for Promoting the Fine Arts in the United Kingdom, and had opened in Pall Mall after 1806. After Angerstein's death (1823), Parliament purchased the collection.

41. In 1780, Blake in Soho was caught up in the Gordon Riots against 'Popery' coming from destruction at Leicester Fields and on the way to Newgate: these riots inflamed London for a week, *SP* 55–7. The riots, subject of *Barnaby Rudge*, led to the place of execution changing from Tyburn to Newgate.

42. 'The Idle Apprentice Executed at Tyburn' (1747) in Joseph Burke and Colin Caldwell (eds) *Hogarth: The Complete Engravings* (London: Thames & Hudson, 1968), plate 213.

43. It included the Pantheon (1772): see Wordsworth, 'The Power of Music'. De Quincey discusses Oxford Street in *Confessions of an English Opium Eater*.

44. *PE* 3 begins with the allegorical significance of Golden Square for Blake: see also 'broad' as opposed to the 'narrows' discussed above. Dickens shows the Square's decline in *Nicholas Nickleby* and *David Copperfield*.

45. On Bunhill Fields, see Sharon Achinstein, *Literature and Dissent in Milton's England* (Cambridge: Cambridge University Press 2003), pp. 43–4.

46. Jean Hagstrum, 'Blake and British Art: The Gifts of Grace and Terror', in Karl Kroeber and William Walling, *Images of Romanticism: Verbal and Visual Affinities* (New Haven: Yale University Press 1978), pp. 61–80 (p. 74).

47. Edward Howard, *Rattlin the Reefer* ed. Arthur Howse (Oxford: Oxford University Press 1978), pp. 12, 13. *PE* 288–91, discusses the area in Blake's time, including the run-down Apollo Gardens.
48. Francis Place, *The Autobiography of Francis Place (1771–1854)* ed. Mary Thale (Cambridge: Cambridge University Press 1972), p. 80.
49. Place, p. 80. Waterloo station supplemented Place's description by opening in 1848.
50. See Tate Gallery Catalogue, *William Blake* (London: Tate Publishing 2000), pp. 72–3.
51. Alexander Gilchrist, *The Life of William Blake (1863)* ed. W. Graham Robertson (New York: Dover 1998), pp. 7–8. See also *BR*, p. 7.
52. *SP* 494. Note: Blake would walk 'to Blackheath, or south-west, over Dulwich and Norwood hills, through the antique rustic town of Croydon ... to the verdant meads of Walton-upon Thames' (p. 28), quoting Gilchrist. Blake's walking compares with Dickens.
53. Quoted, Raymond Lister, *Samuel Palmer and 'The Ancients'* (Cambridge: Cambridge University Press 1984), p. 7.

6 'Forests of the night': Blake and madness

1. E. 510, K. 549. Here, art is the production of madness.
2. Georges Bataille, *Literature and Evil* trans. Alastair Hamilton (London: Marion Boyars 1973), p. 91.
3. Dan Miller, 'Contrary Revelation: *The Marriage of Heaven and Hell*', *Studies in Romanticism* 24 (1985), 491–509, p. 493.
4. See Edward J. Rose, 'The Spirit of the Bounding Line: Blake's Los', *Criticism* 5 (1971), 54–76.
5. See Morton D. Paley, *Energy and the Imagination: A Study of the Development of Blake's Thought* (Oxford: Claredon Press 1970), p. 49, and Phillips, pp. 62–4.
6. Steven Shaviro, ' "Striving with Systems": Blake and the Politics of Difference', *boundary 2* 10 (1982), 229–50, p. 243.
7. David Worrall, Blake and the Night Sky: 1: The 'Immortal Tent', *Bulletin of Research in the Humanities* 84 (1981), 274. There is more on the night sky by Erdman and Paul Miner. For Erdman, Blake's 'art project ... involved turning night into day at least as fast as the tyrannic "Urizen" ... was turning day into night' (p. 296). My interest is in the reverse happening.
8. Walter Benjamin, *The Origin of German Tragic Drama* trans. John Osborne (London: Verso 1977), p. 34.
9. Annotating Lavater's *Aphorisms on Man* (1788), 'Venerate four characters: the sanguine, who has checked volatility and the rage for pleasure; the choleric who has checked passion and pride; the phlegmatic, emerged from indolence; and the melancholy, who has dismissed avarice, suspicion, and asperity', Blake wrote '4 most holy men' (E. 598, K. 86).
10. Thomas Percy, printing six 'mad songs' which these follow, says that 'the English have more songs and ballads on the subject of madness, than any of their neighbours'. *Percy's Reliques of Ancient English Poetry* 2 vols (London: Dent 1906), vol. 2, p. 148.

11. See William Crisman, 'Songs Named "Song" and the Bind of Self-Conscious Lyricism in Blake', *ELH* 61 (1994), 619–63.
12. The ground of Foucault on madness: see Stephen Marcus in 1966 on *Madness and Civilization* comparing it with *The Marriage of Heaven and Hell*, *Representations: Essays on Literature and Society* (New York: Columbia University Press 1990), pp. 156–7.
13. L.C. Knights, 'Early Blake', *Selected Essays in Criticism* (Cambridge: Cambridge University Press 1981), p. 127.
14. Note 'darken'd', and the echo of Christian hearing Faithful sing 'Though I walk through the Valley of the Shadow of Death I will fear none ill, for thou art with me': Bunyan, *The Pilgrim's Progress* ed. Roger Sharrock (Harmondsworth: Penguin 1987), p. 58.
15. Robert F. Gleckner compares the passivity with 'life avoided, not totally unlike Thel's . . .' in 'Antithetical Structure in Blake's *Poetical Sketches*', *Studies in Romanticism* 20 (1981), 143–62 (p. 158). See also Gleckner's *Blake's Prelude: Poetical Sketches* (Baltimore: Johns Hopkins University Press 1982), and Margaret Lowery, *Windows of the Morning: A Critical Study of William Blake's Poetical Sketches, 1783* (New Haven: Yale University Press 1940). For the Muses, see Preface to *Milton* E. 95, K. 480.
16. Stuart Peterfreund, 'The Problem of Originality and Blake's *Poetical Sketches*, *ELH* 52 (1985), 673–705 (p. 687).
17. See innocence in the poems written in a copy of 'Poetical Sketches', – 'Song 1st by a shepherd' and in 'Song 2nd by a Young Shepherd', which leads into 'Laughing Song' (*Songs of Innocence* E. 11, K. 124); and the 'Song by an Old Shepherd' which concludes: 'Blow boisterous Wind, stern Winter frown, / Innocence is a Winter's gown; / So clad, we'll abide life's pelting storm / That makes our limbs quake, if our hearts be warm' (see E. 466–7, K. 63–4). 'Pelting storm' quotes *King Lear* III. iv. 29, which speaks also of 'naked wretchedness'.
18. The crisis is national. 'Bards' are eighteenth-century diction: see Gray, Collins's 'The Passions', and Thomson's Ode ('Rule Britannia') at *Alfred: a Masque* (1740) 'sung by a venerable bard':

> The Muses, still with freedom found,
> Shall to thy happy coast repair,
> Blest isle! with matchless beauty crowned
> And manly hearts to guard the fair.
> (Thomson, Works [Oxford 1951], pp. 422–3)

19. See Theotormon's suspicion of this non-rationalist thought, *Visions of the Daughters of Albion* plate 3.22–4.11 (E. 47–8, K. 191–2).
20. Gray, 'On the Spring' (1742); see also in this poem the line 'Brushed by the hand of rough Mischance'.
21. See EV, pp. 33–4, and Christopher Z. Hobson, *Blake and Homosexuality* (London: Palgrave 2000), pp. 133–8. See plate 41 (Milton with [probably] Urizen), and plates 29 and 33 (the star reaching William and Robert Blake, and causing orgasmic ecstasy).
22. See Andrew M. Cooper, 'Blake and Madness: The World Turned Inside Out', *English Literary History* 57 (1990), 585–642.

23. *BR* 232 (Cary, to Flaxman) and 251. See Blake's poem to Flaxman, E. 507, K. 539. In a letter, 12 September 1800 (E. 708, K. 799), Blake's angels had said 'that seeing such visions I could not subsist on the Earth / But by my conjunction with Flaxman, who knows to forgive Nervous Fear'.
24. *BR* 231; Alicia Ostriker, *Vision and Verse in William Blake* (Madison and Milwukee: University of Wisconsin Press 1965), pp. 203–4. Crabb Robinson in 1852 recorded Wordsworth's 'there is no doubt that this poor man was mad, but there is something in the madness of this man which interests me more than the sanity of Lord Byron & Walter Scott', *BR* 536.
25. Quoted, Robert Brittain (ed.), *Poems by Christopher Smart* (Princeton: Princeton University Press 1950), p. 39. See Roy Porter, 'The Hunger of Imagination: Approaching Samuel Johnson's Melancholy', in W.F. Bynum, Roy Porter and Michael Shepherd (eds) *The Anatomy of Madness: vol. 1: People and Ideas* (London: Tavistock 1985), pp. 63–88.
26. 'An Invite to Eternity', *John Clare: Selected Poems* ed. Geoffrey Summerfield (Harmondsworth: Penguin, 1990), p. 334.
27. David A. Cross, *A Striking Likeness: The Life of George Romney* (Aldershot: Ashgate 2000), pp. 131, 188, on pp. 141–2, melancholia relates, possibly, to homosexuality. See 'Melancholy' (1770) (plate 12). For melancholy themes, see also Alex Kitson, *George Romney 1734–1802* (London: National Portrait Gallery 2002); no. 7, 'King Lear in the Tempest Tearing off his Robes' (a 'night-thoughts' scene), no. 8, study of an old man, perhaps King Lear, no. 47, King Lear, Edgar and the Fool, and no. 48, 'King Saul'. See also no. 137, the portrait of William Cowper. See Jean H. Hagstrum, 'Romney and Blake: Gifts of Grace and Terror', in Robert N. Essick and Donald Pearce (eds) *Blake in his Time* (Bloomington: Indiana University Press 1978), pp. 201–12.
28. William L. Pressly, *The Life and Art of James Barry* (New Haven: Yale University Press 1981), pp. 187–98.
29. On Hayley see Morchard Bishop, *The Life, Works and Friendship of William Hayley* (London: Victor Gollancz 1951), and Warren Stevenson, *Poetic Friends: A Study of Literary Relationships During the English Romantic Period* (New York: Peter Lang 1990), pp. 5–70. See also Joseph Anthony Wittreich Jr, *Angel of Apocalypse: Blake's Idea of Milton* (Madison: University of Wisconsin Press 1975), pp. 229–36, and on Blake's engravings for Hayley's *The Life, and Posthumous Writings, of William Cowper* (1803), see Robert N. Essick, *William Blake's Commercial Book Illustrations* (Oxford: Clarendon Press 1991), pp. 85–90. Blake's couplet on Hayley: 'Of Hayley's birth, this was the happy lot, / His Mother on his Father him begot' (K. 539) may make him hermaphroditic.
30. E. 867 notes the title began as 'Epitaph for William Cowper Esqre'. The first two words, and a first stanza, were deleted: see Erdman, *The Notebook of William Blake: A Photographic and Typographic Facsimile* (Oxford: Clarendon Press 1973), N. 50.
31. OED 'Evangelical' 2b cites Southey, the *Quarterly Review* 1.95 1809: 'The Wesleyans, the Orthodox dissenters of every description, and the Evangelical churchmen may all be comprehended under the generic name of Method-ists.' Ford K. Brown, *Fathers of the Victorians: The Age of Wilberforce* (Cambridge: Cambridge University Press 1961), distinguishes Methodism from the Evangelicals led by Wilberforce (1759–1833). 'The sole purpose of Evangelicalism ... from 1787 to 1825 was to reform the manners and morals

of the English people by combating the infidelity that is the cause of vice and sin' (385). He sees little altruistic in the abolition of the slave-trade, but a 'by-end, a subsidiary or instrumental cause that could be made into a crusade, inspiring large numbers of moral and earnest men and women to share in an emotional and spiritual undertaking identified with Evangelical leadership' (114). Brown, exonerating Newton from causing Cowper's depression (406–8), differentiates between the Evangelicals of Wilberforce's generation, such as Hannah More (1745–1833) and the next, epitomized by William Carus Wilson (1791–1859) (i.e. Mr Brocklehurst), pupil of Charles Simeon (1759–1836) of Trinity Church, Cambridge (teacher of Amos Barton in *Scenes of Clerical Life*, set around 1837). See pp. 448–86. For distinctions in Anglican Evangelicalism, see Boyd Hilton, *The Age of Atonement* (Oxford: Clarendon Press 1988), pp. 8–15. On Dissent and the Evangelical revival see Donald Davie, *A Gathered Church: The Literature of the English Dissenting Interest, 1700–1930* (Oxford: Oxford University Press 1978), pp. 55–72.

32. *The Letters and Prose Writings of William Cowper: vol. 4, 1792–1799* ed. James King and Charles Ryskamp (Oxford: Clarendon Press 1984), p. 297. For Cowper on Milton, see Dustin Griffin, *Regaining Paradise: Milton and the Eighteenth Century* (Cambridge: Cambridge University Press 1986), pp. 217–28.

33. See Morton D. Paley, 'Cowper as Blake's Spectre', *Eighteenth-Century Studies* 1 (1968), 236–52; Harold Bloom, *The Ringers in the Tower: Studies in the Romantic Tradition* (Chicago: University of Chicago Press 1971), pp. 65–79.

34. *The Poems of William Cowper* 3 vols ed. John D. Baird and Charles Ryskamp (Oxford: Clarendon Press 1995), vol. 3, pp. 214–16.

35. Quoted, Vincent Newey, *Cowper's Poetry: A Critical Study and Reassessment* (Liverpool: Liverpool University Press 1982), p. 6.

36. *Poems* 1, pp. 209–10. For Abiram, sent below 'quick' and 'howling', see Number 16. For Judas who also went to hell alive, see Psalms 55.15. Cowper, letter of 16 October 1785 to John Newton, describes the circumstances of this poem: 'I had a dream 12 years ago, before the recollection of which, all consolation vanishes, and, as it seems to me, must always vanish', *The Letters and Prose Writings of William Cowper: vol. 2, 1782–1786* ed. James King and Charles Ryskamp (Oxford: Clarendon Press 1981), p. 385. The dream said 'Actum est de te periisti' – 'It is all over with thee, thou hast perished' – and happened in early 1773, after which he never attended public worship. James King, *William Cowper: A Biography* (Durham: Duke University Press 1986), pp. 86–9.

37. Michel Foucault, *Maurice Blanchot: The Thought from Outside* (with Maurice Blanchot), *Michel Foucault as I Remember Him* trans. Jeffrey Mehlman and Brian Massumi (New York: Zone 1990), p. 25.

38. Cowper, 'On the Ice-islands Seen Floating in the Germanic Ocean', *Poems* vol. 3, pp. 212–14 (first published 1803).

39. See Martha W. England, 'Apprenticeship at the Haymarket', in David V. Erdman and John E. Grant (eds) *Blake's Visionary Forms Dramatic* (Princeton: Princeton University Press 1970), pp. 3–29, for Foote. If she is correct about the carnivalesque in Foote, Blake's response becomes obsessional.

40. *The Letters and Prose Writings of William Cowper: vol. 3, 1787–1791* ed. James King and Charles Ryskamp (Oxford: Clarendon Press 1982), p. 107.

41. Paul Youngquist, *Madness and Blake's Myth* (Philadelphia: Pennsylvania State University Press 1989), p. 158. He sees the Spectre in the 'Mad Song' speaker (p. 152).

42. See Morton D. Paley, 'The Truchsessian Gallery Revisited', *Studies in Romanticism* 16 (1977), 165–77. For the Spectre and the father, see Margaret Storch, 'The "Spectrous Fiend" Cast Out: Blake's Crisis at Felpham', *Modern Language Quarterly* 44 (1983), 115–35.

43. This (Butlin 301), of the colour prints of 1795, needs comparing with: 'Elohim Creating Adam' (Butlin 294), 'Lamech and his Two Wives' (297), 'Naomi Entreating Ruth and Orpah to Return to the Land of Moab' (299), 'Christ Appearing to the Apostles After the Resurrection' (325). Non-Biblical ones: 'Newton' (306), 'Pity' (305), 'The House of Death' (320), 'The Good and Evil Angels' (323), 'Satan Exulting Over Eve' (291), 'Hecate' (306). For George III as Nebuchadnezzar, see Jon Mee, ' "The Doom of Tyrants"; William Blake, Richard "Citizen" Lee and the Millenarian Public Sphere', in Jackie DiSalvo, G.A. Rosso, Christopher Z. Hobson (eds) *Blake, Politics and History* (New York: Garland 1998), pp. 97–114.

44. Joseph Burke and Colin Caldwell (eds), *Hogarth; The Complete Engravings* (London: Thames & Hudson 1968), plate 162.

45. Raymond Lister, *The Paintings of William Blake* (Cambridge: Cambridge University Press 1986), no. 13.

46. Sir Joshua Reynolds, *Discourses* ed. Pat Rogers (Harmondsworth: Penguin 1992), p. 101.

47. See Jean H. Hagstrum, *William Blake: Poet and Painter: An Introduction to the Illuminated Verse* (Chicago: University of Chicago Press 1964), pp. 65–6; Hagstrum reprints Mortimer's engraving.

48. *PE* p. 193 connects Nebuchadnezzar's portrait with Rousseau's 'Discourse on the Origin of Inequality' where the prehuman state is 'confined to a horizon of a few paces'.

49. Emmanuel Levinas, *Existence and Existents* trans. Alphonse Lingis (The Hague: Martinus Nijhoff 1978), p. 58.

7 Dante's 'deep and woody way'

1. The numbering of Albert S. Roe, *Blake's Illustrations to the Divine Comedy* (Princeton: Princeton University Press 1953), referred to in the text as Roe, followed by page-number. See also Milton S. Klonsky, *Blake's Dante* (New York: Harmony Books 1980), and Butlin, vol. 2, pp. 554–94. For criticism: Rodney M. Baine, 'Beatrice's Dante in a Different Light', *Dante Studies* 105 (1987), 113–36, which contests the view that Beatrice is to be seen as the Female Will (the essay concentrates entirely on the last two *cantiche*, and has nothing to say about *Inferno*); David Fuller, 'Blake and Dante', *Art History* 11 (1988), 349–73, which argues against Roe; Jeanne Moskal, 'Blake, Dante and "Whatever Book is for Vengeance" ', *Philological Quarterly* 70 (1991), 317–35. See Eugene Paul Hassar, *Illustrations to Dante's* Inferno (New Jersey: Associated Universities Press 1994) and Steve Ellis's *Dante and English Poetry: Shelley to T.S. Eliot* (Cambridge: Cambridge University Press 1983). For Flaxman's

Dante, see David Irwin, *John Flaxman, 1755–1841: Sculptor, Illustrator, Designer* (New York: Rizzoli 1979), pp. 94–105.

2. The Concordance under the heading 'Money' shows some nine references in Blake before the *Laocoon* and the 'Annotations to Dr Thornton' (1827); and about nine in these two alone. (I exclude the letters from consideration.) The point about the newness of the attention to money is not provable, but I find it suggestive. See also *PE* 491–5.

3. Linda Colley, *Britons* (New Haven: Yale University Press 1992), p. 323.

4. Asa Briggs, *The Age of Improvement* (London: Longman 1959), p. 211. On the relation of the Romantics to politics, see Marilyn Butler, *Romantics: Rebels and Reactionaries* (Oxford: Oxford University Press 1981).

5. For the speculation and financial collapse of these years see Norman Russell, *The Novelist and Mammon* (Oxford: Clarendon Press 1986), pp. 43–59.

6. Charles Dickens, *Bleak House* (Harmondsworth: Penguin 1971), p. 49.

7. Links between Utilitarian and radical thought and the Evangelical ascendancy are made by Elie Halévy, *England in 1815* trans. E.I. Watkin and D.A. Barker (1913, 2nd rev. edn 1949, London: Ernest Benn 1949), pp. 585–7; compare Humphry House, *The Dickens World* (Oxford: Oxford University Press 1942), pp. 74–6; Valentine Cunningham, *Everywhere Spoken Against: Dissent in the British Novel* (Oxford: Clarendon Press 1975), pp. 91–105. The reference to 'surveillance' recalls Michel Foucault, *Discipline and Punish* trans. Alan Sheridan (Harmondsworth: Penguin 1979).

8. William Hazlitt, *The Spirit of the Age* (1825), *The Complete Works of William Hazlitt* ed. P.P. Howe, after A.R. Waller and Arnold Glover vol. 11 (London: J.H. Dent 1932), p.13.

9. Roe, p. 49, and Butlin, p. 555, compare the animals with the 'Accusers of the Moral Law' in *Jerusalem* plate 93 (see E. 253, K. 740).

10. See Andrew Wright, *Blake's Job* (Oxford: Clarendon Press, 1972) for the 21 engravings plus title-page. Commissioned by Linnell, *Job* was published in 1826.

11. Norman Gash, *Mr Secretary Peel: The Life of Sir Robert Peel to 1830* (London: Longman, 2nd edn 1985), p. 479. For forgery, see pp. 478–85.

12. Charles Dickens, *Sketches By Boz* ed. Dennis Walder (Harmondsworth: Penguin 1995), p. 74.

13. Charles Dickens, *David Copperfield* ed. Jeremy Tambling (Harmondsworth: Penguin 1996), 47, p. 626.

14. De Quincey refers to Clare's 'dejection' in 1824 in London: *London Reminiscences and Confessions of an Opium-Eater, Collected Writings of Thomas de Quincey* vol. 3 ed. David Masson (Edinburgh: Adam & Charles Blakc 1890), p. 145.

15. Louis Crompton, *Byron and Greek Love* (London: Faber 1985), pp. 33–8. See on Crompton Robert J. Corber, 'Representing the "Unspeakable": William Godwin and the Politics of Homophobia', *Journal of the History of Sexuality* 1 (1990), 85–101.

16. Northrop Frye, *Fearful Symmetry: A Study of William Blake* (Princeton University Press 1947), p. 199. On Blake and Byron, see Leslie Tannenbaum, 'Lord Byron in the Wilderness: Biblical Tradition in Byron's *Cain* and Blake's *The Ghost of Abel*', *Modern Philology* 72 (1975), 350–64; and Leslie Tannenbaum, 'Blake and the Iconography of Cain', in Robert V. Essick and Donald Pearce (eds) *Blake in his Time* (Bloomington: Indiana University Press 1978), pp. 23–34.

17. Quoted, David D. Cooper, *The Lesson of the Scaffold: The Public Execution Controversy in Victorian England* (Athens, Ohio: Ohio University Press 1974), p. 37.
18. See V.A.C. Gattrell, *The Hanging Tree: Execution and the English people, 1770–1868* (Oxford: Oxford University Press 1994), p. 20. (I cannot reconcile Gattrell's figures with those that Gash gives in his biography of Peel, p. 486. In the seven years after 1822, in England and Wales, according to Gash, 433 people were hanged; in 1829, 17 in London and Middlesex, a figure which was steadily declining (from 56 in 1783, and from 731 overall in the seven years prior to 1822). Gash's figures seem considerably lower, but I have chosen to opt for Gatrell.)
19. J.S. Mill, *Autobiography* ed. Jack Stillinger (Oxford: Oxford University Press 1971), p. 61. See also Gash, p. 334.
20. Byron on Dante is discussed by both Ellis and Pite; for the iconic value of Dante's head, see Carlyle's lecture, 'The Hero As Poet: Dante; Shakespeare' (1840) in *On Heroes and Hero-Worship* (Centenary Edition, vol. 5 London: Chapman & Hall), p. 86.
21. R.D. Laing, *The Divided Self* (1959, Harmondsworth: Penguin 1990), p. 162.
22. John Forster, *The Life of Charles Dickens* ed. J.W.T. Ley (London: Cecil Palmer 1928) 1.2., p. 25. See Michael Allen, *Charles Dickens's Childhood* (London: Macmillan 1988).
23. Deborah Dorfman, *Blake in the Nineteenth Century: His Reputation as a Poet from Gilchrist to Yeats* (New Haven: Yale University Press 1969), Suzanne R. Hoover, 'William Blake in the Wilderness: A Closer Look at his Reputation 1827–1863', in Morton Paley and Michael Phillips (eds) *William Blake: Essays in Honour of Sir Geoffrey Keynes* (Oxford: Clarendon Press 1973) and G.E. Bentley Jr, *William Blake: The Critical Heritage* (London: Routledge & Kegan Paul 1975). In addition, there is Carlyle's knowledge of Blake (he possessed a copy of Wilkinson's edition of the *Songs* (1839)), and Richard Monckton Milnes, who planned an edition of Blake in 1838: see T.Wemyss Reid, *Life, Letters and Friendships of Richard Monckton Milnes* (London 1891), 1, pp. 220–21. He conversed with Crabb Robinson about Blake, evidently planning (see Robinson *Books and their Writers*, 2, p. 717), an edition of Blake in 1852. He was consulted for Gilchrist's and Swinburne's biography of 1869.
24. Steven Marcus, *Dickens From Pickwick to Dombey* (London: Chatto & Windus 1965), pp. 65, 70.
25. F.R. Leavis, Introduction to Peter Coveney, *The Image of Childhood* (Harmondsworth: Penguin 1966). In F.R. and Q.D. Leavis, *Dickens the Novelist* (London: Chatto & Windus 1970), Leavis's chapter on *Little Dorrit* is called 'Dickens and Blake'. See Raymond Williams, *The Country and the City* (London: Hogarth Press 1873), pp. 149, 215–47. For a recent attempt to link Blake and Dickens, see Dominic Rainsford, *Authorship, Ethics and the Reader: Blake, Dickens, Joyce* (London: Macmillan 1997).
26. Pite (note 3) argues one of the importances of Dante for the Romantics: 'Bringing the feelings of childhood into the powers of manhood requires of Wordsworth qualities of mind and of writing that Dante came to exemplify. Dante's directness, the pictorial accuracy and vividness of his writing, correspond to a child's fresh percipience, while the organization of his experience according to self-consciously established categories of judgement reveals the

powers of manhood at work. Both these qualities are discovered in Dante in the Romantic period...' (p. 3).

27. Andrew Elfenbein, *Byron and the Victorians* (Cambridge: Cambridge University Press 1995), pp. 206–29.

28. T.N. Talfourd, supposed to be an original for Traddles, associated with Steerforth at the school, was one of the early (favourable) reviewers of *Cain*, in *The London Magazine* in 1822. See Truman Guy Steffan, *Lord Byron's Cain: Twelve Essays and A Text with Variants and Annoations* (Austin: University of Texas Press 1968), pp. 348–53.

29. See Lawrence Frank, *Charles Dickens and the Romantic Self* (Lincoln: University of Nebraska Press 1984), pp. 60–94.

30. Derrida in *Glas*, quoted Geoffrey H. Hartman, *Saving the Text: Literature: Derrida: Philosophy* (Baltimore: Johns Hopkins University Press 1981), p. 60.

31. Roe (p. 82) compares the Theseus from the Parthenon; Butlin (p. 564) the Nile in the Vatican. For further references to the antique, see Butlin p. 555 on no. 1; p. 559 on no. 9; See generally, Morton D. Paley, 'Wonderful Originals: Blake and Ancient Sculpture' in Essick and Pearce, pp. 170–98.

32. Barbara T. Gates, *Victorian Suicide: Mad Crimes and Sad Histories* (Princeton: Princeton University Press 1988), pp. 3–12, discusses changes in the treatment of suicide: in 1823, Peel passed legislation to end the custom of burying the dead in a public highway with a stake through the heart, a practice literally associating the dead with trees and vegetative existence.

33. De Quincey's 'The Pains of Opium' in the *Confessions of an English Opium Eater* (1821) – evoking Piranesian visions of ascent and descent experienced in opium-dreams – compares for these visions of bridges (nos 34, 40), vertiginous drops (no. 43) and laborious climbings (nos 45, 46).

34. See Hazlitt's account of visits to Bentham, in *The Spirit of the Age*, p. 6.

35. Keith Kyle, 'London: the Unlooked for Conflict', in Seamus Dunn (ed.) *Managing Divided Cities* (Ryburn Publishing: Keele University Press 1994), pp. 53–63.

36. Saskia Sassen, *Cities in a World Economy* (Thousand Oaks, California: Pine Forge Press 1994), p. 154. The post-industrial definition comes from H.V. Savitch, *Post-Industrial Cities: Politics and Planning in New York, Paris and London* (Princeton: Princeton University Press 1988). Manuel Castells's work began in 1972 with *La question urbaine* (Paris: Maspero), and David Harvey's in 1973 with *Social Justice and the City* (London: Edward Arnold). John Friedman discussed what he called 'the world city hypothesis', in Paul Knox and Peter J. Taylor, *World Cities in a World System* (Cambridge: Cambridge University Press 1995), pp. 317–31.

37. Philip Ogden (ed.), *London Docklands: The Challenge of Development* (Cambridge: Cambridge University Press 1992), p. 9.

38. Michael Hebbert, *London: More By Fortune Than Design* (Chichester: John Wiley 1998), pp. 105–6.

39. Anthony D. King, *Global Cities: Post-Imperialism and the Internationalisation of London* (London: Routledge 1990), p. 145.

40. See Deyan Sudjic, 'Sold Down the River', *Observer*, 18 May 2003.

41. Quotations taken from Kevin Robbins, 'Whatever Could a Postmodern City Be?' *New Formations* 15 (1991), 1–22.

42. Peter Ackroyd, *Dickens* (London: Sinclair Stevenson 1990); *Blake* (London: Sinclair Stevenson 1995); *London: The Biography* (London: Chatto & Windus 2000). Jeremy Gibson and Julian Wolfreys, *Peter Ackroyd: The Ludic and the Labyrinthine Text* (London: Macmillan 2000), pp. 170–211, see Ackroyd's work as quasi-deconstructive: 'What Peter Ackroyd strives to make us familiar with is that London remains ineffable. It resists definition, by being nothing other than the voices, the texts, the traces of itself, endlessly reconfigured and performed, time and time again' (210). I see his London as more esssentialist and ahistorical. For a review of *Blake*, see Morton Paley, *Blake: An Illustrated Newsletter* 30.2 (1996), 58–60.

43. Iain Sinclair, *Lights Out for the Territory* (London: Granta 1997), p. 208. Further references in the text. The Blake passage he refers to is *Jerusalem* 31, 14–17. It is discussed by Ackroyd, pp. 315–17.

44. Guy Debord, 'Introduction to a Critique of Urban Geography', in Ken Knabb (ed.) *Situationist International Anthology* (Berkeley: Bureau of Public Secrets 1981), pp. 5, 6–7.

45. On psychogeography, see Simon Sadler, *The Situationist City* (Cambridge, Mass.: MIT Press 1998) and Sadie Plant, *The Most Radical Gesture: The Situationist International in a Postmodern Age* (London: Routledge 1992), pp. 58–60.

46. Salman Rushdie, *The Satanic Verses* (London: Vintage 1988), pp. 327–8.

Index

This index includes Blake's works, but only notes writers with more than a single reference in the text, unless that is held to be significantly material: other names, not referenced, lie buried in footnotes.

Printed in the United States
64401LVS00001B/200